INDIA: ITS LIFE AND THOUGHT

INDIA
ITS LIFE AND THOUGHT

JOHN P. JONES, D.D.

GYAN

Published by

Gyan Publishing House
5, Ansari Road
Daryaganj, New Delhi-110002
Phone: 011-47034999, 9811692060
E-mail: books@gyanbooks.com

Distribution Network
gyanbooks.com
India, USA, Canada, UK, Australia, France

ISBN: 978-81-212-8814-9 (PB)
First Published,1908

2nd Impression 2023

Printed at: Gyan Press, Delhi.

INDIA ITS LIFE AND THOUGHT

Author: john p. Jones

INDIA: ITS LIFE AND THOUGHT

THE MACMILLAN COMPANY
NEW YORK · BOSTON · CHICAGO
ATLANTA · SAN FRANCISCO

MACMILLAN & CO., LIMITED
LONDON · BOMBAY · CALCUTTA
MELBOURNE

THE MACMILLAN CO. OF CANADA, LTD.
TORONTO

A Holy Man of India

INDIA

ITS LIFE AND THOUGHT

BY

JOHN P. JONES, D.D.

SOUTH INDIA

AUTHOR OF "INDIA'S PROBLEM, KRISHNA OR CHRIST,"
ETC., ETC.

New York
THE MACMILLAN COMPANY
1908

Set up and electrotyped. Published October, 1908.

Norwood Press
J. S. Cushing Co. — Berwick & Smith Co.
Norwood, Mass., U.S.A.

Dedicated

TO MY DEAR CHILDREN

WHO HAVE

BRAVELY AND CHEERFULLY ENDURED

THE SEPARATION AND THE LOSS OF HOME

FOR THE SAKE OF INDIA

PREFACE

To the people of the West, the inhabitants of India are the least understood and the most easily misunderstood of all men.

It is partly because they are antipodal to the West —the farthest removed in thought and life. They are also the most secretive, and find perennial delight in concealment and evasion.

According to Hindu teaching, the Supreme Spirit forever sports in illusion. It continuously manifests itself through unreal and false forms, which delude and lead astray ignorant man. In harmony with this philosophy of the Divine—and may it not be as a result of it?—the people of India too often delight in unreal and deceptive exhibitions of themselves. At any rate, it is exceedingly difficult for a man of the West, especially he of the Anglo-Saxon type, to apprehend the full significance and the correct drift of life and thought of this land.

It is amusing, when not discouraging, to witness travellers, who have rushed through India in a winter tour, publish volumes of their misconceptions and ill-digested theories about the people with an oracular emphasis which is equalled only by their ignorance.

The author of this book makes no claim to a right to speak *ex cathedra* upon this subject. Nevertheless, thirty years of matured experience in this land, living in constant touch with the people and studying with eagerness their life and thought, gives him an humble claim to speak once more upon the subject.

Even now, however, his pride of knowledge is chastened by the oft-recurring surprises which the Oriental nature and life still bring to him. And he does not cease to pray, with a western saint, who, at the end of a half century of work for the people of India, daily cried out, —

"O Lord, help me to know these people and to come into intimate relations of life with them!"

If, in these pages, he can help others of the West to come face to face with the immense and intricate problems which confront all who desire to know, to help, and to bless India, and shall enable them to understand better the conditions and characteristics of life in the Land of the Vedas, he will feel amply repaid for his labours.

I express my deep gratitude to the Rev. J. L. Barton, D.D., for his kind encouragement in the publishing of this book; and also to the Rev. W. W. Wallace, M.A., for his generous aid in the proof-reading.

J. P. JONES.

CONTENTS

LIST OF ILLUSTRATIONS

INDIA: ITS LIFE AND THOUGHT

CHAPTER I

INDIA'S UNREST

India has been called the land of quiet repose, content to remain anchored to the hoary past, and proud of her immobility. Invasion after invasion has swept over her; but —

> "The East bowed low before the blast,
> In patient, deep disdain;
> She let the legions thunder past,
> And plunged in thought again."

Yet this same India is now throbbing with discontent, and is breathing, in all departments of her life, a deep spirit of unrest. This spirit has recently become acute and seemed, for a while, in danger of bursting into open rebellion, not unlike the Mutiny of half a century ago.

I

This movement is but a part of the new awakening of the East. The world has seen its marvellously rapid development and fruitage in Japan. It is witnessing the same process in China and Korea. The people of India, likewise, have been touched by its power and are no longer willing to rest contentedly as a subject people or a stagnant race.

This movement is nòt only political, it permeates every department of life; and it partakes of the general unrest which has taken possession of all the civilized nations of the earth. It is really the dawning of India's consciousness of strength and of a purpose to take her place, and to play a worthy part, in the great world drama.

This spirit found its incarnation and warmest expression in the opposition to the government scheme, two years ago, under Lord Curzon, for the partition of Bengal. The Bengalees keenly resented the division of their Province; for it robbed the clever Babu of many of the plums of office. He petitioned, and fomented agitation and opposition to the scheme. Then, in his spite against the government, he organized a boycott against all forms of foreign industry and commerce. This has been conducted with mad disregard to the people's own economic interest, and has, moreover, developed into bitter racial animosity.

The Bengalee has striven hard to carry into other Provinces also his spirit of antagonism to the State. Though he has not succeeded in convincing many others of the wisdom of his method, he has spread the spirit of discontent and of dissatisfaction far beyond his own boundary. Even sections of the land which denounce the boycott as folly, if not suicide, have taken up the political slogan of the Babu (*Bande Mataram* — Hail, Mother!) and are demanding, mostly in inarticulate speech, such rights and privileges as they imagine themselves to be deprived of.

The movement is, in some respects, a reactionary one; and race hatred is one of its most manifest results. It is not merely a rising of the East against the West; it is also a conflict between Mohammedans and Hindus. In Eastern Bengal, where the Mussulmans are in a large majority, and where the Hindus have become the most embittered, the former have stood aloof from the latter and have opposed the boycott. This has led to increasing hatred between the members of these two faiths, — a feeling which has spread all over the country, and which has carried them into opposing camps. This is, in one way, fortunate for the government, since it has given rise to definite and warm expressions of loyalty by the whole Mohammedan community.

Disgruntled graduates of the University and schoolboys take the most prominent place in this movement. The Universities annually send forth an army of men supplied with degrees — last year it was 1570 B.A.'s; and it is the conviction of nine-tenths of them that it is the duty of the government to give them employment as soon as they graduate. As this is impossible, many of them nurse their disappointment into discontent and opposition to the powers that be. Many of them become dangerous demagogues and fomenters of sedition. Not a few such are found in every Province of the country. And they find in the High School and College students the best material to work upon. These boys have been the most numerous and excited advocates of this movement. As in Russia, so in India the educational institutions are becoming the hotbeds of dissatisfaction and opposition to the State. But there is this difference. In Russia the University student is much more truly an exponent of public sentiment, and more ready to suffer for that sentiment, than are the dependent youth of colleges in India.

This movement has not, to any considerable extent,

reached the masses. Nine-tenths of the population of India are satisfied with the government and have no desire to change the present order of things. Indeed, they are deeply ignorant of the grievances which the higher classes nurse into bitterness. And yet it should not be forgotten that the ignorance of the people, coupled with their narrow superstition and lively imagination, make them very inflammable material under the influence of eloquent demagogues.

II

One of the most marked causes of this activity and discontent is the recent victory of Japan over Russia. It is hard for the West to realize how much that event has stirred the imagination and quickened the ambition of all the people of the East. They regard that war as the great conflict of the East and the West. India had not the slightest idea that Japan would come triumphant out of that conflict. But the victory of Japan instantly suggested to all men of culture in India the question, " Why should our land be subject to a far-off, and a small, western country? Why should we be content with our dependence and not reveal our manhood and our prowess, as Japan did?" These are inquiries which have opened up new visions of power and greatness to the people of India. Japan and its people have been immensely popular in India since their recent victory. And Hindus believe that the peace perfected at Portsmouth was the harbinger of a new era of liberty and independence for all the East.

The growing influence of western education in India has had much to do with the present state of things. It is true that India is still a land of ignorance. It is a lamentable fact that only 1 in 10 of the males and 1 in 144 of the females can read. Only 22.6 per cent of the boys of school-going age attend school, and only 2.6 per cent of the girls. And yet the enrolment of more than five million scholars in the public schools is a significantly hopeful fact as compared with the past history of India.

This education is distinctly on *western* lines. And connected with the five Universities of India there are many thousands of young men and women who are devoting themselves to a deep study of western thought and of western ideas of liberty. The Calcutta University alone has, in its affiliated colleges, more students registered than Harvard, Yale, Princeton, and Toronto combined. In that city, which is the centre of the present unrest, there are 12,000 young men in the Colleges, and 30,000 pupils in the High Schools. This host of young men and women are imbibing modern ideas of manliness, independence, and liberty such as India never knew in the past; and they go out into the world with new ambitions for their country and inspired with not a little "divine unrest."

In close connection with this educational influence is that of western civilization and Christian ideals. The government of this land is built upon Christian principles and is animated by that spirit of civilization which dominates the West. And we know that these make for manhood and independence everywhere. It would be a sad thing for Great Britain, as it would be for the Christian missionary in India, if these lofty principles, which they inculcate, did not acquire increasing power over these youth.

And it should not be forgotten that an increasing number of the elect youth of India go to England for the completion of their training, and return well equipped with Anglo-Saxon ideas of human rights and of manhood's claims.

Nor is this merely a movement of the people of India. There is a strong body of Englishmen, several of whom are members of Parliament, banded together in England, for the purpose of promoting the political influence of the people of India in the conduct of the affairs of their own country. These men believe that India has a right to a much larger meed of self-government than she now enjoys. And they seize upon every opportunity to urge upon the Home Government the duty of granting added power to the people, and also to advise the leaders of Indian thought as to their wisest methods of procedure. There are not a few radicals in Britain who believe that India should govern herself as an independent colony. And they rouse within Hindu youth who go to England a radical spirit of discontent and disloyalty. It was only the other day that Lord Ampthill warned these men, because of the insidious influence which they were exercising for the overthrow of the British power in the East.

The National Congress, which has just reached its majority, has a profound influence in the development of a national consciousness, and in the furtherance of the cause of independence and political power in the land. The very existence of this institution is one of the highest compliments to British rule in India. It would be impossible for one to imagine the Russian government permitting such a body of men to gather every year in solemn conclave to devote several days to a vehement criticism of all the principal acts of the

State, to give vent to disloyal sentiments, and to promote the spirit of disaffection throughout the country. This Congress has devoted nearly all its time to a denunciation of the powers that be; and during these twenty-one years the writer has not seen one word of commendation or one vote of appreciation of the State in the reports of the proceedings of the Congress. And the demands of the Congress, inspired as they are by Anglo-Saxon friends in Great Britain, are becoming annually more definite and urgent.

Until the meeting of 1906 there was no divergence of sentiment among Congress-wallahs. No dissentient voice or conflicting opinions were allowed. It is to the honour and highest interest of the Congress that this stage has now been passed and the healthy rivalry of parties is felt and heard in Congress councils. It is to be regretted that at the last Congress meeting, in Surat, these two parties — the Moderates and the Extremists — came into bitter conflict. It was largely due to the past supineness of the Moderates who permitted the other party (which is a small but noisy minority) to resort to bluster in order to force their pet and bitter schemes of disorder upon the Congress. When, ultimately, the Moderates determined to exercise the rights of the majority, the others resorted to force and caused the Congress to be suspended in disorder, thus revealing the sad spectacle of the present incapacity of the leaders of the people to govern themselves and the country.

This is, however, perhaps the best thing that could have happened for the highest interest of the Congress itself. The two parties are now clearly defined — the one seeking, through constitutional agitation, self-government on colonial lines, like Canada; the other determined to overthrow the government of the foreigner and to establish its own upon the ruins. And agitation in this behalf is to be conducted in every possible way, constitutional or otherwise.

The Moderates are now thoroughly roused and have driven out from their councils the irreconcilables and fire-eaters, and can now work with more harmony and success for the attainment of their wiser plans and more reasonable aims.

A few years ago, the State ignored, when it did not ridicule, the National Congress. To-day none recognizes its power more than does the government.

And it is most suggestive and instructive to see this body, of fully three thousand men, gathered together from all parts of this great peninsula — men who represent peoples that speak more than four hundred languages and dialects! They conduct their sessions in English, which is the only universal tongue of the country. And a purer English is hardly spoken in any deliberative or legislative body in any other land; and some of the addresses are delivered with a force, and are adorned with a logic and a rhetoric, which are truly eloquent. Verily, the weapon of popular power, though largely used against the government, is the best compliment possible to the State which has created it.

The Press also has marvellously grown in power and in dignity during the last quarter of a century. At the present time there are scores of dailies, and many more weeklies and monthlies, published in the English tongue by the natives of the land. And they discuss, with intelligence and discrimination, if not with moderation, all matters of State and of political interest. Recently some of these papers have become thoroughly radical and oppose the government at all points.

But it is the vernacular Press, representing, as it does, hundreds of newspapers in all the tongues of India, that carries its influence into the villages and homes of the uneducated millions. The present condition of discontent with the government has been disseminated among the common people more by these vernacular papers than by any other agency. Many of these are thoroughly disloyal and seditious. Very occasionally they are prosecuted for their inflammatory editorials, and their editors are imprisoned.

As a matter of fact, there is hardly any country where the Press has greater liberties than in India; and there is no land on earth where that liberty is more abused. The very toleration of the government is turned as a keen weapon against it.

The same thing is true of the freedom of public speech. There is not another land, save perhaps America, whose citizens have greater privileges in this matter. The seditious speeches which have been made in many parts of India during the last two years, by Bengalees specially, and by a few other radicals, have been such as would in Europe lead to imprisonment if not to deportation. Bepin Chandra Pal, of Calcutta, has just closed a tour during which he has made many addresses, attended, in all cases, by thousands of students and disaffected members of the community, and has not only denounced the government as the very incarnation of unrighteousness and cruelty, but has also urged the people to do all they can, both constitutionally and otherwise, to defeat and overthrow it and to establish a native rule upon its ruin. Any government, in order to ignore such language uttered in immense public assemblies, must feel very secure in its power. Mr. Pal is only one of many who have thus far been granted absolute freedom to sow broadcast the seed of revolution.

III

What is there in the recent condition of the country and of the people, which warrants this unrest and discontent?

Disinterested persons will not say that the State is unprogressive or is administering its affairs unwisely. In its recent Annual Financial Statement we discover evidences of prosperity in all departments of State. There is no extensive famine to distress the people and harass the government. The revenue of the year exceeds, by nearly 30 million rupees, the estimates; there was a surplus at the end of the year of 20 million rupees. Owing to this the government has reduced the opium cultivation, which has wrought, for many years, so much injustice to China. It has also increased postal facilities, which renders them cheaper and more convenient than in any other land. Moreover, the obnoxious salt tax has been reduced by 50 per cent; and it is hoped that the whole tax will be remitted shortly. The grant for education is also much enhanced beyond any former year, and the State is even planning for the introduction of a Free Primary Education, which will be an unspeakable boon to the people.

And when it is said that taxation in India has been reduced, we should also remember that in this land "the taxation per head is lighter than in any other civilized country in the world. In Russia, it is eight times as great; in England, twenty times; in Italy, nineteen; in France, twenty-five; in the United States and Germany, thirteen times." In other words, taxation in India comes to only one dollar, or three rupees, per head.

But it is claimed that India is a land of deepest poverty. This is perfectly true. But it is not true that her poverty is increasing. The Parsee Chairman of the Bombay Stock Exchange, in his last annual address, said that "it was the conviction of merchants, bankers, tradesmen, and captains of industry that India is slowly but steadily advancing along paths of material prosperity, and for the last few years it has taken an accelerated pace." The poverty of the people is a very convenient slogan of the political party; but there is everything to prove that the condition of the people, deplorable though it be, is, nevertheless, slowly improving.

The State is, moreover, constantly yielding to the growing demand of the people for a larger share in the conduct of public business and in the emoluments of office. Even at the present time the Secretary of State for India has introduced a scheme, at the instance of the government, which will add materially to the power of India in the conduct of its own affairs.

The British were never more firmly entrenched and possessed of more power in India than at the present time. The lesson of the Mutiny, of a half-a-century ago, was not lost upon the administrators of India. Since then, no Indian regiment can be stationed within a thousand miles of its own home, and thus be able to enter into collusion with the people. And the artillery branch of the army is entirely in the hands of the British force. Moreover, as we have seen, the Mohammedans and the Sikhs are loyal to the government, and would stand with the British against the Hindus in any conflict of arms.

The Hindus themselves realize this situation perfectly well. One of the best-known Hindu gentlemen recently wrote as follows: "The truth is in a nutshell and may be described in a few words. The British cannot be driven out of India by the Indians, nor by any foreign Power. This fact is known to more than 90 per cent of the people. Of all the foreigners, the British are the best. We, as we are now, are the least able to govern India, being not equal to the worst and weakest foreign Power.

The best class of Hindus are not only sensible of their own weakness, from a military standpoint; they are also dissatisfied with the action of extremists and believe that the present unrest is evil. A well-known Hindu writer describes the situation in the following words: "The class of people the Indian Extremists appeal to, consists of irresponsible and impressionable students and the ignorant populace; and the agitator, who is thoroughly cognizant of this fact, uses it for his purposes. He appeals to their feelings, and succeeds in making them believe in the soundness of his fallacies and mischievous preachings. The authorities have therefore to see that this class of people is protected from the insidious appeals of mischievous pseudo-patriots. After over a century of beneficent British rule in India, it is scarcely necessary to attempt to justify its existence or continuance. At the same time, it has to be recognized that discontent prevails among the people; though, speaking generally, it does not by any means partake of the character of disaffection or disloyalty. Discontent is by no means inconsistent with loyalty to government. On the other hand, it may even be said, with a certain degree of truth, that the deep-rooted and abiding sense of loyalty in the people has engendered the spirit of discontent, the healthy discontent with their lot."

It should also be remembered that the Hindu caste system is an insuperable barrier to the progress of the people toward independence. The unity of the Mohammedans of India, who are only one-fifth of the population, is in healthful contrast to the myriad caste divisions and social barriers which separate Hindus one from another. One must be compelled to deny the sincerity of many who claim that this people is a nation which prides itself upon its patriotism, so long as the caste system dominates them and their ideas. The only tie which binds together these people is the spirit of opposition to this foreign government. Among the classes and the masses there is absolutely no coherence or unity of sentiment in any line of constructive activity. So that in the matter of self-government they would prove themselves to be sadly incompetent.

IV

The action of the Indian government, in view of the present situation, has been the subject of criticism. Anglo-Indians feel that the Viceroy and his Council have, for some reason or other, been too deliberate in their action. For two years things have been going from bad to worse. When, recently, Sir Bampfylde Fuller, the Lieutenant-Governor of East Bengal, took prompt and vigorous action to suppress the uprising in his Province, which was the centre of trouble, the Indian government declined to support him. He therefore resigned, and India lost one of the men who are the most competent to deal wisely and well with sedition-mongers. The State may have thought, and was probably right in thinking, that while the Bengal Babu is capable of unlimited noise, he has a mortal aversion to converting his noise into action. So the government preferred patiently to endure odium rather than suppress the movement.

It was different in the Panjaub, whose people are

less talkative, but are more given to action. These warrior tribes were being rapidly disaffected by political agitators; and they doubtless had definite grievances of their own to agitate them. The time came when government was compelled to do something to suppress the rising tide of feeling. It decided to act upon a law of nearly a century ago, and deported two of the leaders of the movement. They were at once sent to Burma, where they were held in surveillance for six months and then released. This action of the State was effective; for it quieted the people and nipped what promised to be a rebellion, in the bud. But it raised a storm of denunciation from all the Hindu papers, which spoke of it as a violation of the Queen's Proclamation and an act subversive of the most sacred rights of the people of the country and of the most elementary form of justice! One writer claims that "the meanest British subject is entitled to a writ of *Habeas Corpus*, and thus secure an effective protection against arbitrary imprisonment and arrest by the government." This is certainly true in ordinary times of peace; but the government had every reason to believe that the state of things in the Panjaub was anything but peaceable, and that it must act in view of the extraordinary condition of the Province. And its method of procedure has proved itself to be the most bloodless and inexpensive possible. It has been claimed that the chief deported man, Mr. Lala Rajpat Rai, is not an extremist; but this has to be proved, and it may be presumed that the government was more conversant with his acts and their influence upon the people, and the native army, than some of his defenders are. All must regret the necessity of so unconstitutional a method of dealing with this great evil; but when such a man as the Hon. Mr. Morley, the Secretary of State for India, agrees with the Indian government in this matter, it may be presumed to have been necessary.

The government has also proclaimed and prohibited the assembling together of the people for political purposes in the most disaffected parts of the country, and more especially where the Hindus and Mohammedans are fighting each other. None can question the wisdom of thus saving the people from bitter feuds and the power of agitators.

Another very important action of the State has been to warn the students of the Universities against participating in political agitation, and to threaten the withdrawal of affiliation from institutions of learning in which political agitation is encouraged. Nobody will dispute the wisdom of this action; for the schoolboys of India seem as disloyal as they are irresponsible, and are the most pliant tools of radical demagogues.

The Press also is receiving the attention of the government. The vernacular Press is in special need of being taught the lesson of its responsibility to the people and to the State. And the best elements of the community, both Anglo-Indian and Indian, believe heartily that editors and proprietors of papers should be brought to account for their seditious utterances.

V

Many are now asking, "How shall this trouble be removed and peace and good-will be restored to the land?"

Nothing is more necessary than the cultivation of mutual understanding between the two races. It is very unfortunate that, in this matter, the situation has not improved during the last quarter of a century. Indeed, the racial problem is more acute now, as it is in America, than it was ever before. All seem too ready to accept, as conclusive, the statement of Kipling,—

> "O! the East is East and the West is West,
> And never the twain shall meet,
> Till earth and sky stand presently
> Before God's great judgment seat."

And they too easily ignore the other part which conveys his lesson, —

> "But there is neither East nor West,
> Nor border, nor breed, nor birth,
> Where two strong men stand face to face,
> Though they come from the ends of the earth."

The parties concerned in India to-day must learn the lesson of mutual forbearance and study to understand each other's peculiarities and enter more fully into each other's thoughts, sentiments, and idiosyncrasies.

The Anglo-Indian stands most in need of this lesson of aptitude. The Anglo-Saxon is notoriously conceited and given to thinking that he has nothing to learn from other people, especially those who are politically subject to him. He looks with contempt upon the "mild Hindu," and maintains that it is the business of Brahman and Sudra alike meekly to submit to, and obey, his lordship. He tramples upon their sensibilities and declines to learn any lessons of wisdom from them. On the other hand, Brahman and Sudra have ineradicable prejudices, which they nurse with extraordinary fondness and cherish with unyielding tenacity. The leader of this people, the Brahman, is, in his way, even more haughty than the Anglo-Indian.

This situation is full of difficulty. Here we have

two races, the Aryan of the East and the Aryan of the West, standing face to face. Each in its way claims dominance. The Westerner claims superiority by right of conquest and of advanced civilization and general progress. And he is not backward in presenting his vaunted claims! The Easterner, on the other hand, has ruled India by right of intelligence and by every claim of social and religious distinction, for at least thirty centuries. He stands to-day a match for any individual, East or West, in intellectual prowess. But, more than this, socially and religiously he regards himself as the first son of heaven. Contact with an Englishman, even with the King-Emperor himself, is for him pollution, which must be removed by elaborate and exacting religious ceremonies. To eat with any such would be a sin of the deepest dye. How can one expect such a man to meet with a foreigner on even terms, or to treat him with equality and true friendship? Before India loves its conquerors, and sympathy and good understanding are established between them, both parties need to be born again. At least they must endeavour to lay aside their prejudices and to cultivate the kinship of their united destiny. The writer recently listened to an eloquent address delivered by a cultured Hindu gentleman, in which he implored Anglo-Indians to cultivate their friendship and to forget the different shades of their complexion. The prejudice of colour is, he maintains, as strong in India as it is in America, and is perhaps more bitter than ever. A man, said he truly, should not be condemned by his brother because of his slightly different shade of colour, which is only skin deep.

It is also certain that Great Britain should and must give to the inhabitants of this land more influence and higher position in the direction of the affairs of the State. After a training of more than a century by England herself, India is prepared for a larger place in the direction of her own political destiny. Western civilization, western education, and the Christian religion have wrought wonders in India in the development of a new life and a new consciousness among many of the people. There are thousands of men, to-day, who are in every way competent to occupy high positions in government. And it is impossible that they should be kept loyal and contented under a régime which constantly reminds them of their subjection and their lack of worthiness to fill any but subordinate positions. It is true, as we have seen, that government is extending the privileges and multiplying the opportunities of such men.

But it is not doing this with the pace, the grace, and the heartiness that circumstances demand.

On the other hand, Indians must seek, increasingly, to cultivate social and moral aptitude, rather than to be forever claiming and demanding rights. The best friends of India believe that she has just as many political rights as she is able wisely to exercise. Representative Institutions have already been established here both in the conduct of Municipalities, District Boards, and of the Provincial and the Imperial Governments. The people are being trained for the wisest exercise of political rights. But many who have carefully observed the political corruption which they reveal in the exercise of already acquired rights, think that no greater evil could befall India than that of a sudden bestowal, by the State, of a great extension of these privileges.

The root of India's present incapacity for self-government is not intellectual, but social and moral. No one doubts that there is ability enough; but many believe that India must develop much upon the lower ranges of domestic sanity and social ethics before it is prepared for enhanced political privileges. The ignorance and the disabilities of women in India are a crying injustice, whose influence penetrates every department of Indian life, and for the removal of which educated Indians will hardly raise a finger.

The caste system, with its numberless stereotyped divisions, its myriad insurmountable barriers between class and class, and its countless petty jealousies and mutual antagonisms, is well known to all. And so long as Hindus continue to worship this demon, caste, it is impossible for them to become a united body to which, with any courtesy, the name Nation can be applied. Nor can they blend into such action as can in any sense be called National or patriotic. India is wofully lacking in the first essential of self-government — public spirit.

In other words, the most urgent need of India at present is social reform, which depends entirely upon the people, and not political reform, which must come from the State. And yet the social reform movement in India is less rapid to-day than at any time during the last quarter of a century. And those who cry loudest for political rights are the ones who cast a sinister eye upon the social reform movement.

And it must be remembered that the people who cry most loudly for national independence to-day are the very ones whose antecedents and whose fundamental conceptions of life and of society would forbid them to grant even the most elementary social, not to say political, rights to one-half of the population of the land. The way the Brahman and the higher Sudras, who are clamouring for what they regard God-given rights from the British government, deny in principle and practice, to their fellow-citizens, the so-called outcasts and other members of the community, the most elementary principles of liberty and privilege which they themselves now enjoy, is a significant comment upon their political sanity and sense of congruity.

In connection with this same problem, Indians should not forget that in the multiplicity of antipathies which exist between the many races of India, and in the religious conflicts, which too often arise, there is need, and there will be need for many years, of one supreme power which has the ability to hold the balance of justice evenly between race and race, and to command social and religious liberty to the three hundred millions of the land. And this is what Great Britain has done and is doing for India. *Pax Britannica* has been one of the greatest boons that the West has conferred upon the East.

It may also be well to add that Indians should have regard to the limits of the rights of a subject people.

It is useless to talk of self-government, until they are able to exercise the same; and even the most rabid Hindu cannot dream that India is ripe for self-government and could maintain it for a month if the British were to leave the country. And if the British must remain here at all, it must be as the dominant power. Canada and Australia, in their independence, may be ideals for India to pattern after; but India cannot enjoy the rights of those two independent colonies until her character becomes as steady, her ideas of liberty and her practice of social equality and her conception of human rights become as clarified, as they are in those two countries.

The recent proposal of the Government of India to enlarge the Legislative Councils and to create an Imperial Advisory Council reveals the purpose of the State to grant to the people all that is consistent with the paramountcy of the British in India. But it is this very paramountcy which the extremists deny to Great Britain. Herein lies the gist of the trouble. It will erelong create a serious *impasse*.

Great Britain cannot remain in this land and efface herself. At the same time, when India is prepared for absolute self-government, she will receive the blessing, and Great Britain will leave the land with a blessed consciousness that she has wrought for India the greatest blessing and the noblest achievement that any people has wrought for another and a foreign people in all the history of the world. And until that time comes, both India and Great Britain need to thank God that He has so strangely blended together their destinies for the highest elevation of both races.

CHAPTER II

THE HOME OF MANY FAITHS

THE land of the Vedas justly boasts of being the mother, or the foster-mother, of nine great religions. It has given birth to the greatest ethnic religion the world has seen; it is also the motherland of one of the three great missionary faiths of the world. These two religions — Hinduism and Buddhism — count among their followers more than a third of the human race, and are, in some respects, as vigorous now as at any time in their history.

It is the foster-mother of Mohammedanism and counts among her sons and daughters more of the followers of the Prophet of Mecca than are found in any other land.

It has also been the asylum of many followers of the Nazarene for at least sixteen centuries; many even claim that Christianity has found a home here since apostolic days.

There is no land comparable with India in the variegated expressions of its beliefs which add picturesqueness to the country and diversity to the people.

I purpose to take the reader with me on a tour with a view to furnishing glimpses of these religions at those places where they reveal special interest to the tourist.[1]

India is a land of immense distances. But its thirty thousand miles of railroad will enable the traveller, within a couple of months, to scan all its points of interest, and to feast his eyes upon visions of Oriental charm and splendour, of architectural beauty and grandeur, and of such monuments of religious devotion as no other land can present to the traveller and student.

Let not the Westerner indulge his fears about the discomforts and dangers of travel in this tropical land.

[1] The principal faiths of the land, with their adherents, were as follows, according to census of 1901:—

Hindu	207,147,026
Sikh	2,195,339
Jain	1,334,148
Buddhist	9,476,759
Parsee	94,190
Mohammedan	62,458,077
Jewish	18,228
Christian	2,923,241

These figures include Burma.

To an English-speaking tourist there are a few lands only which furnish more conveniences and facilities for travel than this same India; and travelling is cheaper here than in any other country. Comfortable second-class travelling rarely costs more than one cent a mile. And many, like the writer, have travelled thousands of miles in third-class compartments at less than half a cent a mile, and without much other inconvenience than an excess of dust and stiffened bones. The writer has seen many globe-trotters pass through India of whom few were not surprised at the relative comforts of travel here during the winter months, and no other time of the year should be chosen for travelling in India.

It will be convenient to start upon our tour from Madura, the missionary home of the writer. It is a large, wide-awake centre of enthusiastic Hinduism in the extreme south of the peninsula. In the heart of this town, of more than a hundred thousand people, stands its great temple, dedicated to Siva. The principal monuments of South India are its temples. They are the largest temples in the world. The Madura temple is only the third in size; but in its upkeep and architectural beauty it far surpasses the other two, which are larger. It covers an area of fifteen acres, and its many *Gopuras*, or towers, furnish the landmark of the country for miles around. It is erected almost entirely of granite blocks, some of which are sixty feet long. Its monolithic carving is exquisitely fine, as it is most abundant and elaborate. Hinduism may be moribund; but this temple gives only intimation of life and prosperity as one gazes upon its elaborate ritual, and sees the thousands passing daily into its shrine for worship. It represents the highest form of Hindu architecture, and, like almost all else that is Hindu, its history carries us to the dim distance of the past. But the great Tirumalai Nayak, the king of two and a half centuries ago, spent more in its elaboration than any one else. And it was he who built, half a mile away, the great palace which, though much reduced, still stands as the noblest edifice of its kind south of a line drawn from Bombay to Calcutta.

In this same temple we find, transformed, another cult. It is called the Temple of Meenatchi, after its presiding goddess, "the Fish-eyed One." When Brahmanism reached Madura, many centuries ago, Meenatchi was the principal demoness worshipped by the people, who were all devil-worshippers. As was their wont, the Brahmans did not antagonize the old faith of the people, but absorbed it by marrying Meenatchi to their chief god Siva, and thus incorporated the primitive devil-worship into the Brahmanical religion. Thus the Hinduism of Madura and of all South India is Brahmanism *plus* devil-worship. And the people are to-day much more absorbed in pacifying the devils which infest every village than they are in worshipping purely Hindu deities.

The prevailing faith of the Dravidians, therefore, is demonolatry; and the myriad shrines in the villages and hamlets, and the daily rites conducted in them, attest the universal prevalence of this belief and the great place it has in the life of these so-called Hindus.

A run of a hundred and fifty miles directly south brings us to Cape Comorin, the southernmost point of India. It is also the extreme south of Travancore, "the Land of Charity," and one of the richest and most charming sections of India. It is a Native State under the control of the Brahmans.

It is unique in the large proportion of Christians which are among its inhabitants. Though the Christian community in India averages only one per cent of the population, in the State of Travancore it amounts to 25 per cent. It is here that we find the ancient Syrian Church, with its three hun-

THE GOLDEN LILY TANK IN THE MADURA TEMPLE

dred and fifty thousand souls. Though it calls itself "the Thomasian, Apostolic Church," and though the Romish Church accepts the legend, modern historians deny its apostolic origin, and claim that it was founded no earlier than the third century. Even thus, it furnishes an intensely interesting study. The writer was deeply interested to see and enter its two churches at Kottayam, both of which are at least eight hundred years old.

Four centuries ago, Roman Catholicism used all the resources of the Inquisition in order to absorb this Church. They succeeded only too well, and half of the Indian Syrian Church is now subject to Rome. Nearly a century ago, the Church Missionary Society of England lent a helping hand to the Syrian Church, and has brought new life and progressive energy, and a new spiritual power and ambition, into a portion of that decrepit type of ancient Christianity.

Furthermore, a century of work given by the London Missionary Society and the Church Missionary Society has created a Protestant Christian community of more than one hundred thousand souls in that little kingdom alone.

We pass from Travancore into the little State of

Cochin, on the north. We are impressed by the colossal Christian church in the town of Cochin, in which, however, only a small handful of English people worship every Sunday evening. It was erected by the Portuguese four centuries ago, and is a charming study. It is here, shortly after Vasco da Gama had completed the first round-the-Cape journey, that this house of God was erected by his followers. Two centuries later, the Dutch came, conquered the Portuguese, occupied their house of worship, and desecrated their tombs. In that church to-day one can find tombstones inscribed on one side by the Portuguese to their departed friends, and, on the other side, in Dutch, to commemorate departed Hollanders.

But the most interesting sight, by far, in this quiet old Indian town, is the community of white Jews who live on its southern side. No one knows when they came here. They probably arrived at the Dispersion of the first century of our era; or it may be later. But the community must have been reënforced from time to time, as they have maintained, in a marvellous way, the fairness of their complexion. It will not require much imagination, as one enters their synagogue, to think of the synagogue of Nazareth of old. As we ascend the stairway into the little schoolroom above, and hear the little ones reciting, in pure Hebrew, passages from the Pentateuch, we can easily imagine that we are listening to the voice of a dear little Boy, nineteen centuries ago, reciting to His master those same passages in that same tongue in Palestine. There is hardly a place on earth where Judaism has met with fewer vicissitudes and changes than on this western coast of India.

It is only a couple of hundred yards farther away that we find the synagogue of the black Jews — the descendants of those who were given by the ancient king to be slaves to the white Jews. They adopted the religion of their masters, and are still praying, like their masters, for the coming of the Messiah, of whose arrival and triumphs in India they seem to be oblivious.

Leaving Cochin, we pass along the coast as far as Bombay, which has been called the "Eye of India," and also the "Gateway of India," two names which are equally appropriate to this beautiful city. There is hardly another city on earth where more races and religions blend. And its streets are made exceedingly picturesque by the many costumes of its polyglot population. Before the arrival of the plague, some eight years ago, Bombay was perhaps the most populous city in India. But this fell scourge has decimated its population and has robbed it of much of its ambition.

Perhaps the most interesting people that we see here are the Parsees, with their "Towers of Silence." According to their belief, earth is too sacred to be contaminated, and fire too divine to be polluted, by the bodies of their dead, which, therefore, they expose in the towers, erected upon an adjacent hill, to be consumed by a crowd of hungry, expectant vultures. One usually sees forty or fifty of these filthy birds standing around the edge of each tower, watching the funeral cortège as it slowly winds its way up the hill, eager to pounce upon the body as soon as exposed by the bearers in the centre within. And from the time of exposure it takes hardly ten minutes before every particle of flesh has been consumed.

The one hundred thousand Parsees of Bombay are almost the only representatives of the ancient faith of Zoroaster, perhaps the purest of all ethnic religions. They were driven out of their home land of Persia in the early onrush of Mohammedan fury, and fled, twelve centuries ago, to India, where they found asylum.

The Parsees have the distinction of being the most advanced people of India, alike in wealth and philanthropy, in their treatment of woman, and in education and general culture. Their influence throughout the land is far beyond their numbers. And yet they are so narrow in their conception of their faith, that they declined, the other day, to receive into their fold the English bride of one of their number. Thus they decided that there is no door of entrance into their religion for any one who is not a born Parsee.

It is in this city, also, that we find a large representation of another ancient cult—Jainism.

Jainism is closely kin to Buddhism. It represents the same type of reaction from a debased Brahmanism. As its name indicates, it is a cult for the worship of "The Victorious Ones," that is, men who by self-discipline have triumphed over their passions and have attained perfection. Buddhism succumbed to, and was absorbed by, a new militant Brahmanism, which we call Hinduism. Jainism, on the other hand, has maintained itself as a distinct faith and now has 1,334,148 followers. Like Buddhism, it is an agnostic religion, knowing no object of worship save the seventy-two Victorious Ones.

One of the leading characteristics of Jainism is its love of life, even in its lowest manifestation. Their devotion to this article of their faith is carried to such an extent that the devout will sweep the road lest they step upon insects, and cover their mouth with gauze cloth lest they swallow and destroy minute forms of life. In the city of Bombay, Jains have a hospital for animals, for the maintenance of which they spend large sums of money annually. Maimed cattle, stray dogs and cats, and decrepit animals of all kinds are sought and brought here for asylum and care. It is even said, I cannot say with how much truth, that they employ men to come and spend nights here with a view to furnishing food for the many kinds of vermin which infest the place.

In a sumptuous through train we now pass rapidly over nearly one thousand miles of a country which is intensely interesting, historically and ethnologically, and finally arrive in the famous city of Agra, which stands supreme among Indian cities as a centre of architectural beauty. We have here come into a distinctively Mohammedan region; and the edifices which crown the city with glory are not only con-

Taj Mahal, Agra

nected with the Mohammedan faith, they are also the masterpieces of the greatest minds of the Mogul Empire, and culminate in the Taj Mahal, which is the most valued gem of Mohammedan architecture, and, perhaps, the most beautiful edifice in the world. We first turn our face toward the Fort, which is one of the magnificent fortresses of India. Two and a half centuries ago, Shah Jehan was the ruling Mogul. He was not only one of the greatest rulers of the dynasty; he had also a passion for building, and was a man of rare taste as an architect. The Agra Fort, whose stern walls of red sandstone extend about a mile and a half, represents to us, at present, not strength and protection, but an enclosure within which the emperor built his great palace, which is a marvel of beauty and of superb architectural workmanship. The most attractive of the many parts of this palace is the Pearl Mosque, which "owes its charm to its perfect proportions, its harmony of designs, and its beauty of material, rather than to richness of decoration and ornament. In design it is similar to most temples of this kind; a court-yard with a fountain in the middle, surrounded on three sides by arcaded cloisters; while on the entrance side and that facing it are exquisitely chaste marble screens." "Into the fair body of the

India marble the Moguls could work designs and arabesques borrowed from the Persia of ancient history, and flowers of exquisite hue and symmetry suggested by the more advanced and civilized Florentine artists, who were tempted over by the well-filled coffers of Shah Jehan." As the Pearl Mosque was a part of the palace, it was only used by the royal court. Days of pleasure and improvement could be spent in the study of the various parts which have been preserved of this ancient palace. But we pass on a few miles to the Taj Mahal, which, like most of the best buildings of Mohammedan art in North India, is a mausoleum and was erected by Shah Jehan to his favourite wife, Mumtaz-i-Mahal. The Taj is erected in a beautiful garden, the gateway into which is perhaps the finest in India and is "a worthy pendant to the Taj itself." The garden is exquisitely laid out, with a view to setting off the unspeakable charms of that "dream of loveliness embodied in white marble." The Taj has well been described as a work "conceived by Titans and finished by jewellers." The grandeur of the conception and the wonderful delicacy of the workmanship cannot fail to impress even the most unlearned in the architectural art. Much has been written, and all in unstinted praise, of this incomparable edifice; and

Marble Screen in Taj Mahal

yet, like the writer, every visitor comes to its presence, feels the growing thrill of its beauty, and exclaims, "The half was never told!" And few leave the place without returning to be enthralled once more by a moonlight view of this thing of beauty. How great, indeed, must have been the love of that otherwise cruel monarch for his departed empress that he should have exhausted so much of wealth (some say that the Taj cost thirty million rupees) and conceived so much of beauty wherewith to embalm her memory. And as we enter the mausoleum and stand in the presence of the lovely shrines which it encases,—that of Mumtaz-i-Mahal, and that of the emperor himself,—the mind is awed and may find expression in Sir Edwin Arnold's poetic fancy,—

> "Here in the heart of all,
> With chapels girdled, shut apart by screens,
> The shrine's self stands, white, delicately white,
> White as the cheek of Mumtaz-i-Mahal,
> When Shah Jehan let fall a king's tear there.
> White as the breast her new babe vainly pressed
> That ill day in the camp at Burhanpur,
> The fair shrine stands, guarding two cenotaphs."

And upon a panel of his own shrine the mourning emperor had inscribed these significant words from ancient traditions: "Saith Jesus, on whom peace be, this world is a bridge. Pass thou over it, but build not upon. This world is one hour; give its minutes to thy prayers, for the rest is unseen."

We cannot but feel that the Taj is the highest expression of art that human affection and domestic affliction have ever achieved. This is not religion; but it is closely kin to it.

Not far from the Fort is found another great mosque, or *musjid*, where the Mohammedans crowd for worship. This, also, is a wonderful specimen of art, and in its combination of simplicity and beauty is well calculated to rouse to enthusiasm the many worshippers of Allah.

About six miles away from Agra is another specimen of architectural genius. It is the tomb of Akbar the Great. Some believe it to be almost equal to the Taj. It commemorates with great beauty the noble name of that most distinguished man of the whole Mogul dynasty,—a man who was famed for his breadth of view and sympathy, his wise statesmanship, and religious tolerance. He did more than any other to create sympathy between Hindus and Mohammedans. It was in this mausoleum that the famous Kohinor diamond found its place and was exhibited for years. It is a striking fact that this precious stone

Shah Jehan's Fort, Agra

was undisturbed there, in the open air, for over seventy years, until the Shah of Persia, in 1739, invaded India and sacked the palace of the Moguls, and, with other fabulous wealth, carried this diamond also back to his own country.

Delhi is only a few hours' ride to the north from Agra. It is perhaps the most interesting city in all India. From the earliest times of Brahmanic legends down to the present, it has been the centre of war and conflict, of royal display, extravagance, and treachery. Here, again, Mohammedanism has, from the first, exercised its power and revealed its religious warmth and enthusiasm. The Mohammedan mosques are equal to any in the land. And though the Persian sacked the city a hundred and seventy years ago, and robbed it of most that was beautiful and valuable, there still remains a part of what was probably the loveliest palace that was ever erected. It reveals to us also "the imperial grandeur of the Moguls, whose style of living was probably more splendid than that of any monarchs of any nation before or since that time. Their extravagance was unbounded. Their love of display has never been surpassed." It is claimed that the Peacock Throne of this Delhi Palace was of sufficient value to pay the debts of a nation. The marble walls are richly adorned with exquisite mosaics. Indeed, they are regarded as incomparable specimens of the art. One can pardon the builder who engraved over the north and south entrances to this palace of the Moguls the following lines:—

> "If there be a Paradise on Earth,
> It is This! It is This! It is This!"

Eleven miles from the city are found splendid ruins which are crowned by the celebrated tower known as Kutab-minar, which is another of the most ancient and interesting monuments of India. Originally, this remarkable structure was a Hindu temple, and was erected probably in the fourth century of our era. But upon the invasion of the Mussulmans the temple was converted into a Mohammedan mosque, and the famous tower, which is 238 feet high, and is one of the most beautifully erected in the world, was allowed to stand. "The sculptures that cover its surface have been compared to those upon the column of Trajan in Rome and the Column Vendome in Paris; but they are intended to relate the military triumphs of the men in whose honour they were erected, while the inscription on the Kutab-minar is a continuous recognition of the power and glory of God and of the virtues of Mohammed, his Prophet."

Akbar's Tomb

It is in this city that one is impressed most thoroughly with memorials of the great Mutiny of half a century ago, where the British were so hard pushed and suffered so terribly in those days of bitterness which tried men's souls. And there is no memorial of this bitter struggle, to which the British refer with so much of pride and glory, as they do to the Cashmere gate, which they blew up and thereby forced an entrance into the city, with a loss of much precious blood.

But it was not the Mutiny nor the massive and gorgeous emblems of Mohammedanism which impressed the writer most in this city. It was a vision just outside the walls of the city — a vision of great simplicity — which thrilled his heart a few years ago. It was a very unattractive little ruined tower, from the centre of which rose a polished granite pillar, some thirty or forty feet high. It was inscribed from top to bottom, and the inscription was quite legible. It spoke not of the triumphs of war nor of the glory of human rule and conquest. It is one of the most eloquent testimonies to the nobility of the Buddhist faith. It was carried here only a few centuries ago by an enlightened Mohammedan monarch from the far-off plains of the north. It is one of the celebrated "Asoka Pillars."

Asoka was the emperor of twenty-two centuries ago who wrought for Buddhism what Constantine the Great, at a later day, wrought for Christianity. He was converted to Buddhism and at once became the devout propagator of that faith. As the great emperor of his time, he exalted Buddhism and made it the State religion of India. He not only sent his missionaries all over the land; he decreed that its principal teachings should be everywhere inscribed upon rocks and upon pillars; and that these pillars should be erected in public places for the instruction of the people. This pillar in Delhi is one of about a dozen already discovered and preserved in North India. And it is, perhaps, the most fully inscribed of all that have been found. And of the fourteen Asokan edicts inscribed, most of them inculcate a high morality, and some of them a noble altruism. For instance, the first is a prohibition of the slaughter of animals for food or sacrifice. The second is the provision for medical aid for men and animals, and for plantations and wells on the roadside. The third is a command to observe every fifth year as a year of mutual confession of sins, of peace-making, and of humiliation. The ninth is the inculcation of true happiness as found in virtue. In all these inscribed edicts of that most tolerant and cos-

KUTAB-MINAR, DELHI

mopolitan Buddhist emperor, we see nothing of which Buddhism should be ashamed, and much of which it may be proud, in the way of ethical injunction. It is more than ten centuries since Buddhism, which had been the common faith of India for a thousand years, was absorbed into a new militant Hinduism and ceased to exist as a separate faith in this land. To-day, India proper has hardly half a million Buddhists. And yet we behold these mute prophets of far-off days scattered in many parts of the land, still pressing their message, but vainly, indeed, upon a people of unknown tongues. Buddha himself is now a part of the Hindu Pantheon; and his principal teachings have become an essential part of the faith which he tried to overthrow. But these pillars stand for Buddhism that was tolerant toward all save, perhaps, the Brahmanism which it existed to overthrow.

From Delhi we pass on northward to the beautiful city of Amritsar, which is comparatively a modern town of one hundred and fifty thousand people. In the heart of this town stands the far-famed Golden Temple of the Sikhs, built by Ranjit Singh, — "The Lion of the Panjaub." The temple is not a large one, being only fifty-three feet square, and is built in the centre of a water tank, called "The Pool of Immortality." The peculiar external feature of the temple is that it is largely covered with gold plate; hence its name. It is a beautiful object to behold; and we are in haste to take off our shoes, which are prohibited in the sacred precincts, and to put on the shapeless holy slippers presented to us! We enjoy perfect freedom in passing through all parts of the temple, while devotees, under the guidance of the priests, sing their songs of praise with devout impartiality to their god and to their bible.

The temple is the centre and inspiration of the Sikh religion. The Sikhs are an interesting people. They rallied round one of the multitude of the Hindu religious reformers, named Nanak Shah, who established this cult about the end of the fifteenth century. It may be called an amalgam of Mohammedanism and Hinduism. It unites the monotheism and the stern morality of the former with much of the petty ritual of the latter. It does not observe caste. Still, in outer matters of observances, Sikhs are not easily distinguishable from ordinary Hindus. They, also, have bound themselves into a military order, which gives them almost the distinction of a nation. For this reason they are among the very best material which the country furnishes for the native army, and

CASHMERE GATE, DELHI

are worthy to stand shoulder to shoulder with European soldiers.

This religion is peculiarly a *book* religion. It has degenerated into a species of bibliolatry. Their bible contains the teachings and sermons of the founder of the faith; and it presents the highest standard of morality and courage, and appeals with special power to this sturdy tribe of the north. This book is called "Granth," and is generally spoken of as "Granth Sahib," which we may translate as "Mr. Book"! That is, they give it a dignity and a personality which is unique in any faith; and the Golden Temple is largely used as the receptacle of the "Granth," of which they keep a few copies protected by covers, which, however, they remove in order to show them to us as we pass by.

In several particulars this faith is unique. They have no idols or altars, but meet once a week for prayer and praise. Their preacher reads passages from the "Granth" and prays to their god, who may be reached through the intercession of Nanak Shah, his prophet and their redeemer. They sing hymns similar to those used in Protestant worship, and celebrate communion by partaking of wafers of unleavened bread. Their congregation do not object to the presence of strangers, but usually invite them to participate in the worship. There are about two and a quarter million Sikhs in the Province of the Panjaub, — the land of the "five rivers."

While in this city, one is tempted to look at the Khalsa College, one of the institutions established by government in different parts of the land for the suitable training of native princes. Here one may find young Sikh nobles and wealthy landlords, to the number of five hundred, being qualified for the high responsibilities which are before them.

We hurry back from the north in a southeastern direction over a distance of eight hundred miles and reach the city of Benares, on the river Ganges. There is hardly a river in the world which produces more fertility and which brings sustenance to more people than the divine Ganges. The river is not only deified, but is regarded as one of the most potent deities of India.

From time immemorial, Benares, or "Kasi," which is built upon the banks of the Ganges, has partaken of the sanctity of the river, and is regarded by devout Hindus as the most sacred spot in the world. To die within the radius of ten miles from its centre is sure and eternal bliss, even to the outcast and the defiling white man! Many thousands are brought annually from all parts of the land to die at this sacred place, and have their ashes scattered upon the waters of the holy river. Many thousands of others who die in all parts of the land have their bodies burned and their ashes brought, by loving relatives upon pilgrimage, to this city to be sprinkled upon the tides of the Ganges, which insures eternal rest to the departed souls.

What Mecca is to Mohammedans, more than Jerusalem is to Jews, is Benares to devout Hindus. It has more temples and shrines than any other equal area in the world. Its priests, who are called *Gangaputhira* ("the Sons of the Ganges"), are legion. They have their emissaries at principal railway stations for hundreds of miles from the city, always on the lookout for pilgrims, and gathering up pilgrim bands to lead them on with ever increasing numbers to their temples. The idols of this city are legion.

But there is nothing here which impresses one more than its squalid filth, and the abject degradation of the people which crowd its streets. The temples are extremely dirty. There is not one of imposing size or of decent attractiveness. There stands the monkey-temple, where scores of mangy, tricky brutes are daily sumptuously fed by devout pilgrims. On one side of the precinct a clever butcher-priest severs with one stroke the heads of goats which are brought for sacrifice to the thirsty deity. As in Madura, so in Benares, the great god of the Hindu is Siva. But the character of the worship which is rendered to him and to others of his cult is far from ennobling when not actually revolting. And the phallic emblem of this god is everywhere found in his temples and is suggestive of definite evils connected with his worship.

The saddest and most grewsome of all objects which impress one in this centre of Hinduism is its burning Ghaut. To the side of the river many bodies are brought daily, each wrapped in a white cloth, and are deposited just where they are half covered by the water. Within ten feet of this place we see parties of pilgrims bathing in and drinking of the sacred water of the river, utterly regardless of the proximity of corpses above stream! From time to time corpses are picked out of the water and placed upon piles of wood near by. Each pile is ignited and the body reduced to ashes. These ashes are carefully collected, later on, and sprinkled, with appropriate ceremonies, on the face of the river. Day after day, and year after year, this ceaseless procession of the dead takes place, while up stream and down stream the bank of the river is covered with men and women who fatally believe that by bathing in this dirty stream they are washing away their sins and preparing themselves for final absorption and eternal rest in Brahm!

Benares reminded the writer of Rome. He never realized the degradation possible to Christianity until he visited "The Eternal City," with its huge shams and ghastly superstitions. He never saw Hinduism with its myriad inane rites and debasing idolatry half so grotesque, idiotic, and repulsive, as in this city of Benares, where one ought to see the religion of these two hundred odd million people at its best, and not at its worst.

It is a positive relief to go out of the city, a distance of four miles, to Sarnath, where the great Buddha — "The Enlightened One" — spent many long years in establishing his faith and in inculcating his "Doctrine of the Wheel." It is a beautiful drive to the birthplace of one of the greatest world faiths. Very little but ruins meets the inquiring gaze of the visitor. Some of these, however, are very impressive, especially the great *stupa*, or tower. It now stands a hundred and ten feet high and ninety-three feet in diameter. It was very substantially built, the lower part faced by immense blocks of stones which were clamped together with iron. And this facing was covered with elaborate inscriptions. The upper part was built of brick. At the foot of this striking ruin, built in the remote past as a monument to an ancient faith, devout Buddhists from all parts of the world come for worship and meditation upon the vanity of life. The day before the writer arrived, the Lama of Tibet spent here a few hours worshipping and seeking the blessing of the "Enlightened One." Near by, government is making a series of excavations and is discovering very interesting relics connected with this ancient monastery founded by the Buddha. Already a beautiful specimen of an Asoka pillar and a variety of interesting sculptures have rewarded their industry. One can imagine no place more dear to the contemplative Buddhist than this centre of the activities of his great Master, where he spent many of the best years of his life in expounding the teachings of his new cult, and in leading many souls toward the light for which he had struggled with so much of heroic self-denial, and which had ultimately dawned upon him under the sacred Boh tree at Buddha Gaya.

In this extended pilgrimage, during which we have sought ancient and modern expressions of the many faiths which have dominated, or which now dominate, the people of this land, we have come into touch not only with those tolerant faiths which have found their origin here, or which have found refuge and popularity in this peninsula,—such as Hinduism, Demonolatry, Buddhism, Jainism, Zorastrianism, and Sikhism. We have also come into touch with the three most intolerant faiths of the world,—Christianity, Mohammedanism, and Judaism. There is no land where these three religions have suffered less of opposition than in India. Indeed, it is not from persecution and opposition that they have stood in most danger, but from fraternal contact, growing appreciation, and ultimate absorption. The Hindu mind, like the Hindu faith, has a fatal facility for accepting, semi-assimilating, and finally absorbing, all of religious belief and conviction that may come into contact with it. And this never necessarily involves the abandoning of the old beliefs.

CHAPTER III

BURMA, THE BEAUTIFUL

In order to appreciate the wide extent of the British Empire in the East, one needs to travel over the main lines of India and then steam a thousand miles across the Bay of Bengal to Burma. Landing at Rangoon, which is the doorway of the land, he reëmbarks upon one of the sumptuous Irrawady River boats and steams northward another thousand miles into the very heart of the country. Thus without leaving the eastern empire one can spend weeks of most interesting travel, and pass through territories inhabited by peoples of separate racial types and of totally different tongues. Perhaps no other region of the world can furnish such a variety of climes and such marked contrasts of national habits and costumes. And yet, all this vast territory has been brought into subjection to the British crown and furnishes facilities and conveniences of travel which are really marvellous in the East. Burma is politically and industrially a part of India.

It is a rich country, with four magnificent rivers reaching nearly its whole length, furnishing abundant facilities for cheap travel and commerce, and carrying fertility into all sections of the land.

It is the land of rice, of teak, and of oil. These are the triple sources of Burmese industry, commerce, and wealth. Never was a land richer than this in alluvial soil, in refreshing rains, and in bountiful rivers. It is one great expanse of living, paddy green. The teak timber furnished by the mighty forests of this land is carried to many lands. The extent of this trade may be imagined from the statement that the Bombay-Burma Trading Company in Burma employs three thousand elephants for hauling its timber to the river. Every two elephants are under the care of three men; so that there are forty-five hundred men in charge of these animals alone.

Burma is called the "Land of Pagodas." The first object which attracts the eye soon after the ship enters the river, and while still twenty miles from the harbour, is the far-famed pagoda of Schwey Dagon, in Rangoon. Buddhism is preëminently the faith of Burma. All the people have been for many centuries its adherents. And the pagoda is the outward emblem of that faith. What the church is to Christianity, and the temple is to Hinduism, the pagoda (sometimes called "dagoba") is to Buddhism. It is the farthest removed from the Christian conception of a place of worship. In Christianity, large edifices are erected where the multitude can meet to unite in public worship. In Hinduism, a temple is largely the abode of the idol, which is the outward emblem of their god. In it there is no place for public worship or for an assembled audience. In Buddhism, there is not even a god to worship, so that there is no interior to the pagoda. It is like the pyramid of Egypt, one massive solid structure, but of an elongated bell shape. The highest part of it, corresponding to the handle of the bell, is called "hti," and is usually covered with precious metal. It is a reliquary rather than a place of worship; and every pagoda of note is supposed to be the receptacle of a few hairs or bones of the Buddha! Indeed, if one believe the members of that faith, the anatomy of that great man was marvellous and is still very promiscuously distributed through various lands of the East!

The Schwey Dagon pagoda is a very prominent object; for it is not only three hundred and seventy

Schwey Dagon Pagoda, Rangoon

feet high, but is also built on an artificial mound which is a hundred and seventy feet in height. It is elaborately decorated, and its "hti" is mostly of solid gold, encrusted with precious stones presented to the pagoda by King Mindoon Min. But while the pagoda itself impresses one with its massive proportions, it is the exquisite group of numberless little shrines or temples which surround the pagoda, every one of which holds one or more large images of the great Buddha, that furnish the rich sense of beauty and charm which prevail. These little shrines are either built of marble or of richly carved teak, or of glass mosaic; and every one tries to excel every other in its delicate charm. And upon nearly every one of these shrines there are sweet little bells, which, as the wind blows, seem to respond to spirit hands and ring forth their gentle peals of sacred music to the great founder of the faith.

Here, also, is a massive bell of forty tons, — the third in size in the world. It was once carried away by the British and lost in the Rangoon River. But the people later received permission to search for it. They found it, and with genuine pride and triumph raised it and restored it to their pagoda.

It is one of the peculiar ironies of history that

in this land of the Buddha, who was the greatest iconoclast, and who not only abhorred idolatry but also ignored deity, there should exist to-day numberless images of him in every town and hamlet. These are of all sizes, from the immense reclining Buddha of Pegu, which is a hundred and eighty-two feet long, and is built of brick and mortar, down to the tiniest figures carried on the persons of individuals. There is no pagoda or shrine in Burma around which is not found a large number of these images. They have not the hideous deformity of Hindu idolatry; but present either the benign and complacent, or the calm and contemplative, expression which cannot fail to impress itself upon the national character of the people. And one may say, with confidence, that in this matter the truth of the proverb is verified, — "Like god, like people."

One may leave Rangoon in a comfortable train, and in about eighteen hours reach the old capital of Upper Burma, the beautiful Mandalay, which is nearly four hundred miles distant. The same journey may be taken by the river Irrawady if one has more leisure and means; and he may thus enjoy one of the most beautiful and sumptuous river journeys in the world.

It was only twenty years ago that this part of the country was seized by the British without bloodshed, and the foolish and dissolute King Theebaw was made prisoner for his stupid insolence, and deported, with his two wives, to India, where they are still spending their days in retirement. Upper Burma has, however, put on new beauty and prosperity since the British have taken it over; and the people are abundantly satisfied with the new régime. Mandalay has also its famed Arrakan pagoda, which claims to have the only contemporary likeness of Buddha on earth. It is an immense brazen image; and it is the occupation of the devout to gild the same with gold-leaf. At least a dozen men and women can be seen thus constantly expressing their devotion. In a few years there will be tons of gold thus pasted upon his sacred body! But alas for the vandalism which lights up its shrine and the calm face of Buddha by electricity!

Another famous pagoda of Mandalay is the so-called "Four Hundred and Fifty Pagodas of the Law." This is a kind of Buddhist bible in stone. It has four hundred and fifty small shrines, every one of which has a large polished granite slab, upon which is engraved a precept of the faith; and the whole make up a complete body of the law, which every member of the faith may come and read at his leisure.

Here, as at all shrines, we notice the beautiful custom of these Burmese people in practising their public devotion with bouquets of flowers in their hands. It is touching to see this constant blending of beauty with piety. The abundant use of the candle, also, in their worship reminds us of the Romish ritual.

We are taken through the royal gardens and the deserted palaces of Mandalay, which are constructed largely, as many of the houses of Burma are, of exquisitely carved teak, rising here and there in pointed spires, which are indeed beautiful, but which give the impression of the so-called gingerbread style of architecture.

Upon one who has lived for many years in India there are two things in Burma which make a deep and a very pleasing impression.

In the first place, the charm of the Burmese woman is marked. She has none of the cringing, retiring, self-conscious mien of the Hindu women. She is possessed of liberty and of equality with man.

THEEBAW'S PALACE, MANDALAY

Her appearance in society is both modest and self-respecting. She is conscious of her own beauty, and knows how to enhance it with exquisite taste. She is a great lover of colours, as is the Hindu woman. But the latter loves only the primitive and elementary colours; the former, on the other hand, cultivates the delicate shades, and adorns herself with silks of various tints, such as attract and fascinate. It is for this reason that Burma is called "The Silken East." Her dress is clumsy and uncouth in form, and, in this respect, is incomparably inferior to the graceful cloth of India. But the woman herself is lovely, and the taste which she displays in her personal adornment is very attractive. It does not surprise one to know that not a few Europeans marry these Burmese ladies of beauty. But above her beauty is that pose of freedom and self-respect which commends her everywhere. Nor is this assumed. The woman of Burma is "the man of the family." In business, and in all forms of trade, she is far superior to her lord, and much of the support and the honour of the family depends upon her industry, cleverness, and independence. Certainly Buddhism has produced, in many respects, a higher type of womanhood than has Hinduism.

Another aspect of life in Burma is one that instantly captivates one who goes there from India. It is a land free from the trammels of caste. The trail of this serpent is upon all things in India. It divides men at all points, and robs social life of much that is sweet and beautiful in other lands. The great Gautama vehemently attacked the Brahmanical caste system, and one is glad to see in Burma that that faith has adhered to this primitive enmity. One rejoices to see at the temples and on the public streets, everywhere, common eating and drinking houses, where the people meet for refreshment and for quiet social chat, without any thought of caste to disturb their relationship and mar their convivial pleasures.

That which impresses the observant Christian visitor to that land is the triumph and wonderful achievement of missionary effort there during the last half century.

All know the works, the sufferings, and the results attained by that great prophet of Burma, Adoniram Judson. He was a saint of the heroic mould, and his influence will affect the history of that people for centuries to come.

The American Baptist Mission overshadows, by

its numbers and success, all other bodies of missionaries in the land. And at the present time their splendid force of workers is making a deep impress upon the community.

But their success has been mostly achieved among a very peculiar hill-tribe of that country,—the Karens. It was long after the Baptists had begun work there that this low hill-tribe, of less than two million people, was in the lowest depths of barbarism. Their language was not reduced to writing, and consequently, they had no literature whatever. But they had one interesting tradition. It had come down to them, generation after generation, that their bible had been lost, and that some day the Great Spirit would send a fair brother from the West to restore unto them the message of God which had disappeared. The "Fair Brother" came in the person of the American missionary; and his message was received in the assured faith that it was divinely sent and was the long-lost tradition of their tribe. From that day forward, thousands of the Karen tribe have everywhere accepted the Gospel of the Christ, until there are, at the present time, connected with that mission alone, more than one hundred and fifty thousand Karen converts.

And this is by no means all of the wonderful story of the regeneration of this barbarous tribe. Either by a very wise missionary statesmanship, or by a rare inspiration, such as we do not see elsewhere in the East, these people have almost entirely assumed the financial burdens of their own religious training and institutions, and are always quick, even beyond their means, to respond to every Gospel claim upon their purse. The story of their offerings, in view of their extreme poverty, is marvellous in its self-denial and outgoing generosity. The writer spent a few days at the missionary centre in the outskirts of Rangoon. Upon that compound there was a memorial church that had cost $30,000, of which the Karen Christians had given all, save a grant made by government for a few adjoining class-rooms. Three bungalows and other buildings of value are also found there, and the whole property is owned, not by the mission, but by the Karens themselves. Ten miles away from this is the largest theological seminary in the East, with more than one hundred and forty students under training. For the maintenance of this, again, those poor Karen Christians gladly impose upon themselves a family tax, and have the sweet consciousness that their youth are being trained for Christian service through their own self-denying endeavour.

These people were in social scale so low that they had practically no music of their own. They have therefore readily taken to western music. And it is astonishing to hear how well they sing our western tunes, and even render solos and quartettes at public European functions in a way that calls forth hearty encores. It is verily the birth of a nation in a day. So that in this land of many wonders the movement among the Karen people seems to be the most wonderful of all.

Among the Karens, Ko San Ye stands forth as a unique figure of intense interest. He has been called the "Moody" of Burma. He is absolutely illiterate. When about thirty years old, he lost his wife and his only child; and finding no comfort in his ancestral demonolatry, he turned to Buddhism for relief and retired to a mountain retreat and became known and esteemed among his people as a devout ascetic and a holy man. With the offerings of his people he built two pagodas and a monastery. But his soul found no rest there. In 1890, he was baptized as a Christian, with one hundred and forty of his followers. He then obtained a grant of twenty thousand acres of waste land from government, and established a village which now numbers several hundred houses. His influence over his own people is amazing, and is the result of superstitious reverence and awe.

He regretted that his ignorance prevented him from preaching the Gospel; but he thought that his influence over the people should be rightly used in the Lord's service. So he devoted himself to the collection of funds for religious purposes among his people. And in this work he has had almost fatal success, for his fellow-Christian Karens have responded to his appeals for money to the extent of at least $130,000. In view of the exceeding poverty of the people, this sum seems almost fabulous. Mr. Ko San Ye is known by all to be perfectly disinterested in the use of the money intrusted to him. Not a cent sticks to his hands; and he reverently and truthfully speaks of it as the "Lord's money." But his judgment is not commensurate with his piety. Even the most friendly cannot say that he has wisely administered this sacred trust of his poor brethren. He has erected churches, schools, and rest-houses which are altogether too sumptuous for the people. He spent thousands in the purchase of a fine steam-launch for the convenience of his people on the river side. He then purchased a rice-mill which brings a fair income to the mission. He has added to these two fine and expensive automobiles, in the smaller of which the writer had, for him, the unique pleasure of a delightful spin through the city of Rangoon and its suburbs, under the guidance of a Karen chauffeur! It was his first automobile ride; and to think of it as being enjoyed in a vehicle bought by poor Christians of Burma! Strange to say, the people continue to repose implicit confidence in him, even to the extent of mortgaging their property, in order to add to this public fund. It is to be hoped that this good man may soon submit more to missionary guidance.

Ko San Ye is but an interesting episode in the wonderful progress of a nation from the depth of barbarism to Christian privilege and civilized life. The missionaries often dare not have him present during the baptism of new converts, lest they should think that they were baptized in the name of Ko San Ye rather than in the name of Christ! And yet it is said that the two leading characteristics of this strange man are his humility and his unselfishness!

The Karens, with all their lowliness and barbarous antecedents, are excellent material to work upon, and are responding with wonderful eagerness to the missionary endeavour made in their behalf, and are already, in many noble qualities, revealing to the native Christians of the East the way of ascent to nobility of character and to the highest Christian possession.

CHAPTER IV

THE HINDU CASTE SYSTEM

THE word "caste" is derived from the Latin term *castus*, which signified purity of breed. It was the term used by Vasco da Gama and his fellow-Portuguese adventurers, four centuries ago, as they landed upon the southwestern coast of India and began to study the social and religious condition of the people. The word expressed to them the remarkable bond which held the people together; the subsequent generations of foreigners and English-speaking natives have adopted it as the most appropriate term to express the unique system which prevails all over India. No other people, in the history of the world, have erected a social structure comparable to this of India. For twenty-five centuries it has controlled the life of nearly one-sixth of the human race. Other countries have, or have had, tribal connections, class distinctions, trade unions, religious sects, philanthropic fraternities, social guilds, and various other organizations. But India is the only land where all these are practically welded together into one consistent and mighty whole, which dictates the every detail of human relationship and controls the whole destiny of man for time and eternity. For it should be remembered that India has consistently declined to recognize any distinction between the social and the religious. These are the reverse and the obverse of life; they are brought to the same rules and must yield obedience to the same authority. Religion, to the Hindu, permeates the whole social domain; and social order draws its sanctions from, and is enforced by the penalties of, religion. To marry outside one's caste, to eat food cooked by an outcast, to cross the ocean, to delay unduly the marriage of a daughter, — these, and a thousand other delinquencies which may seem absolutely harmless to a Westerner, are not only regarded as social irregularities, but also as sins whose penalties will harass the soul beyond the grave or burning-ground. Herein does caste reveal its uniqueness, and from this does it pass on to the exercise of its extraordinary tyranny over the people.

I

The origin of caste is a subject of much uncertainty and debate. In ancient Vedic times, caste was unknown. Society, in those days, was more elastic and free, and resembled that of other lands. And yet it showed a tendency toward a mechanical division which later grew into the caste system. It was not until the time of the great lawgiver, Manu, about twenty-five centuries ago, that the system crystallized into laws, and the organization became so compact as to force itself upon all the people and become an integral part of recognized Hindu law. Manu and other lawgivers found the basis of caste rules in the traditions of an ancient Brahman tribe. These they elaborated and enforced.

The ancient name for caste was *varna*, which means "colour." This name is suggestive, and has led many authorities to trace back the whole system to original race-purity, as indicated by the colour of the skin. The first incursion of the fair Aryans from the northwest settled down, it is claimed, in the northern portions of the country. They gradually mingled and intermarried with the dark-skinned Dravidian and aboriginal population, with the natural consequence of a loss of race-purity and of whiteness of complexion. A subsequent descent of a new Aryan host upon the plains of northern India found the descendants of their predecessors of darker hue than themselves, which bespoke their race degeneracy; so they kept aloof from them. Later, however, they began to mingle with the former inhabitants, so that their descendants partly lost the ancestral complexion. A still later Aryan incursion declined to have intercourse with the descendants of those who last preceded them. Thus we have four classes divided upon the basis of colour, or *varna*, which may correspond with the four great original castes of India.

The traditional theory of the Hindus themselves, in reference to caste origin, is admirably simple and quite adequate to satisfy ninety-nine per cent of the devotees of that faith to-day. Brahmâ, the first god of the Hindu triad, the Creator, was the immediate source and founder of the caste order; for he caused, it is said, the august Brahman to proceed out of his divine mouth, while the warlike and royal Kshatriya emanated from his shoulders, the trading, commercial Vaisya, from his thighs, and the menial Sudra, from his feet. And from these four primal classes have descended, through myriads of permutations and minglings, the present hydra-headed caste organization.

But modern and scientific students of the social order of India entirely discard and ignore all Hindu mythical explanations and *Puranic* legends concerning this subject, and endeavour to trace the present system to its sources and primal causes through patient historic research and through a most elaborate system of anthropometric and ethnographic examinations conducted all over the land. The subject, however, is so vast and complicated that authorities upon the subject are still considerably at variance in their theories of origin. We may conveniently classify the prevailing theories, according to their emphasis, as follows:—

(*a*) *The Religious Theory.*—This gives emphasis to the religious influence as the dominant one in the formation of the social order of the land. It is maintained that the clever and unscrupulous Brahman has, to a large extent, originated it and nursed it into its present wonderful proportions, in order to create and perpetuate his own supremacy among the people of India. As the spiritual head of Hinduism, and the recognized source of religious power among its devotees, he required and devised this organization, with himself as its undisputed head, and with a distinct recognition by all others of his supremacy in the Hindu faith as a *conditio sine quâ non* of their admission as castes into the Hindu system. Up to the present day, the public acceptance of the supreme religious authority of the Brahman is one of the two conditions which qualify any people to admission into the sisterhood of Hindu castes. The other condition is separation from all other peoples in matters which will be hereafter mentioned.

There are potent reasons for accepting this theory; for the strongly entrenched position which religion still holds in the system, both as a basis and as a regulator, notwithstanding other antagonizing influences, is a testimony to its original place and power therein. Any social order whose direction is regulated by social injunctions and whose forms and ritual are enforced by religious penalties must be recognized as a mighty religious system.

(*b*) *The Tribal Theory.*—Moreover, there were many aboriginal tribes which entered the ranks of Hinduism through the formation of new castes. Mr. Risley, in the Census of 1901, refers to such. (See Vol. I, p. 521). They gradually abandoned their old tribal customs and entered upon new paths which brought them into conformity with Hindu usages. Or in some cases they preserved tribal habits and even their tribal *totems*, and baptized them into the new faith and thus became separate castes in the Hindu order.

As in the past, so "all over India at the present moment there is going on a process of the gradual and insensible transformation of tribes into castes. The stages of this operation are in themselves difficult to trace. . . . They usually set up as Rajputs, their first step being to start a Brahman priest, who invents for them a mythical ancestor, supplies them with a family miracle connected with the locality where their tribes are settled, and discovers that they belong to some hitherto unheard-of clan of the great Rajput community." (Census 1901, Vol. II, p. 519.) It is precisely the same process which brought the many Dravidian and even more primitive tribes of South India into the Hindu fold; and it is a curious fact that these same people are to-day the greatest sticklers in the land for caste and its myriad rules.

(*c*) *The Social Theory.*—Some hold with Sir Denzil Ibbetson, in the Census Report of 1881, "that caste is far more a social than a religious institution; that it has no necessary connection whatever with the Hindu religion, further than that under that religion certain ideas and customs common to all primitive nations have been developed and perpetuated in an unusual degree." This is acknowledged to be an exaggerated statement. It may possibly be true that "caste has no *necessary* connection with Hinduism," but it is emphatically true that caste, as understood by all, does not exist apart from that faith.

It is, however, a fact that divisions have occurred within castes, owing to the development of slight social differences between the members. For instance, several castes have been created by the degradation of members of the existing castes on account of their marriage of widows. The Pandarams of South India are held in distinction among the begging castes because of their abstention from meat, alcohol, and widow marriage. Indeed, it is interesting to note that a former caste status has been more frequently lost by, and degradation to a new caste has been consequent upon, the adoption of widow marriage, than through almost any other act. And, at present, this prohibition of the marriage of widows, including child widows, is the most tenaciously and unrighteously enforced caste custom in India.

(*d*) *The Occupational Theory.*—All regard fellowship in the same trade, or occupation, as the most prolific source of caste alignment, in modern times at least. Ibbetson contends that "the whole basis of diversity of caste is diversity of occupation. The old division into Brahman, Kshatriya, Vaisya, Sudra, and Mlechha, or outcast, who is below the Sudra, is but a division into the priest, the warrior, the husbandman, the artisan, and the menial. . . . William Priest, John King, Edward Farmer, and James Smith are but the survivals in England of the four *varnas* of Manu." (Census of 1881.) This statement needs serious qualification. Farming, which is followed to-day by a majority of the population of India, is an occupation which is subsidized by no caste and is followed practically by the members of all castes. The Brahmans are the only ones who are degraded by following the plough. And there is a growing number of trades, introduced by modern civilization, which have not yet been touched by the caste system, and which the enterprising youth of different grades of Hindu society are entering with eagerness. And yet, while this is a fact, it is equally true that the functional type of castes is developing and spreading much more rapidly than any other. In the town of Madura, a few of the families, from the weaver caste, opened a remunerative trade in the manufacture of fireworks. They at first began it as an extra, to add to their very meagre income. Gradually it encroached upon their time until it became their sole occupation. To-day they are prospering in their new trade. But to them and their castemen their change of trade involves the transfer of caste relations. No longer being weavers, they do not see how they can continue to be bound by ties to their former castemen or former fellow-tradesmen; hence the old connubial and convivial bonds of caste are relaxing, and the weavers decline to have fellowship with them as formerly on these lines. Thus, in all parts of the land, we have present-day illustrations of the creation of functional castes. And it is an interesting inquiry whether this mania for creating a new caste for every rising trade and occupation will finally overcome and absorb all occupations created by the demands of modern life and advancing civilization, or whether it will in time succumb to the spirit of modern progress until all occupations shall be emancipated from the tyranny of caste and shall be open to all men who desire to enter them.

(*e*) *The Crossing Theory.*—According to Manu's *Dharma Sastra* one might be led to believe, as Hindus do stoutly maintain, that nearly all modern castes have been created by interbreeding. Those caste laws of twenty-five centuries ago taught that the offspring of the union of a woman of higher with a man of lower caste could belong to the caste of neither parent, and therefore formed a new and a separate caste. The names of castes thus formed are given with much detail in Manu's works. But it does not require much wisdom for one to perceive the absurdity of the working out of such a system, and the impossibility connected with it as an adequate basis for the caste organization of the present day. Yet interbreeding has doubtless been an important element in the elaboration of the stupendous caste organization. We have abundant illustration of this very process and its results in modern times. Among the Dravidians, especially, there are many castes which trace their origin to miscegenation. Among the Munda tribe we find nine such divisions; also five among the Mahilis, who themselves claim their descent from the union of a Munda with a Santhal woman.

This will not be unexpected when it is remembered that endogamy is the prime law of most Hindu castes; and this, too, in a land where immorality and adultery are so prevalent. Other sources of Hindu castes are mentioned. Some, like the Mahrattas, have behind them national traditions, and a history to which they refer and of which they are proud. Others, still, have, by migrating from the home of the mother caste, severed their connection from the parent stock and have formed a separate and independent caste.

It is unnecessary to state that not one of the above theories is adequate to account for all the existing castes of the land. These forces have entered, with varying degrees of efficiency, into their structure,—one being dominant as a causal power in one, and another in another. And yet it may be stated that of all these caste-producing forces religion and occupation have had marked preëminence; and they are more influential to-day than ever before.

II

We shall next consider the various Characteristics or Manifestations of Caste. The system is a very flexible one; and yet its characteristics are practically the same in all parts of the country. Perhaps the best way to clearly describe these to a western reader is to quote at length what we may call Mr. Risley's capital western paraphrase of the system in *Blackwood's Magazine*, a decade ago. "Let us," he writes, "imagine the great tribe of Smith . . . in which all the subtle *nuances* of social merit and demerit have been set and hardened into positive regulations affecting the intermarriage of families. The caste thus formed would trace its origin back to a mythical eponymous ancestor, the first Smith, who converted the rough stone hatchet into the bronze battle-axe and took his name from the 'smooth' weapons that he wrought for his tribe. Bound together by this tie of common descent they would recognize as the cardinal doctrine of their community the rule that a Smith must always marry a Smith, and could by no possibility marry a Brown or a Jones. But, over and above this general canon, two other modes or principles of grouping within the caste would be conspicuous. First of all, the entire caste of Smith would be split up into an indefinite number of in-marrying clans, based upon all sorts of trivial distinctions. Brewing Smiths and baking Smiths, hunting Smiths and shooting Smiths, temperance Smiths and licensed victualler Smiths, Smiths with double-barrelled names and hyphens, Smiths with double-barrelled names without hyphens, Conservative Smiths and Radical Smiths, tinker Smiths, tailor Smiths, Smiths of Mercia, Smiths of Wessex,— all these and all other imaginable varieties of the tribe Smith would be, as it were, crystallized by an inexorable law forbidding the members of any of these groups to marry beyond the circle marked out by the clan name. . . . Thus a Hyphen-Smith could only marry a Hyphen-Smith, and so on. Secondly, and this is the point which I more especially wish to bring out here, running through this endless series of clans we should find another principle at work breaking up each clan into three or four smaller groups which form a sort of ascending scale of social distinction. Thus the clan of Hyphen-Smiths, which we take to be the cream of the caste — the Smiths who have attained the crowning glory of double names securely welded together by hyphens — would be again divided into, let us say, Anglican, Dissenting, and Salvationist Hyphen-Smiths, taking ordinary rank in that order. Now the rule of these groups would be that a man of the Anglican could marry a woman of any group, that a man of the Dissenting group could marry into his own or the lowest group, while the Salvationist Smith could only marry into his own group. A woman could, under no circumstance, marry down into a group below her. Other things being equal, it is clear that two-thirds of the Anglican girls would get no husbands, and two-thirds of the Salvationist men no wives. These are some of the restrictions which would control the process of match-making among the Smiths if they were organized in a caste of the Indian type. There would also be restrictions as to food. The different in-marrying clans would be precluded from marrying together, and their possibilities of reciprocal entertainment would be limited to those products of the confectioners' shops into the composition of which water, the most fatal and effective vehicle of ceremonial impurity, had not entered. Fire purifies, water pollutes. It would follow in fact that they could eat chocolates and other sweetmeats together, but could not drink tea or coffee, and could only partake of ices if they were made without water and were served on metal, not porcelain, plates."

Mr. Risley might have added considerably to these restrictions and limitations without exhausting the catalogue.

Let us briefly enumerate those elements which enter into caste. The first and the most important is intermarriage within the caste. None except members of totemistic castes can, with impunity, look beyond the sacred borders of their own caste for conjugal bliss. So long as castes remain endogamous they will preserve their integrity, and their foundations will never be removed. This is the *fons et origo* of caste perpetuity. All other characteristics may pass away; if this remain, all is well with the organization. And it is this which remains with devilish pertinacity and mischief-working power in the infant Native Christian Church of India. It is this same extreme evil which the social reformers of India are trying to puncture. But all that they dare to struggle and hope for is the right of members of subdivisions of any caste to intermarry. A generation ago, there were 1886 divisions in the Brahman caste alone, no two of which could enjoy connubial or convivial privileges together. It is not up to the most sanguine reformer of India to seek that all Brahmans enjoy the right of intermarrying,—he only asks that the divisions among the Brahmans may be reduced, and intermarriage may be sanctioned among subdivisions. Yet even this meagre quest is not likely to be gratified. This is not surprising, for the defenders of the system well know that if this stronghold of caste is at all weakened, the whole will speedily yield to modern attack. This, doubtless, is the reason why orthodox Hindus are so vehement in their opposition to any and all endeavour to remove the many disabilities and cruelties which the marriage regulations of the land inflict upon Hindu women. There is no land under the sun whose weaker sex suffer more from marital legislation than India; and yet the people can do nothing practically to remedy the crying evils of the same, simply because the mighty engine of caste is arrayed against them. Its perpetuity is linked closely with the resistance of all efforts at reform.

Next in importance to the connubial is the convivial legislation of caste. It is the business of every member of a caste to conserve the purity of his *gens* by eating only with his fellow-castemen. Under no circumstance can he inter-dine with those of a caste below his own. The dictates of caste in this matter are sometimes beyond understanding. Not only must a man eat with those of his own connection; he must be very scrupulous as to the source of the articles which he is about to eat; he must know who handled them, and especially who cooked them. Some articles of food, such as fruit, are not subject to pollution; while others, preëminently water, are to be very carefully guarded against the polluting touch of the lower castes. The writer has entered a railway car and accidentally touched a Brahman's water-pot under the seat, whereupon the disgusted owner seized the vessel and immediately poured out of the car window all its contents. It has been truly said that that monster of cruelty, Nana Sahib of Cawnpore, was able, without any violation of caste rules, to massacre many innocent English women and children at the time of the great Mutiny; but to drink a cup of water out of the hand of one of those tender victims of his treachery and rage would have been a mortal sin against caste, such as could be atoned for only in future births and by the fiery tortures of hell! The rationale of this interdiction is doubtless the desire to preserve the purity of caste blood. As food becomes a part of the body, and, as the Hindu thinks, of the life, it is imperative that all the members of a caste shall eat only the same kind of food, and also that which has not been subjected to the ceremonially polluting touch of outsiders.

This urgency is increased by the fact that different castes proscribe different articles of diet. The *Sivar*, so-called, are strict vegetarians, and will have absolutely no communion in food with meat-eaters, even though the latter may belong to a higher caste than themselves. Meat of any kind is an abomination to them. Other respectable castes will touch only chicken meat, others mutton, a very few pork, while no caste will permit its members to eat beef. No sin is regarded by the orthodox with more horror than that of killing and eating the flesh of the cow,—the most sacred and most commonly worshipped animal of India.

These convivial rules of caste are the greatest obstacles to social union and fellowship among the people of India. Westerners hardly realize the extent to which their communion is based upon the convivial habit. Many times a friendship which lasts a lifetime is formed by strangers sitting together at the common dinner table. And, in the same way, are the old friendships of life generally renewed and cemented in the West. And it is a significant fact that the Christian faith antagonizes Hinduism at this very point by enacting that its great Sacrament of love and communion of life in Christ be embodied in a perpetual and universal "drinking of the same cup and eating of the same bread." In nothing is Hinduism becoming more manifestly a burden to the educated community than in this restriction about interdining; and in nothing are they more ready, as we shall see later, to violate caste customs than in this matter.

Then comes, as a natural consequence of the above, limitations to the contact of persons of differing castes. If a Brahman cannot eat with a Sudra, because it supposedly brings a taint to his pure blood, no more can he, with impunity, come into personal contact with him. The touch of such is pollution to his august and pure person; and the very air the low castes breathe brings to his soul and body taint and poison. This idea of ceremonial pollution by contact causes great inconvenience and trouble, and for that reason has been considerably mitigated or modified in recent times. The Rajah of Cochin, who lives temporarily near the writer, and who is evidently a stickler for caste observances, receives calls from European friends only before nine o'clock in the morning, for the obvious reason that that is the hour of his daily ablution. The Maharajah of Travancore bathes at 7 A.M. daily; hence, intending European guests find reception only before that early hour. In the State of Travancore, in which Brahmanical influence is great, even the high caste *Nair* cannot touch, though he may approach, a Namburi Brahman. A member of the artisan castes will pollute his holiness twenty-four feet off; cultivators at forty-eight feet; the beef-eating Pariah at sixty-four feet. Like the Palestinian leper of old, the low-caste man of that part of India was, until recently, expected to leave the road when he saw a Brahman come, and remove his polluting person to the required number of feet from his sacred presence. Low-caste witnesses were not allowed to approach a court of justice, but standing without, at the requisite distance, to yell their testimony to the Brahman judge who sat in uncontaminated purity within. The falling of the shadow of a low-caste person upon any Brahman in India necessitates an ablution on the part of the latter. It is this frequency of contaminating and polluting contingencies in the life of the Brahman which requires of him so many ablutions daily, and which renders him perhaps the cleanest in person among the sons of men. So many are the dangers of contamination which daily beset him in the ordinary pursuits of life that relief in the form of dispensations is granted him, so as to reduce the ceremonies and diminish the extreme burden of religious observance. This law of contact and pollution must weigh heavily upon any genuine Hindu of high caste. The relation of the Maharajah of Travancore to his Prime Minister, who is a Brahman, is an interesting illustration. The Rajah is not a born Brahman; he is by many of his people regarded as a manufactured Brahman. But His Highness himself does not regard himself as equal, in sacred manhood, to his Brahman Prime Minister; hence he will never be seated in his presence. Nor will the Brahman

Dewan deign to sit in the presence of his royal master, the Maharajah. Hence all the business of State (sometimes requiring conferences of three hours a day) is transacted by them while standing in each other's presence.

Occupational limitations are observed, as we have already seen, by many modern castes. Trade castes not only prescribe the one ancestral occupation to their members; they also, with equal distinctness and severity, prohibit to all within their ranks any other work or trade. So in all those legion castes not only has a man his social sphere and status assigned to him, he is also tied to the trade of his ancestors; yea, more, he is expected to confine himself to ancestral tools and methods of work in that narrow rut of life. One day the writer was accosted by a weaver who was in a famishing condition. He made a pathetic plea for charity. Manchester cloths were flooding the market; they therefore could not sell the products of their labour at living rates. It was suggested that they take up some other trade that could furnish them a decent living. He lifted up his hands in horror at the impious suggestion, that they abandon their caste-prescribed occupation! He felt that he and his were ground between the upper and nether millstones. To suggest to him that they even change the kind or style of article which they prepared upon their looms for the market would have been equally impossible. Out in the villages, where these people live, it would seem almost as absurd for the weaver to become a carpenter as for the weaver who uses only cotton thread to become a silk-weaver, or for those who weave coarse white cloths to produce the finer coloured cloths worn by the women. No; for generations their people have given themselves to the production of only one article. "It is the custom of our people" is the final word. And what has become customary is by caste enactment made obligatory. And woe be to him who defies caste. And thus the caste-prescribed trade becomes the be-all and the end-all of life.

These four — the connubial, the convivial, the contactual, and the occupational — are the constant factors of the caste existence and activity in India. But in addition to these, caste takes other functions and assumes other forms in certain localities and under certain circumstances. Definite forms of religious observance are often enjoined, certain places of pilgrimage are sanctioned, marriage forms prescribed, marriage obligations defined, divorce made possible or impossible, and the limit of marriage expenses set. There is hardly a department of life or a duty which men owe to their dead which does not enter the domain of caste legislation somewhere or other.

A strange and very interesting peculiarity of certain castes is their totemistic aspect. This characteristic has only recently been discovered. "At the bottom of the social system, as understood by the average Hindu, we find, in the Dravidian region of India, a large body of tribes and castes each of which is broken up into a number of totemistic septs. Each sept bears the name of an animal, a tree, a plant, or some material object, natural or artificial, which the members of that sept are prohibited from tilling, eating, cutting, burning, carrying, using, etc." (See Census of 1901, Vol. II, pp. 530–535.)

Mr. J. G. Frazer, in the *Fortnightly Review*, gives the following description of the totem: "A totem is a class of natural phenomena or material objects — most commonly a species of animals or plants — between which and himself the savage believes that a certain intimate relation exists. . . . This relation leads the savage to abstain from killing or eating his totem, if it happen to be a species of animal or plant. Further, the group of persons who are knit to any particular totem by this mysterious tie commonly bear the name of the totem, believe themselves to be of one blood, and strictly refuse to sanction the marriage or cohabitation of members of the group with each other. This prohibition to marry within the group is now generally called by the name Exogamy. Thus totemism has commonly been treated as a primitive system, both of religion and of society."

In absorbing the Dravidian tribes, Brahmanism appropriated the totemistic cult and incorporated it into the caste system. And many Dravidian castes which are identified with this cult have the striking peculiarity of being exogamous as contrasted with the endogamy of the Aryan section of Hindu castes.

III

The penalties which are inflicted by caste for violation of its rules are many and very severe. It is hardly too much to say that there is not on earth an organization more absolute in its power, more wide-reaching in its sweep of interests, and more crushing in its punishment, than is caste. In the first place, it so completely hems in the life of a man, imperatively prescribes for him the routine of life, even down to the most insignificant details, and thus shuts him up to his own clan, and with equal completeness cuts him off from the members of other castes, that it can reduce any recalcitrant member to certain and speedy obedience, simply because there is no one to whom he can flee for sympathy and refuge. Even if this whole system had not, as its first aim and achievement, the alienation of members of different castes, who is there among Hindus that would interfere with this function of a caste to discipline its members? For is not "Thou shalt obey implicitly thy caste," the first law of the Hindu decalogue, and the one most sincerely believed by all Hindus? The following are among the penalties inflicted upon one who is under the ban of his caste:—

All the members of his caste are prohibited from accepting his hospitality. Not even his own household are permitted to dine with him. He is boycotted, absolutely, by all his best friends, associates, and companions. Not one of them dares, under penalty of complete ostracism, to harbour or favour him. Nor will he be invited to their homes. They dare not receive him under the shelter of their roofs nor offer him food. More than once the writer has seen the bitter tyranny of caste brought to bear upon those who had abandoned caste by becoming Christians. Here is a youth known to the writer. He is a member of a respectable caste. He accepts the religion of Christ publicly as his own. His parents and brothers and sister will cling to him with the hope of bringing him back to the ancestral faith. But caste authority steps in. It forbids the family to receive the son and brother, or to offer him a morsel of food. In that household a sad war of sentiment is inaugurated. Parental love and family tenderness cling to the Christian youth; and is he not the hope of the family for the years to come? But to harbour him means to be outcast as a family; and how can they endure that? And are they not at heart loyal to the caste of their fathers? So the conflict runs on for months. One night only the tender heart of the sister compels her to defy caste to the extent, not of eating with the dear brother and companion of her youth, but so far as to bring him the remnant of their meal, not in one of the home vessels from which he had eaten so often as a Hindu in the past, but on a plantain leaf and behind the house!

Then, of course, comes the connubial ban whereby all the members of the caste are prohibited from giving any of their children in marriage to those of his household. To the Hindu who believes that marriage is not only the God-given right of every human being, but who also implicitly believes that it is a heavenly injunction whose fulfilment rests as a duty upon every father in behalf of his children, this interdict is the most oppressive of all. But it is enforced with heartless severity in every case; and any family which may defy the caste in this respect by entering into conjugal relationship with that of the one under ban, is at once outcast.

Another mighty resource of the organization, in this connection, is to interdict to the recreant member the use of all caste servants. For instance, the caste barber and washerman are commanded to serve him and his no longer. The severity of this interdiction cannot possibly be realized by westerners, who are not always dependent upon these functionaries. But in India every one depends upon the barber and washerman for their service even more than a westerner does upon the service of the butcher or the doctor. The Hindu never dreams of the possibility of doing for himself the duties performed by these caste servants for him. Moreover, the barbers and washermen of other castes would, under no circumstance, be allowed to render him the service thus prohibited to him by his own caste.

Add again to these inflictions the further one of complete isolation in times of domestic bereavement. Should a member of his family die, not one of the caste members is permitted to help in the last sacred rites for the dead. Even at that moment, when one would expect the icy barriers to melt away, the heart of caste is as hard and its severity as rigid as ever. The helplessness of a family under these circumstances is, to any one who is not a slave to the whole accursed system, most pitiful and heartrending.

Another caste penalty which has received undue public prominence of late is called *prayaschitta*, which means atonement. It is usually applied as punishment to those who have had the temerity to cross the ocean for foreign travel, business, or study. More correctly, it is rather a process of cleansing and ceremonial rehabilitation than an act of punishment. The exclusiveness of caste delighted in calling all foreigners Mlechhas, which, though perhaps not as vigorous a term as the Chinese sobriquet, "black devils," connoted, and still connotes, to the caste Hindu, "unclean wretches," contact with whom brings ceremonial pollution and sin. He who crossed the ocean would necessarily be debased by these defiling ones and would be, as a matter of course, engulfed in the pollutions of their life! To prohibit travel, which necessarily involved such sin and degradation, became therefore the concern of the ancient lawmakers of India. Hence the *prayaschitta*, under which the educated community of India chafe so much at the present time. For many of the best and most promising youth of India travel abroad or reside temporarily in England, with a view to perfecting their educational training so as to qualify themselves for highest positions of usefulness in the homeland. Others go abroad on business or to behold and study the wonders of western life and civilization. All men of culture and power in India, at the present time, are convinced of the evil and absurdity of this caste law, which is common to all castes, because it is a part of the general legislation of their religion. They decline to believe that it is either sin or pollution to go in search of the best that the West and the East have discovered and can bestow upon one, and that which is to-day doing most in the elevation and redemption of India herself. And many of them are defying this obsolete and debasing law of their faith. Many others are crying for a modern interpretation of the law—an interpretation which will explain away its bitterness and render it innocuous. For it is not simply or chiefly the reactionary and absurd character of this legislation which exasperates the intelligence of the land; it is the very offensive and revolting *nature* of the expiation which preëminently stirs up the rebellion. In former centuries of darkness, Hindus may have been willing to submit to the humiliation of eating the five products of the cow as an atonement for the supposed sin of sea-travel. The culture and intelligence of the present time is neither so abject nor so superstitious as to submit to this, without, at least, a vigorous protest. And yet, what the culture of India seeks to-day is not the abolishing of this law, which is equally repulsive to their taste and to their intelligence; it asks only that some way of avoiding the penalty may be found! And all that Hinduism and caste require of these foreign-travelled men is not an intelligent submission to its behests, but an outward observance of them. So the faith and its conservative defenders are satisfied to see these men of culture, as they return with the acquired treasures of the West, submit outwardly to this offensive rite, while their sensitive nature rises in rebellion against it. And these young scions of the East willingly practise this hypocrisy and submit to this indignity in order to live at peace with, and indeed to live at all in, their ancestral caste! It is only an illustration of the hollowness of the major part of the life of the educated community in this great land. Well may one exclaim, what can be expected from a people whose leading men of culture are living this double and mean life! This is verily "peace with dishonour"!

CHAPTER V

THE HINDU CASTE SYSTEM (*continued*)

IV

THE agency through which, and the occasion upon which, caste penalizes its members are manifold.

Formerly, Hindu kings, under instruction from their pandit ministers, would enforce caste observances. But under the present non-Hindu State no such action could be expected. In many instances pandits have to be consulted both as to whether a member has really violated *shastraic* injunctions and as to the penalty which should be inflicted in that special case. In doubtful cases, pandits of various trainings and leanings are called who present conflicting opinions which end in confusion.

In Southern India important cases of caste violation among non-Vishnuvite Hindus are under the jurisdiction of the Superiors of Sankarite monasteries. Some of these assume and exercise Papal authority in such matters among their people. Usually, however, each local caste organization deals directly with infractions of its own rules, and is competent to deal drastically, and as a court of final resort, with all cases of caste infringement within its own membership. It may be done in public assembly, when all male members are present and have a voice; or the caste *panchayat*, or council of five, may sit in judgment upon the case and have right of final action. This latter tribunal is the more common in South India, and is more in harmony with the spirit and methods of the land.

There are a number of courses of action which are adequate as causes of removal from caste.

One of these is a change of faith. The abandonment of the ancestral religion, which is the mother of caste spirit and organization, especially when the newly accepted faith repudiates openly caste and all that belongs to it, inevitably leads to expulsion from caste. In most cases this has resulted upon conversion to either Christianity or Mohammedanism. But this is not as universal as we could wish or as many suppose, as we shall see later on. It may be seen how, in a mass movement of a large body of men toward Christianity, for instance, the people may easily, and would naturally, carry with them into the new faith many of their old customs and habits, including much that pertains to, and is of the essence of, caste.

Roman Catholicism has interpreted caste chiefly from a social standpoint, and has therefore regarded it as a social institution which can be adapted to, and adopted into, the Christian religion. Protestantism, or, at least, Anglo-Saxon Protestantism, has regarded caste as primarily and dominantly a religious institution, whose spirit antagonizes fundamentally our faith, and which must be opposed at all points. Hence it is a part of the pledge of every one who enters into the Protestant fellowship in India that he will eschew and oppose caste at all times. And it may be said that, though Hinduism loves dearly compromise and evasion, it has in the main held that a man who has accepted the Christian faith and has been publicly baptized into its conviction of the "fatherhood of God and the brotherhood of all men," has no place in its own caste system, and it consistently deals with him as with an outcast. As we have already seen, every man who has travelled abroad has lost thereby caste and has to undergo expiation before reinstatement. It matters not how thoroughly he has tried to preserve caste customs during his travels and in the foreign land, he is regarded by all as a *de facto* outcast.

Marrying a widow is also an act which severs caste ties and places a man under the ban. Of course, this applies not to the few castes which allow widow-remarriage. But as the bulk of Hindus deny the right of a widow to remarry (though there is no caste obstacle to a widower taking unto himself a new virgin wife every year of his life), a man cannot enter into an alliance with a widow without losing caste thereby.

Beef-eating is regarded as so heinous a sin that no member of a respectable caste would expect consideration for a moment. And yet Dr. J. H. Barrows has said that the famous Swamy, Vivekanantha, when with him at Chicago, ate a whole plateful of beef in his presence and with a great deal of relish. But he, of course, had graduated out of the ordinary level of Hindu-hood into the sacred heights of Swamyhood, in which a man is exempt from the mean limitation of caste, and when the vulgar sins of common Hindu life are transmuted into the ordinary blessings and privileges of saintdom.

In like manner, vegetarian castes punish their members for the eating of any meat. The Hindu aversion to meat is very common; it is also sanitary and wholesome; for meat-eating in the tropics is neither necessary nor conducive to health. And yet the Pariah outcast has no scruples in this matter. It is indeed true that he would deem it a sin to butcher a cow or an ox; but he will not hesitate to poison his neighbour's cattle, that he may thereby have enough carrion to eat. For the carcases of the dead cattle of the village are the perquisite of the Pariah; and it is upon finding such that he enjoys his only feasts of plenty. But to the ordinary Hindu all bovine kind are divine, and the flesh of the same is strictly and vehemently tabooed.

Punishment is also dealt out, as we have seen, to those who eat any food cooked by an outcast, whether he be Christian, Mohammedan, or Pariah. And the same is true of eating with an outcast, or with one who is of a lower caste than himself. Indeed, so far is this spirit carried by certain high castes that to be seen eating by a member of a lower caste, or to allow the shadow of a stranger to fall upon one's prepared food, is pollution. Hence the care with which all Hindus seek privacy and avoid the gaze of men during mealtime.

Officiating as a priest in the house of a low-class Sudra is strictly prohibited to a Brahman, and he loses caste thereby. He and other "twice born" are also driven out of caste if they throw away the sacred thread which is the outer badge of their second birth and dignity.

A woman, when found in open sin with a man of another caste, and a widow, when she can no longer hide the consequence of her immorality, are no longer in caste.

It is hardly necessary to mention that marrying outside of one's own caste is a sin which finds no countenance, but severest punishment, in nearly all castes.

Generally speaking, we may say that caste authority is exercised only in cases where ceremonial observance and social usages are violated. In matters that are purely ethical, and which bear upon the character and moral elevation of the individual and the clan, caste rarely acts; for it does not consider that its honour is compromised or its organic life impaired by such conduct.

It should also be mentioned that caste is not even in the distribution of its dispensations and punishments. A man of wealth and social influence succeeds in staving off many acts of caste displeasure which would fall heavily upon the poor and friendless man. Such a man may, and often does, trample under foot every command of the decalogue, and at the same time defy and violate a good moiety of the injunctions of his caste. And yet, because of his wealth and general importance in caste councils, he stands unimpeached and unrebuked.

In matters of caste observance and discipline, villages are much more conservative and strict than cities. In the latter, as we shall see, caste observance is much relaxed, and life is more on modern lines.

V

The results of the caste system in India are many and manifest. It has sown its seed for many centuries and to-day reaps a rich harvest in life and conduct. It should not be assumed, and it cannot be asserted, that this great system has always been an unmixed evil to the people of this land.

No organization which has bound by its fetters for eighty generations nearly a sixth of the population of the globe, and which continues to grip them to-day with tyrannical power, can be devoid of any redeeming feature. The very perpetuity and prosperity of the scheme argues for its possession of some rational features, originally connected with it, which gave it sanction to the myriads who have submitted to its reign over them. But it is exceedingly difficult to discover that excellence which originally commended it to the people of this land. Nor do the writings of those who have striven to defend the system assist us in making this discovery. A modern Brahman defence by Jogendra Nath Bhattacharya (see "Hindu Castes and Sects," pp. 1–10) gives only one ray of light upon the subject when he observes that "the legislation of the Rishis was calculated not only to bring about union between the isolated clans that lived in primitive India, but to render it possible to assimilate within each group the foreign hordes that were expected to pour into the country from time to time." In those remote days when weakness through isolation threatened their very existence, and when there was no possibility of a general union of all the people for defence, thorough organization of clans into castes brought strength and confidence and was a conspicuous blessing. It was in those days a convenient and effective way of enforcing religious obligations upon the heterogeneous clans. It also was then probably useful in preserving purity of blood among the higher races, and in conserving the nobility of the Aryan who was destined to rule the mixed races of India for many centuries.

Nor is the system without possibilities of good in modern times, as was illustrated recently by the action of a prominent North India caste in prohibiting large expenses in marriage and in raising, by legislation, the limit of the marriageable age of its girls.

But, alas, any good that may possibly inhere in the system has largely remained *in posse* rather than *in esse*. The history of caste has been one of evil, and it is no wonder that such a fair-minded writer as Mr. Sherring, who has probably made a more thorough study of the subject than any other man, should call the organization "a monstrous engine of pride, dissension, and shame" (see Preface to his "Hindu Tribes and Castes"). Considering the subject, therefore, in its bearing upon the life of India to-day, and studying its results as we now find them among all classes of the people and in their definite bearing upon the future of the land, we are compelled to pronounce against it at all points.

It is, in the first place, the source of interminable discord and dissension all over the land. It not only arrays caste against caste; but bitter animosity is the order of the day among the subdivisions of castes. In every one of the numberless castes in the land there are divisions and subdivisions galore. And while the Sudras acknowledge the supremacy of the "twice born," among the myriad clans of the Sudras themselves there is endless assumption and contention, every one, fomented by pride, claiming primacy and distinction above the others. Recently, in South India, this feeling led to a serious riot, in which not a few lives were lost and villages devastated.

It also narrows the sympathies of the people in a most lamentable way. Among the common people of India it is held that a man's duties to his caste embrace his whole obligation. When a fellow-being is in difficulty and his condition strongly appeals for sympathy, the first, and often the last, question asked is, "Is he a member of my caste?" If not, like the priest and the Levite of old, his conscience allows him to "pass by on the other side." Recently a woman perished in the streets of a town near Madura. She was a resident of a village some twenty-five miles away, and was, therefore, a stranger in this town, where she sickened and was carried to a public rest-house. But when her condition became serious and no relatives or caste friends came to her support, she was put out into the street, where she lay helpless for three days in the rain and sunshine. Hundreds of people saw her dying agonies as they passed by during those days; but no heart of sympathy went out to her; for was she not a stranger? And it was left to an American, who happened to pass that way on the third day, to demand of the town officer that she be put back in the rest-house, where she shortly afterward died. Let it not be thought that this is an isolated case. He who is familiar with Indian life knows it is not, for daily he has to witness the woful limitations which caste imposes upon human sympathy.

Caste has also degraded manual labour. The loss of caste by any Brahman who follows the plough is only an application of this rule in the highest quarters. Caste has taught the people of this land that humble toil, however honest it may be, is more than mean; it is sinful. There are millions of the higher castes of India who deem it honourable to beg, and dignified to spend their years in abject laziness, but who would regard it as unspeakable degradation to take a hoe or a hammer and earn an honest living by the sweat of their brow. Nor will their caste rules permit of their undertaking such work. And this spirit has passed down the ranks until it pervades the whole of society in India, with the consequence that manual labour is universally regarded as degrading, and with the further natural result that a horde of five and a half millions of lazy, wretched, immoral, able-bodied, religious beggars are burdening this land. And thus mendicancy is made honourable at the expense of honest toil. It should be further remarked that there are a number of begging castes, in which all work is proscribed and mendicity exalted into a divinely ordained profession!

Moreover, caste makes it impossible for India to become a commercial country. So long as foreign travel is banned and contact with other lands is regarded as a sin against heaven and caste, there is little hope that the people of this land will distinguish themselves in that kind of trade and commerce which has made India's mistress, Great Britain, so illustrious in wealth and dominion.

And it is this caste spirit which so easily made the great peninsula of India a prey to the "tight little island" many thousands of miles away. For not only has caste made the Hindus an insular people, it has also so divided them that they do not realize any common sentiment, save that of opposition to the State, or seek any common good. Hence they have for many centuries been the easy prey of any adventurers who sought to overcome and despoil them. A genuine national feeling and a patriotic sentiment are all but impossible in the land. And all intelligent Hindus acknowledge this sad condition at present, and many of the best of them publicly maintain that national consciousness, self-rule, and a glowing, triumphant patriotism can be built only upon the ruins of the caste system.

And even as it is a foe to nationality, so is it the mortal enemy of individualism. The caste system is really a glorification of the multitude as against the individual. Individual initiative and assertion, liberty of conscience, the right of man to life and the pursuit of happiness, — all these are foibles of the West which it has been the chief business of caste to crush; and upon their ruin it has erected this mighty tower of Babel. In India, it has been the business of men, from time immemorial, not to do what they think to be right, nor to find out, every one for himself, what they consider to be the best and to act according to the dictates of conscience; it has rather been submission to caste dominance. And it is the unblushing teaching of the *Shastras* that obedience to caste is the fulfilment of duty and the *summum bonum* of life. So omnipotent and omniscient is the arm and head of caste that men dare not defy it. Hence we are compelled to look in India to-day upon the saddest spectacle of abject manhood the world has known. To those who, like the writer, have spent a lifetime in trying to raise the outcasts and the lower strata of Indian society, the most difficult and discouraging obstacle is the inertia and the abjectness of the people themselves. Through a bitter experience of many centuries they have learned that it does not pay for the individual to assert himself against the dictates of the caste, or for the lower castes to rise in rebellion against their lot. They discovered that they were merely butting their heads against an adamantine rock. So they have lost every ambition and hope; and he who would lift them up must first remove that leaden despair which rests upon them like a mighty incubus.

Nor is it much better with the educated classes of India. There are hundreds of thousands of these men of western university training who annually assemble in Congress and in Convention, and who in spotless English of Addisonian accent and in the sonorous phraseology of a Macaulay, discourse upon human rights and who denounce the bondage of caste tyranny. And yet they submit, in their own homes, to that same accursed tyranny and are in life as abject as the meanest Pariah in the face of caste edicts which they know to be unrighteous and demeaning to the core.

It should also be remembered that caste is the foster-mother of all the manifold social evils of the land. In pre-caste days in India such evils as child marriage, prohibition of widow remarriage, temple women, excessive marriage expenses, etc., did not exist. They are a part of the caste régime supported and perpetuated by its authority. Remove this mighty compulsion, and these institutions would soon become things of the past.

Another evil of this organization is that of ignoring the ethical and spiritual standard and of measuring everything from a purely formal and ceremonial standpoint. All life is reduced into an unceasing ritual under the perpetual priestly surveillance of caste. All that it asks of man is outward conformity. He may disbelieve and hate every commandment of his faith; but if he conforms, he is a faithful son. On the other hand, he may be a man of unblemished character, and he may even intend to be obedient to caste; but if, some night, a few enemies were to thrust into his mouth and compel him to swallow a piece of beef, no power could save him from the dreadful punishment that would follow. A man may write a tract in condemnation and ridicule of all the gods of the Hindu pantheon and still remain an acceptable Hindu; but if, in the agony of a burning fever, he should drink a spoonful of water from the hands of a Christian or of a Pariah, his caste would doom him to perdition for it.

In other words, the whole system directly cultivates, in all the people, a hollowness of life which does more than anything else to rob India of her manhood and which makes nobility of character and ethical integrity most difficult things among the Hindu community. A Brahman gentleman described the whole system as a "vast hollow sham." And such it is.

VI

Paradoxical though it may seem, caste spirit is more prevalent and its influence more dominant in India at the present than in the past; yet there is more defiance and violation of caste rules and more frequent and sure evidences of the speedy termination of its reign than at any previous time.

It has ruled so long and so supremely in this country that the Hindu accepts it without questioning; and it has become more than a second nature to him, even a necessity of his being. What would be intolerably irksome to a Westerner is to the Hindu a matter of course. To the rank and file of the Hindus, caste has ceased to be a matter of question. It is the only order of life with which he is conversant; and while he may be convinced by arguments which prove its cruelty and its many evils, he still clings to it as the only system under which he knows how to live and which he cares to obey.

As we have already seen, the ramifications of caste are more numerous and its authority more general to-day than at any former time. Many Hindu reformers, especially of the Vishnu sects, have followed in the steps of the great Buddha, by denouncing caste, root and branch, and have established their own sects during the last ten centuries on a non-caste basis. But they have all succumbed to the demon which they antagonized and now generally observe caste rules with the same devotion as other Hindus.

The lower the caste spirit has descended to the "submerged tenth" of the land, the more vehemently have they become inoculated with its virus. The outcast Pariah is not to be outdone in this matter; and so we have Pariahs and Pariahs. Many divisions are found among this wretched class, and they are more exclusive in their divisions and more rigid in their narrowness than are many of the high castes.

Even those who have abandoned the Hindu faith and professed another, do not leave behind them this divisive spirit. Perhaps the converts from Mohammedanism have eschewed Hindu caste more than converts to other faiths.

Among Christian converts, though caste is professedly abandoned, it clings with vital tenacity and almost unconquerable persistence to their sense of the fitness of things. Their deepest prejudices and unconscious tendencies, even against their intellectual convictions and sincere professions, unceasingly sway the vast majority of them and lead them into affiliations and narrow sympathies which are Hindu and not Christian. It is true that the oldest Christian community in India, the Syrian Church of Malabar, has long abandoned the Hindu caste organization, with even its mean remnant of caste titles. And yet

Jungle People of India

that community settled down for many centuries into the conviction that it was merely one caste among the many of that region and must keep itself aloof from and untainted by the surrounding castes. Roman Catholicism, which has still the most numerous Native Christian community in India, has largely adopted the Hindu system and tries to utilize it in the furtherance of Christianity in the land! No greater mistake was ever made than this of trying to uphold and promulgate the meekness, the humility, the love, and the fellowship of Christ by means of the haughty pride, the cruel hate, and the bitter divisiveness of caste.

Protestant Christianity is to-day the pronounced foe of caste. It is war to the death between them, and the missionaries have not yet found a foe to their cause so subtle, deceptive, deep-rooted, persistent, and pervasive as this. It is fortified by a thousand ramparts and presents more discouragement to the Christian worker than all other obstacles combined. Even Buddhism and Jainism, the former of which was the ancient protest against Hindu caste, have fallen ofttimes a prey to the subtle and damning wiles of this system. In Bengal, a number of Hindu castes are known to have been formerly members of the Jain and Buddhist communities (see Census 1901, Vol. II, p. 523).

However, notwithstanding this growing prevalence and the marvellous tenacity of caste throughout the land, there are encouraging signs of its decadence. Its grip is certainly relaxing in many ways, and its asperities are softening.

It may not untruthfully be said that the growing multiplicity of castes is one of the sure harbingers of the downfall of the system. For the divisions of caste are already beyond computation. The population is cut up into so many minute sections that the caste edifice overtowers everything else, so that it is in imminent danger of toppling over. It is claimed that war among civilized nations will soon become an impossibility because of the growing devastating power of modern weapons of warfare. In like manner, caste is speedily passing through its very excesses to a *reductio ad absurdum;* its spirit is so rampant, and its gross evils are becoming so intolerable, that even the patient inhabitants of India will soon cease to endure the ruin which this monster of their own creation carries on among them.

Educated Hindus are already denouncing it with great vehemence and with considerable unanimity. They are convinced that India can never win independence and power under the régime of caste;

and they proclaim their convictions upon the housetop. It is true, as we have seen, that caste has so powerfully thrown its spell over them, its own children, that they are too abject to withstand it openly and unitedly. But I believe that they will erelong be driven to action. Further, obedience and submission will mean ruin to them, their families, and their country.

Even now, among the educated, especially in Bengal, caste restrictions upon dining are being increasingly ignored. A Bengalee gentleman enjoys ordinary hotel fare with apparently none to interfere with his liberties. In Madras, the writer has more than once rubbed shoulders with Brahman lawyers and others eating together the common fare of a well-known restaurant of the city. And he has known Brahman patients, high in society, who did not object even to buy and use nourishment in the form of "Liebig's Beef-extract," so long as they could cover its offensiveness to the women of their household by the euphemistic name "meat-extract."

And to this they are being rapidly carried by a conjunction of many forces which are increasingly dominating the land.

In the first place, they have the potent example

of a host of western lives among them. This body of white people, from the far-off lands, is distributed all over India. They are the rulers of the land. A Brahman may deem their touch pollution. But that same Brahman is often glad to undergo that ceremonial taint if thereby he can only enjoy the white man's cultured society. He beholds in these people from the West a freedom from irksome caste restraints. He notices conjugal relations among them, such as furnish richest home blessings. Their social relations are untrammelled and abound in convivial privileges such as are denied to Hindu society. All this creates in him an uneasiness. If he is a man of culture and resides in some city of importance, he will wish to meet English friends upon lines of social equality; but this he will find to be impossible apart from his defiance of caste rules; for, to the man of the West, the common cup and the festal board are the essential conditions of true friendship and intimacy. Thus the life of the ruling race in India is a constant rebuke to the narrowness of caste and a source of discontent to the caste-ridden people, because it reveals to them a different and a better way of living.

Nor is it merely this new type of non-caste

western life that appeals to them. The modern civilization of the West, with its humanizing laws, its exaltation of the individual, its religious freedom, its new and broadening education and culture, its equal rights to every man, its many institutions through every one of which there breathes the Anglo-Saxon's blessed love of liberty, the home with its sanctified affection and its glorified womanhood, philanthropy which carries with an even hand its sweet services to the high and the low—to Pariah as to the Brahman,—all these institutions and influences are at work like a mighty leaven in the mind and heart of India. And the people cannot be blind to this influence; and it is gradually transforming their ideals and ambition.

Connected with these more subtle western civilizing agencies are found the material agencies which are the dread foes of caste exclusion. The chief among these is the railroad, the thirty thousand miles of which are so many tongues to proclaim the doom of past narrowness. The Brahman, with all his mean pride, cannot forego the wonderful conveniences of the "iron road and the fire-carriage"; but in order to avail himself of them, he must sit an hour at a time cheek by jowl with a low-caste—

it may be a Pariah—fellow-passenger. The railroad gnaws at the vitals of caste life and convictions.

Next to it come the schools. Millions of youth are trained in them daily to regard caste as an unworthy classification. All sections are taught in the same classes; they play in the same playground. In both places the lower often excels the higher caste boy. The seeds of equality and a common regard are thus constantly sown among the youth of all sections of the land. If it astonished the recent educational (Moseley) Commission which went from England to the United States to study the educational conditions there, when it saw the children of the President of the country studying side by side with the children of day-labourers, so must it seem wonderful, and wonderfully good, to a student of social conditions in India, to behold the child of a Pariah and that of a Brahman preparing, side by side, in the schoolroom, for the responsibilities and the blessings of life.

Many other agencies similar to the above are doing their benign levelling work.

The government, however, is the great leveller. In all its gifts of offices, in all posts of honour and influence, it distributes its blessings with strict impartiality, so far as caste is concerned. It wisely ignores all social distinctions and depends upon qualifications of culture and character when it seeks men to conduct its affairs. This is something unprecedented in the land of Manu. That the outcast should stand an equal chance with the high castes for positions of honour and emolument was unknown in this land of sharp distinctions.

And even more fundamental than this is the blessing of equal personal and political rights. In ancient India, such an idea was never entertained. Before British rule entered the land it was never dreamed that priest, prince, and beggar—and that Brahman and Pariah—had equal rights before the law. To-day they all recognize the justice of this and expect it.

Finally, the advent of Christianity, with power, into the land has brought a new death-knell to caste supremacy. We have seen that Indian Christian converts abandon all other customs and superstitions with greater facility than they do those of caste. Its roots have sunk deepest into the soil of their nature. But let it not be thought that they do not grow stronger against caste than they used to be. In the Indian Christian community there is developing a most encouraging movement toward the complete eradication of caste sentiment and observance within the Church itself. They are more sensible than ever before of the gross inconsistency of a man's taking upon himself the sacred name of Christ and at the same time submitting to the dominance of caste. Indian Christian anti-caste organizations are now at work seeking to drive out of the Church of God in India this Antichrist, and to cultivate the true spirit and amenities of Christian fellowship and fraternal communion.

The spirit of Christ is abroad in the land in regenerating and transforming power. His great message to the world was the common fatherhood of God and the brotherhood of man. And the Christian Church is growing increasingly true to the message of its Leader and Lord in this country. Men may not accept the Christian call to believe and to be baptized; but they cannot be blind and deaf to the work and call of the Spirit of Christ in these modern times of thrilling changes and opportunities.

It is this Christian ideal which is running athwart the most ancient and cherished institutions and customs of India, and has precipitated a conflict such as the land has never before known.

But the end is not yet, and caste will not be hurled down from its high pedestal in a day. It is a mighty institution which has its root in deepest sentiments and is sustained by cherished antiquity and by the strongest passions and prejudices. These will not succumb in a brief generation. And even when Christianity shall have triumphed and shall have driven out its rival faith from the land, as we have every reason to believe that it will, let it not be supposed that the Christianity of the East will have the social complexion of that of the West. In the earliest days of Christianity, we are told by the great Apostle to the Gentiles that there were "heresies" in the Church. These were *social* heresies or class divisions. It was later in the West that "heresy" became an error of *belief*. The Indian Church will also have heresies of life rather than of thought. The caste spirit will not vanish entirely from India, even when it becomes Christ's land; because while India is always indulgent and tolerant concerning beliefs, she is particular about class distinctions. And this, doubtless, will be the weakness of the Indian Church of the future. But she will have her strong points, also, and in these she will glory and through them glorify her exalted Lord.

CHAPTER VI

THE BHAGAVAD GITA — THE HINDU BIBLE

The Bhagavad Gita (translated "The Song of the Adorable One" and "The Divine Lay") is rightly regarded as the gem of all Hindu sacred literature. Hindus maintain (and few will question them) that in beauty of language and in elevation of thought it stands supreme among their *Shastras*, or sacred writings.

Educated Hindus proudly claim for it superiority to all sacred books of other faiths.

Of all ancient Brahmanical writings it is to-day the most cherished by the members of that faith. The ancient Rig Veda is at present only a book of antiquarian interest. The Upanishads, which are the fountainhead of Hindu thought and philosophy, are only the text-books and treasure-houses of philosophers and metaphysicians. But the Divine Lay is extolled and used alike by men of western culture, by conservative pandits, and by the masses as their highest book of doctrine and their richest treasury of devotion.

Even many Hindus who have come under the fascination of the Christ, carry with them upon their journeyings the New Testament in one pocket and the Bhagavad Gita in the other, as the common guide and inspiration of their quiet hours of meditation.

It is thus universally recognized that there is no book which wields a larger influence than this in the religious life of the two hundred and thirty millions of Hindus to-day; and there is none which is more worthy to be called the Hindu Bible.

I

In strange contrast with the bulky tomes of Brahmanism and of the great epic, Mahabharata (which, with its two hundred and forty thousand lines, is the longest epic ever written, being eight times as long as the Odyssey and the Iliad put together), the Bhagavad Gita contains only seven hundred *slohams*, and is not as long as the Gospel of St. Mark.

The date of the origin of the Song is very much disputed. There are Hindu authorities who would carry it back to the fifth century B.C., the time which is assigned for the first recension of the Mahabharata, of which the Bhagavad Gita is a very small part. But the highest authorities find conclusive proof that it originated about the second or third century of our era, and was then inserted as a part of an episode in the narrative of the great epic.

The Mahabharata is a great poetic narrative of a conflict between the two branches of the Bharata family—the Pandavas and the Kauravas—for the petty kingdom of Hastinapura, near the modern city of Delhi.

The two forces are already, in counter array, eager for the fray on the battle-field of Kuruchetra. The call to battle has already been blown upon the miraculous conchs of the leaders of both sides, who are seated in their chariots drawn by white horses. Over each one waves his personal ensign. Arjuna, the noblest of the five brave Pandava leaders, is a man of heroic traits of character; and yet within him breathes the tenderest sentiment of humanity. He pauses a moment ere he leads his mighty hosts against the enemy; and, as he looks upon his own kith and kin in the opposing ranks, he is overcome by the stern voice of conscience blending with humanitarian impulses. Is it right, can it *possibly* be right, for him to go forth to destroy his own friends and relatives; shall he shed the blood of those who are nearest and dearest to him upon the earth? This is the agonizing doubt which seizes upon him at this time. And in his distress he turns to his friend and relative, Krishna, who has declined to participate in the war, but who had volunteered to act as Arjuna's charioteer. And he says unto him: "Seeing these kinsmen, O Krishna, standing (here) desirous to engage in battle, my limbs droop down; my mouth is quite dried up; a tremor comes on my body; and my hairs stand on end; the Gandiva (bow) slips from my hand; my skin burns intensely; I am unable, too, to stand up; my mind whirls round, as it were. Even those for whose sake we desire sovereignty, enjoyments, and pleasures, are standing here for battle, abandoning life and wealth — preceptors, fathers, sons as well, grandfathers, maternal uncles, fathers-in-law, grandsons, brothers-in-law, as also other relatives. These I do not wish to kill, though they kill me, O destroyer of Madhu! even for the sake of sovereignty over the three worlds, how much less than for this earth (alone)?"

Krishna replied, with a view to soothe Arjuna's perturbed mind, and to urge him on to battle.

It is this dialogue between the hero and the god which constitutes the Bhagavad Gita. And yet one can hardly call it a dialogue, since Krishna's remarks make up more than nine-tenths of the book.

The dialogue is one of the favourite forms of Hindu literature. Most of the Puranas and the Tantras are cast in that form.

It seems very strange that this book, which is the favourite exponent of a faith whose very essence is non-resistance, whose genius is to inculcate the passive virtues, should have found its motive in the purpose of the god Krishna to overcome, in the warrior Arjuna, those worthy, humane sentiments of peace and kindness and that noble resolution to forego even the kingdom rather than to acquire it through the shedding of the blood of his relatives. How incongruous to build up the lofty structure of a faith upon so unethical, unsocial, and cruel a foundation!

II

The Song evidently belongs to the *tendensschrift* school of literature. It is written with a definite aim and purpose. It is the highest exponent of Hindu Eclecticism. The three great schools of Brahmanical thought and philosophy — the Sankya, the Yoga, and the Vedanta — were founded more than twenty-five centuries ago and have wielded resistless power in the shaping of religious thought in India. And perhaps this power was never more manifest than at the present time.

But these schools are, in their main issues, mutually antagonistic. The Sankya philosophy is severely dualistic and even has little use, if indeed it has any place, for the Divine Being. On the other hand, the Vedanta is uncompromisingly monistic. Its pantheism is of the highest spiritualistic type and is radically opposed to the materialism of the Sankya school. In one school the Divine Being is nothing and materialism has full sway; while in the other Brâhm is everything, and all that appears to men — the phenomenal — is false and illusive.

Again, as to the method of redemption, the Yoga philosophy advocates renunciation, self-effacement, and all the forms of asceticism. On the other hand, the Sankya philosophy inculcates action as the embodiment of the duty of man, through which alone he can attain unto absorption.

Even to the present time these different schools of thought not only prevail; they have also begotten and are nourishing different schools of religious life and practice which present different ideals and enforce different methods.

The Brahman author, or authors, of the Bhagavad Gita was inspired with the laudable ambition of harmonizing these conflicting teachings and of blending their peculiarities into one consistent whole, which would appeal to all the followers of the many-sided Brahmanical faith. This he accomplished with rare beauty of language, and with a success which has won admiration and acceptance by nearly all the people of India. And this is the more remarkable since the worship of Krishna is distinctly a part of the Vaishnavite cult of Hinduism, and as such does not appeal to the Saivites, or the worshippers of Siva.

But the author, naturally and inevitably, failed to produce a congruous scheme of saving truth and religious appeal. The result is that we see, on almost every page, contradictory teachings and conflicting methods of salvation. This, of course, is by no means fatal to it in the estimation of Hindus, with whom consistency has never been a foible, and in the eyes of whom two mutually contradictory teachings can rest peacefully side by side.

Here we find dualism and monism locking hands together, and the three ways of liberation — that of ritual, of asceticism, and of knowledge — not only find full expression, but are also supplemented by the inculcation of faith and of the obligations of caste. To a Westerner, this jumbling together of such antagonistic ideas and methods would be as repulsive as it would be absurd. But the Oriental mind works on different lines from the Occidental, and is never hampered by logical inconsistency.

The Song of the Adorable One is divided into three chapters, of six divisions each.

The first extols the benefits of the Yoga method; but it also adds that action should be supplemented to Yoga for the speediest attainment of beatification.

In the second part, the pantheism of the Vedanta is inculcated, and Krishna identifies himself with the universal Spirit and claims adoration as such.

In the third part, an effort is made to blend the Sankya and the Vedanta conceptions, an effort which largely permeates the whole book. That is, it claims that *prakriti*, or elemental nature, and the soul, or *âtma*, find their source in Brâhm; and thus it practically vitiates the fundamental teachings of both systems. At the same time, it also teaches the separate existence of individual souls, which is anti-Vedantic.

As we study carefully the contents of this remarkable work, we are impressed equally with its excellences and defects, with its sublime teachings and absurd contentions. Generally speaking, it may be said to be characterized by notions which are, at the same time, supremely attractive to the East and unintelligible and repellent to the West.

1. Considering first its teaching concerning God, we find emphasized that monistic teaching of Hindu Pantheism which has been the dominant note in the faith of India from the first. But it is not the strictly spiritual and the unequivocal Pantheism of Vedantism, which is purely idealistic and which bluntly denies the existence of everything but Brâhm itself. It is rather a mixture of the dual and the non-dual teaching of the two dominant, contending philosophies of the land. Krishna tells us that he is not only the supreme Spirit, but also that the material universe is a part of himself. "O Son of Pritha! I am the Kratu, I am the Yagna, I am the Svadha, I am the product of the herbs, I am the sacred verse. I too am the sacrificial butter, I the fire, I the offering. I am the father of this universe, the mother, the creator, the grandsire, the thing to be known, the means of sanctification, . . . the source and that in which it merges, the support, the receptacle, and the inexhaustible seed. . . . All entities which are of

the quality of goodness, and those which are of the quality of passion and of darkness, know that they are, indeed, all from me; I am not in them, but they are in me. The whole universe, deluded by these three states of mind, develops from the qualities, does not know me who am beyond them and inexhaustible; for this delusion of mine, . . . is divine and difficult to transcend."

"There is nothing else higher than myself; all this is woven upon me like numbers of pearls upon a thread. I am the taste in water, I am the light in the sun and the moon."[1]

These and many other similar expressions represent an evident effort to graft the materialistic conceptions of the Sankya upon the Vedanta, which is in nothing more emphatic than in denying the existence of all that is phenomenal and material.

Krishna gave to Arjuna, at the latter's request, a vision of his true Self separate from, and infinitely higher than, the humble and illusive garb of his incarnation. And it was to him "as if in the heavens the lustre of a thousand suns burst forth all at once."

[1] The translation which I follow here is that of Mr. Telang, in "The Sacred Books of the East," which is, on the whole, both exact and more intelligible than most other translations.

And what a vision! Gazing upon it, Arjuna exclaims, "O God! I see within your body the gods, as also all the groups of various being; and the lord Brâhm seated on his lotus seat, and all the sages and celestial snakes. I see you, who are of countless forms, possessed of many arms, stomachs, mouths, and eyes on all sides. And, O Lord of the Universe, O you of all forms! I do not see your end, middle, or beginning. . . . I believe you to be the eternal being. I see you void of beginning, middle, or end — of infinite power, of unnumbered arms, and having the sun and the moon for eyes, and having a mouth like a blazing fire and heating the universe with your radiance. For this space between heaven and earth and all the quarters are pervaded by you alone. Looking at this wonderful and terrible form of yours, O high-souled one! the three worlds are affrighted. For here these groups of gods are entering into you. . . . Our principal warriors, also, are rapidly entering your mouths, fearful and horrific by reason of your jaws. And some with their heads smashed are seen stuck in the spaces between the teeth. As the many rapid currents of a river's waters run toward the sea alone, so do the heroes of this human world enter your mouths blazing all around. As butterflies, with increased velocity, enter a blazing fire to their destruction, so too do these people enter your mouths with increased velocity, only to their destruction. Swallowing all these people, you are licking them over and over again from all sides with your blazing mouths!"

Here we verily have a fine combination of the sublime and the ridiculous! The Apostle of Jesus was given to witness a vision of heavenly things such as could not be uttered. This disciple of Krishna does not hesitate to paint in such glowing terms a vision of the divine, that, to all but a Hindu, the picture seems not only incongruous but highly absurd and disgusting. One can hardly imagine that any mortal, to whom a vision of the divine being had been granted, could fail so utterly to furnish us with an edifying description of the same.

In this Song, Krishna claims to be, at the same time, absolute Deity and the supreme incarnation. In nothing do the East and the West differ more radically than in their teaching concerning incarnation or "descent." In Christianity, God only once became incarnate; and in that Incarnation every believing soul has found its needs fully satisfied. Never, in all these two thousand years, did our Lord Christ satisfy more completely the human soul and bring rest to more human hearts than at the present time.

To the Christian, Jesus represents the ultimate of God's earthly manifestation, as He does the complete realization of human salvation.

But in Hinduism, incarnation is presented as a continuous passion of the Deity. The absolute Spirit forever amuses itself with the "sacred sport" of ever changing emanations and manifestations. Myriads of "descents" are recorded in their sacred books, of all degrees and forms of grotesqueness, and not a few of unblushing vileness. It is an interesting fact that the same Krishna who poses, and by millions of Hindus is accepted, as the Supreme Deity, is nevertheless represented in the most popular books of Hinduism to-day—the Puranas, which are known in their legends to all Hindus and which wield a supreme influence over them in their life—as a very different being. In these books the story of Krishna is one of fetid, unblushing immorality and voluptuousness. The publishing of these narratives in the English language in a western land at the present time would be considered a crime punishable with imprisonment. And thus this Hindu god, who is the most popular in India and who appeals most to the imagination of the people, led a life upon earth whose record is a story of immorality which brings a crimson blush to the pure.

But, to return to the Hindu conception of incarnation, it must be remembered that it is unique in this particular; viz. that it regards the Deity as continually returning to the world to visit and to help human beings. In the Gita, Krishna remarks: —

"Whensoever, O Descendant of Bharata! piety languishes and impiety is in the ascendant, I create myself. I am born, age after age, for the protection of the good, for the destruction of evil-doers, and the establishment of piety."

The inadequacy of any one incarnation is here proclaimed, and the idea of constant communication with and impartation of himself to humanity through repeated *descents* is here inculcated. And it is a fundamental conception of Hinduism — a conception which differentiates it essentially from the Christian religion.

From this remark of Krishna, who speaks here as the Supreme Being, one would suppose that Hindu incarnations have been, and still are, definitely intended to enhance human piety upon earth, and have been such as to accomplish this purpose. As a matter of fact, the historic or legendary incarnations of India, as they are now recorded in their sacred books, have practically no ethical or spiritual content. I defy any Hindu to take the narratives of these descents, as found in the Puranas and other books, and show from them that there was anything more than physical and social relief to men intended by them or accomplished through them. I have yet to find, in those narratives, the conception of human sin and moral depravity and of the purpose of the incarnation to break the fetters of sin and to bring spiritual light and moral beauty to those among whom it manifested itself. The gulf which thus stands between the Hindu ideal of incarnation and the real incarnations which are recorded in Hindu literature, including that of Krishna himself, is wide and impassable. One has well said that the incarnation of Krishna is an incarnation of lust, and the record of his 16,100 wives and 180,000 sons is but a suggestion of the correctness of this estimate. Even the incarnation of Buddha, which, doubtless, is the highest and best among those incorporated into the Hindu Pantheon, is expressly stated by Hindu authorities to be for the purpose of deceiving and destroying the people.

When one begins to compare the picture of the Christian Incarnation with that of any and of all those that occupy the Hindu mind, and fill many volumes of Hindu literature, we pass from noon-day light into Egyptian darkness.

2. The doctrine of *âtma*, or the human self, or soul, is more in accordance with the Sankya than the Vedantic school. The individual soul is represented, not as a part of the Supreme Soul, which is the distinct doctrine of the *Adwaitha* philosophy, but as a separate entity which is immutable and eternal. Listen to Krishna's argument to Arjuna, in order to urge him into battle and to shed the blood of his friends: "Learned men grieve not for the living nor the dead. Never did I not exist, nor you, nor these rulers of men; nor will any of us ever hereafter cease to be. As in this body, infancy and youth and old age come to the embodied self, so does the acquisition of another body; a sensible man is not deceived about that. . . . There is no existence for that which is unreal; there is no non-existence for that which is real. . . . These bodies, appertaining to the embodied self

which is eternal, indestructible, and indefinable, are said to be perishable; therefore do engage in battle, O descendant of Bharata! He who thinks it to be the killer and he who thinks it to be killed, both know nothing. It kills not, is not killed. It is not born, nor does it ever die, nor, having existed, does it exist no more. Unborn, everlasting, unchangeable, and primeval, it is not killed when the body is killed. . . . But even if you think that it is constantly born, and constantly dies, still, O you mighty man of arms! you ought not to grieve thus. For to one that is born, death is certain; and to one that dies, birth is certain."

There is a great deal more in this line of the indestructibility of the soul; but nothing is said of the Vedantic idea that the soul has no real, separate existence, and that even this illusory existence, in human conditions, will terminate when the self shall be recognized to be, as it really is, an unsevered and inseparable part of the Supreme Soul.

The eternal existence of the soul is posited by every school of Hindu thought. In the Sankya philosophy, the human self, as we have seen, is a separate, uncreated entity; and the teaching of the Divine Lay concerning it is in harmony with this. And it must be confessed that in many respects this doctrine is inferior to the Vedantic, which emphasizes the spiritual character, and the divine origin and destiny, of the soul.

3. The doctrine of Liberation, or of Redemption, as found in the Bhagavad Gita, is a strange combination of all the ways which Brahmanism has inculcated through its many schools, with other ways here added. "In every way men follow in my path," declared Krishna. In the pursuance of any religious practices whatever, men were assured that they would be acceptable if they were only Krishna-olaters.

(1) But the highest path which leads unto God is the path of knowledge (*Gnana*). "Sacrifices of various sorts are laid down in the Vedas. Know them all to be produced from action, and knowing this you will be released from the fetters of this world. The sacrifice of knowledge is superior to the sacrifice of wealth, for action is wholly and entirely comprehended in knowledge. . . . Even if you are the most sinful of all sinful men, you will cross over all trespasses by means of the boat of knowledge alone. As a fire well kindled, O Arjuna! reduces fuel to ashes, so the fire of knowledge reduces all actions to ashes. For there is in this world no means of sanctification

like knowledge, and that one perfected by devotion finds within one's self in time. He who has faith, whose senses are restrained, and who is assiduous, obtains knowledge. Obtaining knowledge he acquires, without delay, the highest tranquillity. . . . Therefore, O descendant of Bharata! destroy with the sword of knowledge these misgivings of yours which fill your mind, and which are produced from ignorance." "He who is possessed of knowledge, who is always devoted, and whose worship is addressed to one only, is esteemed highest. For to the man of knowledge I am dear above all things, and he is dear to me. All these are noble, but the man possessed of knowledge is deemed by me to be my own self."

From time immemorial Indian sages have looked upon God as the Supreme Intelligence; He is the absolute Wisdom, and to know Him or it, and to know that "I am it" (*Tat twam asi*), this is the highest wisdom (*Brahma Gnana*), and it gives immediate entrance into the heaven of beatification or of absorption. And the only sin which such a man, and which this system of thought, recognizes is the sin of ignorance (*Avidia*); that is, the folly, or stupidity, of thinking that one's soul is separate from the divine Soul. To know, under these mundane conditions of delusion (*Maya*), and while under the tyranny of passion and of action (*Karma*), that I am, after all, identical with the divine Spirit, and that the thought of a separate existence is a snare and a bondage, — this is the immediate shattering of my earthly bondage and the full entrance of my soul (like a drop of water to its mother ocean) into the eternal peace and tranquillity (*Sayutcha*) of the godhead — a state of unconscious calm which shall never after be disturbed.

Thus the highest way of salvation, as taught by Hindus of all classes, is the way of knowledge. It is the highest step in the progress of human redemption. All other ways of salvation are but preliminary, or stepping-stones, to this. There is no return to the bondage of this world of Him who has crossed the river of death "in the boat of knowledge." All others must again return and further, by new births, the cause of the soul's emancipation.

(2) The second path of liberation here inculcated is that of self-restraint, of asceticism. From time immemorial the ascetic has been India's ideal of a man of piety. He is a man who has turned his back upon the pleasures of the world, even its harmless amusements and physical enjoyments, and has given himself to stern rigid self-denial. By thus denying himself

every pleasure that body can bring and every satisfaction that human society can furnish; yea, more, by a renunciation of everything worldly to the extent of supreme physical pain and social deprivation, he separates and weans himself from all that is temporal, that he may pass on in sadness up the pathway of redemption. This is the way of Yoga; and the Yogi to-day finds highest admiration in India as its ideal of life.

In the Divine Lay also this pathway of Yoga finds emphasis and exaltation.

"The devotee whose self is contented with knowledge and experience, who is unmoved, who has restrained his senses, and to whom a sod, a stone, and gold are alike, is said to be devoted. . . . A devotee should constantly devote himself to abstraction, remaining in a secret place, alone, with his mind and self restrained, without expectations and without belongings. Fixing his seat firmly in a clean place, not too high nor too low, and covered over with a sheet of cloth, a deerskin, and kusa grass—and there seated on that seat, fixing his mind exclusively on one point with the working of the mind and sense restrained, he should practise devotion for the purity of self. . . . Thus constantly devoting himself to abstraction, a devotee whose mind is restrained attains that tranquillity which culminates in final emancipation and assimilation with me. . . . The self-restrained, embodied self lies at ease within the city of nine portals, renouncing all actions by the mind, not doing or causing anything to be done."

This path of abstraction and asceticism leaves the soul to theosophic knowledge, which is consummated in the supreme bliss of assimilation with the Divine.

So enamoured has India been of this method of life throughout the centuries that Yoga has been reduced to a science, and has been elaborated to a degree which is ridiculous and almost idiotic. Listen, for instance, to Krishna's instructions where he speaks of the ascetic as "holding his body, head, and neck even and unmoved, remaining steady, looking at the tip of his own nose," etc. These ridiculous posturings and idiotic attitudes cannot, as has been well said by Barth, but lead to idiocy or to a loss of all mental aptitude.

The ultimate aim of Yoga is to reduce the soul to tranquillity and quiescence, by abstracting the mind from all things earthly, and thus leading to cessation from action; for action is said to lead to new fruit, which must be eaten by the soul; and for this purpose new births are necessary, which delay final absorption in the deity.

The spirit of Hinduism is thus evident in its exaltation of this method of life. It has made the path of abstraction and the elimination of every thought, emotion, and ambition, its ideal. In other words, man, by self-repression and the effacement of every faculty of mind and body, is to attain unto final beatification or emancipation. This is an end in itself, according to the Hindu plan of life.

In Christianity, on the other hand, self-realization and not self-effacement must be the consummation of life. The way of the Cross, that is, the path of self-denial, is indeed most rigidly enjoined; but it is the denial of the lower self, the meanest passions of the soul, in order that the highest faculties may find complete realization. Thus, in Christianity, also, asceticism has a place of value; but it is as a means to a higher end, and that is, perfect growth and development of the man unto the "measure of the stature of the fulness of Christ."

(3) It also possesses the distinction of emphasizing works or action as necessary to salvation. Indeed, the Bhagavad Gita is unique among the books

of India in teaching that action is superior to renunciation.

Sri Krishna says: "Renunciation and pursuit of action are both instruments of happiness. But of the two, pursuit of action is superior to renunciation of action."

This is, indeed, strange teaching in the realm of Hindu literature, where action is universally taught to be both in itself an evil and to be the cause of sin. Krishna, by some magic of his own power, here reverses the ordinary Hindu teaching. "He who has controlled his senses and who identifies his self with every being, is not tainted, though he performs actions." "He who, casting off all attachment, performs actions, dedicating them to Brâhm, is not tainted by sin, as the lotus leaf is not tainted by water." Indeed, we are told that some "perform actions for attaining purity of self." Thus we see inculcated the peculiarly un-Hindu doctrine that he who works for God is for that reason absolved from the fruit of his action; yea, more, by his very acts attains unto purity, and approaches the consummation of absorption. Still more, the very motive of Krishna, in this Divine Song, is to stir up the warlike courage of Arjuna and to lead him into the bloody activities of war. "Therefore do you, too, perform actions, as was done by men of olden times."

But action, in order that it may be effective, must be according to prescribed rules. Any work which is inculcated in the sacred books is both sacred and useful in the scheme of redemption. And among these prescribed works, few are more useful than the performance of sacrifice. Men "have their sins destroyed by sacrifice. Those who eat the nectar-like leavings of the sacrifice prepare for the eternal Brâhm. This world is not for those who perform no sacrifice. Thus sacrifices of various sorts are laid down in the Vedas. Know them all produced from action, and knowing this you will be released from the fetters of this world."

Idolatry, also, is a part of this sacred duty. "Desiring the success of action, men in this world worship the divinities, for in this world of the mortals, the success produced by action is soon obtained." "Those who worship the divinities go to the divinities, and my worshippers, too, go to me." "Even those, O Son of Kunti, who being devotees of other divinities worship with faith, worship me only, but irregularly. For I am the enjoyer as well as Lord of all sacrifices. But they know me not truly, therefore do they fall," *i.e.* they return to the world of mortals. This teaching may be called polytheism rather than idolatry. And yet at the time this book was written, polytheism had already degenerated into idolatry.

The most definite and multitudinous courses of action are those enforced by the caste system. And these also are emphasized in this song. Krishna here informs us that he is the author of the caste system. "The four-fold division of castes was created by me according to the apportionment of qualities and duties." Elsewhere, in Hindu writings, we are abundantly informed that Brâhm created these four divisions of men from his head, his shoulders, his loins, and his feet, respectively.[1]

He only lives well and works worthily who lives in strict accordance with caste rules, and who works in obedience to the dictates of caste tyranny. We are here informed that "one's own duty, though defective, is better than another's duty well performed. Death in performing one's own duty is preferable; the performance of the duty of others is dangerous." Here, of course, "one's own duty" is the duty prescribed to a man by the Hindu caste

[1] See Chapters IV and V, on Caste.

system. "The duties of Brahmans, Kshatriyas, and Vaisyas, and of Sudras, too, O terror of your foes, are distinguished according to the qualities born of nature. Tranquillity, restraint of the sense, penance, purity, forgiveness, straightforwardness, also knowledge, experience, and belief in the future world, this is the natural duty of the Brahmans. Valour, glory, courage, dexterity, not slinking away from battle, gifts, exercise of lordly power, this is the natural duty of Kshatriyas. Agriculture, tending cattle, trade, this is the natural duty of Vaisyas. And the natural duty of Sudras, too, consists in service. Every man intent on his own respective duties obtains perfection." And, again, "One's duty, though defective, is better than another's duty well performed. Performing the duty prescribed by nature one does not incur sin. One should not abandon a natural duty though tainted with evil."

Thus the most stupendous system of social and religious evil that the world has ever known—the Hindu caste system—is here boldly taught and inculcated as the most sacred duty of life. One man is born for pious leadership, another born to fight, another born for menial service; and woe be to any one of them who abandons this so-called "natural duty" and strives for a betterment or a change of life! This is the divinely inculcated system of bondage which has enthralled India for twenty-five centuries.

But it is gratifying to know that, though taught and inculcated in this highest book of their faith, Hindus are beginning to denounce the whole system. Both a social and a religious consciousness are beginning to rebel against its very existence.

But we pass from this lowest aspect of "action" to the highest when we remark that all acts should, according to Krishna, be free from attachment. No duty is more frequently enforced in the Bhagavad Gita than that of detachment in religious activity; nor is there any higher than this within the whole compass of this Song. It is the duty of man to work out righteousness and to exercise virtue without regard to the results or the fruits of his action. It is the high-water mark of the teaching of the book.

"Your business is with action alone; not by any means with fruit. Let not the fruit of action be your motive to action." "Wretched are those whose motive to action is the fruit of action." Therefore, perform all action, which must be performed, without attachment. For a man, performing action without attachment, attains the Supreme. "Forsaking all attachment to the fruit of action, always contented, dependent on none, he does nothing at all, though he engages in action. Devoid of expectations, restraining the mind and the self, and casting off all belongings, he incurs no sin."

We must not, however, give to this detachment a Christian value. For it is a part of Hindu thought to condemn every emotion and sentiment, however lofty as an asset of life. It regards every desire, however noble in itself, and every sentiment, however exalted, as essentially evil; for it is a momentary barrier to that equilibrium and quiescence of soul which the Hindu has always maintained to be the highest cultivation of the self. Therefore, action, in order to be of any permanent value, must be severed from every passion, desire, or expectation. And thus the Hindu does not here seek so much the existence of pure altruism as he does the absence of desire, which means soul unrest and the removal of one of the barriers to soul emancipation. It is, he says, when love and every other passion cools off into a quiet intellectual calm, and the soul is animated, not by sentiment, but by clear vision, that *Sayutcha*, or absorption into the Brâhm, is attained.

If, then, detachment is a keyword to Higher

Hinduism and man is forbidden to seek after any good, even the highest, in connection with his religious activities, what then can be an adequate motive to a religious life of good works?

Here is introduced another keyword of this Eclecticism — the word *Bhakti.*

The doctrine of Bhakti finds a supreme place in the Divine Song. *Bhakti* means devotion or love to Krishna himself. Perhaps the Christian word "Faith" best expresses the full meaning of the word *Bhakti.* Krishna says, in substance, Have no attachment to the results of your acts; but be attached to me who am the supreme God, and live and act according to the noble impulse of that attachment.

"Among all devotees, he who being full of faith worships me, with his inmost self intent on me, is esteemed by me to be the most devoted." "Even if a very ill-conducted man worships me, not worshipping any one else, he must certainly be deemed to be good, for he has well resolved." "Place your mind on me, become my devotee, my worshipper; reverence me, and thus making me your highest goal, and devoting yourself to abstraction, you will certainly come to me." "On me place your mind, become my devotee, sacrifice to me, reverence me, you will certainly come to me. I declare to you truly, you are dear to me. I will release you from all sins. Be not grieved." "No one amongst men is superior to him in doing what is dear to me."

It is probable that the Bhagavad Gita was the first to introduce this doctrine of faith. It is, of course, a doctrine possible only in connection with a *personal* God, and was doubtless introduced through the new cult of Krishna-olatry. It is foreign to Vedantism, whose God is the Impersonal and the Ineffable One; foreign also to the Sankya school, where God is neither known nor needed. It is essentially a new teaching, and is a peculiar feature of the worship of the incarnations of Vishnu.

But, introduced by this Song of the Adorable One, it has been incorporated into the Hindu religion, and figures now as one of the most powerful motives of that faith. And this new doctrine brings the Hindu religion into warmer relationship to Christianity than at any other point. Sir Monier Williams truly claims that Hinduism, in no other teaching, so closely approaches Christianity as in the doctrine of faith.

But, like all other teachings of Hinduism, this doctrine also has been considerably distorted in the process of appropriation; so that "faith" in the worship of Vishnu's incarnations, to-day, is more potential as an act than is "faith" in Christianity. For, in Hinduism, it matters not on what god or ritual the *Bhakthan* places his faith, it has power to redeem him from all troubles.

It should be remembered that *Bhakti* is perhaps the most distinctive and mighty influence in Vaishnavism, if not in all Hinduism, at the present time.

(4) Little is said in Hinduism with a view to inculcate and to reveal the efficiency of altruism, or the love of man for man. In the Bhagavad Gita hardly any reference is made to this which is so dominant a note in the Christian faith. Krishna does remark that one should have "regard also to keeping people to their duties," in performing action. "Whatever a great man does, that other men also do; . . . wise men should not shake the convictions of the ignorant who are attached to action, but acting with devotion should make them apply themselves to all action." "He who identifies himself with every being is not tainted, though he performs actions." "The sages who are intent on the welfare of all the beings obtain the Brahmic bliss."

This certainly is neither very clear, nor at all adequate, as the inculcation of the most fundamental of all duties, the love of our fellow-men and the sacrifice of self in the interest of common humanity. The Vedantin claims that the unity of all being, as taught by him, is a strong injunction upon him to love all the parts of that unity. But the Bhagavad Gita does not teach clearly even this Vedantic doctrine. Selfishness is too much stamped upon the Hindu faith. It is too exclusively an individualistic religion. It is every one for himself in the great struggle of man for redemption. It preeminently tends to cultivate in man both pride in his own achievement and an exclusively selfish devotion to the consummation of his own redemption.

4. In the Bhagavad Gita little is said of the character of the salvation which is to be achieved by the devotee of Krishna. Indeed, the nature of this consummation is left very much in mystery. We are told that Krishna's worshipper will come to him. "He who, with the highest devotion to me, will proclaim this supreme mystery among my devotees will come to me freed from all doubts." Again we are taught that such a devotee, "understanding me, truly enters into my essence." This carries the definite and universal thought of Hinduism, that man will be absorbed in the Deity. In another

place we are told that the worshipper "who is purified by the penance of knowledge has come into my essence."

This is the eschatology of all Hindu *Shastras.* The peculiar teaching of the Bhagavad Gita concerning action and its emphasis upon a strenuous life in this world would have led us to expect the teaching of a future of some kind of activity. Instead of that, it falls back upon the old and hackneyed pantheistic idea, that the human soul, being ultimately divested of its human bodies, both gross and fine, passes on in its nakedness into oneness with the Absolute, and thus loses all the faculties which, so far as we know, constitute its greatness, power, and glory. In this condition of absorption the human soul is not only deprived of its separate existence, but also of all self-knowledge, which is the true basis of personality.

As to the process of this salvation we are here taught, as in all Hindu writing, that it is attained through metempsychosis, or reincarnation. The human soul, like the divine, in Brahmanism, passes through many incarnations (some writers say 8,400,000) before it receives the crown of perfection, or of absorption. Krishna says: "As a man, casting off old clothes, puts on others and new ones, so the embodied self, casting off old bodies, goes to others and new ones." "I have passed through many births, O Arjuna, and you, also," says Krishna; "I know them all, but you, O terror of your foes! do not know them."

This devious and tedious path of reincarnation is the one over which every soul must pass. And between every incarnation and that which follows, the soul, clothed upon with a subtle body, passes through many heavens and hells in order to eat the fruits of its past actions. And there is a remnant of these fruits left which necessitates the return to a new body and a new human existence.

These upper and nether regions through which the soul passes and settles its accounts with the past, are not in any sense permanent. Concerning this, the Bhagavad Gita says that men, "reaching the holy world of the Lord of Gods, they enjoy in the celestial regions the celestial pleasures of the gods. And having enjoyed that great heavenly world, they enter the mortal world when their merit is exhausted." After, perhaps, millions of these human incarnations (and, indeed, the incarnation may be of lower animal and of vegetable), the self will gradually be perfected, they say, and will pass on into the calm essence of the supreme Soul, as a drop of water descends in rain and blends again with the ocean. I see absolutely no reason why this interminable process of metempsychosis should lead to the perfection of the soul rather than to its complete demoralization. Indeed, there is nothing ethical at all in the character of these reincarnations, so far as they are described by Hindu writers.

III

This, then, is the "Divine Lay" of the Hindu religion, the book most cherished and most highly extolled by more than two hundred and thirty million Hindus.

We are, first of all, impressed by the many contradictions which disfigure the book. Hardly a page is free from conflicting doctrines and methods of life. It could not be otherwise in any effort to harmonize the mutually contradictory teachings of the conflicting schools of religious thought and practice in this complicated faith.

On the other hand, we see in this Song an honest and an able attempt to bring the many tenets of that faith into a consistent whole. And we cannot help feeling that, while the view of God and man here presented, and the ways of salvation here enunciated, are not satisfactory, yet we find scattered through its pages gems of thought and beauties of religious conceptions and instruction which are beyond cavil, and which to-day *seem* to satisfy many millions of our fellow-men.

But, at the close of a careful perusal of the book, one feels that it is radically unsatisfying.

In the first place, it is wanting in any power for life. In order to feel this, one has only to compare it, for a moment, with the Gospels of Christianity. We find here philosophical disquisitions on the Divine Being which few men can understand and none can hope to harmonize. In the Gospels, on the other hand, we see presented a scheme of life which, at the same time, satisfies the highest philosophy and is perfectly intelligible to the most simple-minded. Here a bewildering number of mutually contradictory ways of life are urged upon us, not one of which can appeal in fulness and power to the common man. There do we find one clear way of salvation — the way of faith in Christ; and in order to walk in that way the power of the Divine Spirit is promised to every one, even to the humblest soul and to the greatest sinner, that he might accept the Christ and live in and through Him a holy and a righteous life.

Above all, we have here represented an incarnation the records of whose doings, in the sacred writings of the Hindus, shock us by their immorality and disgust us by their coarseness. And yet he arrogates to himself the nature and the functions, as he makes upon us the demands, of the supreme Deity. There, on the other hand, we witness the spectacle of the Christ who so lived the divine life, and whose immaculate holiness is so overwhelming, that His claim to be one with the Godhead brings no shock or sense of incongruity to any one to-day. He has so impressed men of all generations that untold millions, in all lands, have felt no hesitation in believing Him when He says, "He that hath seen me hath seen the Father." Here do we indeed find the supreme contrast between the manual of Hindu faith and the Gospels of Christianity; and it is a contrast at the most vital point of religion.

CHAPTER VII

POPULAR HINDUISM

In the last chapter we dwelt upon what may be called the Higher Hinduism—that system of thought and religious exercise which engages the attention, attracts the thought, and invites the devotion of the thinking classes of the Hindu fold. The Bhagavad Gita is only one of many writings which seriously present to the thoughtful Hindu some of the higher conceptions and deepest yearnings of the soul. Of all the faiths of the "Far East" none dwells so much upon these profound religious realities, or engages in such lofty flights of spiritual aspiration, as does this religion of the Brahmans. And no one can study these products of the greatest minds and most sensitive religious souls of India without entertaining a great and growing admiration for them.

But it is well to remember these are not all of Hindu literature; nor do they represent the current thought or the general religious life of the people.

A Dravidian Shrine, South India

They indeed reveal the highest and the best that has ever come to light in the thought and spiritual culture of this people. For that reason, the Bhagavad Gita is worthy of the name we gave it — the Hindu bible.

In view of all these things, who would say that God did not visit this people, or left Himself without witness among them? While He was leading the Hebrews in the time of Moses, He was also stirring this people through its old rishis, or sages. While He was rebuking the degenerate Jewish people through their later prophets, He was raising and inspiring the great prophet of India, the Buddha, to protest against a debased Brahmanism.

But let it not be supposed that this literature of "Higher Hinduism" is, in any sense, popular in India. Those religious books which engage the mind of the masses are of a very different class. They are the wild legends of the Puranas, and inane dialogues and lying incantations of the Tantras — two classes of works which are both the most popular and are lowest in the range of their ideas and most demoralizing in the cults which they present.

These books were ostensibly written for the common people and for women. And the common people delight in them and are intoxicated by their religious exaggerations and excesses.

Thus the faith of the people, as a whole, is far removed, in its grovelling thought, its idolatrous practices, and its thousand-headed ritual, from the teaching of Higher Hinduism.

Above all, we must remember that the Hinduism of to-day is not the Brahmanism of thirty centuries ago. It has been the passion of that faith, from the beginning, to absorb all cults and faiths that have come into contact with it. Hinduism is an amorphous thing; it has been compared to a many-coloured and many-fibred cloth, in which are mixed together Brahmanism, Buddhism, Demonolatry, and Christianity. And all these, utterly regardless of the many contradictions which they bring together, form modern Hinduism.

This is true also of the gods of India. The earliest of the Vedic gods had elements of nobility in them. The most universally recognized of their divinities in primitive times, Varuna, is free from the vain passions and moral obliquities of more recent gods. Indeed, as one follows the course of time and the consequent multiplication of deities in India, one sees in their pantheon a steady deterioration of character, until we come to the most popular of modern Hindu deities, Krishna and Kali, the one well-called "the incarnation of lust," and the other "the goddess of blood." One is the deification of human passion, while the other is an apotheosis of brute force. And yet the cults of those two deities have attained, at the present time, the maximum of popularity throughout the land.

The same fact is manifest in connection with the customs of the people. In early Vedic times, hardly one of those institutions which now so disfigure this religion existed among the people. Idolatry, the caste system, and the many forms of degradation of women are of later growth. Never, in all the history of the country, did they exist and flourish as they do at the present time.

Thus it will be seen that, while the religion of the Brahmans in its earliest, primitive stage was merely an ethnic faith and largely the echo of the spiritual yearning of the human soul, its development has neither added to its power nor broadened its horizon. On the contrary, it grows weaker and has, age after age, added superstition to superstition, until it has reached its maximum of error and of evil at the present time.

It is wise neither to ignore nor to underestimate the

best that is in a faith; nor is it fair to shut one's eyes to its achievement as revealed in the life of the common people.

Indeed, the religious life of the masses is the truest index of the real value of a religion, if it has wrought upon them many centuries, as Hinduism has, in this land.

I

In the West the national evolutionist says to us, "Let the people of India alone, that they may evolve their own faith. It is not by cataclysmic change, but by growth, that they will ultimately find their true redemption." Others, who have listened perhaps to the pleasing words of a clever, yellow-robed Hindu Swami, ask the question, "Why should we spend our money in sending the Gospel to these wonderfully bright people of the East; are they not able to take care of themselves; and is not their faith adequate to their needs?"

To this we simply say: "Come with us to India and see for yourselves. Live, as some of us have, for a third of a century in this land, and see, hear, feel, and understand what this Hinduism is. And, having understood the situation, ask yourselves whether this ancestral faith of India has in itself real saving power and redeeming efficacy for any one. I maintain that, to know Hinduism, is to feel a deep sympathy with the people who have inherited it as their faith, and to desire to bring to them the Gospel of life and of salvation in Christ Jesus. The people of India are, perhaps, the most religious upon earth. In this respect they are very unlike the Japanese and Chinese, who are worldly, prosaic, practical. Hindus are poetic, other-worldly, and spiritually minded. They have a keen instinct for things of the spirit. They are, also, very unlike the people of the West. Among Westerners, religion is largely an incident in life. It has for them a separate department, a small corner, in the life. In the East, on the other hand, religion enters into every detail of life. There is hardly a department or an interest in life which is not subsidized by faith and which has not to be conducted religiously.

Moreover, the people of India thought out and elaborated most profound systems of theosophic thought in the far, remote past. When our ancestors were in the depths of savagery, Indian sages were indulging in metaphysical disquisitions which are even to-day the admiration of western sages. And there were many among those ancient Hindu rishis whose self-propelled flight toward God and divine things, and whose spiritual aspirations and yearnings were so beautiful that we can but speak with profound respect and entertain the highest admiration of them. Religion is not merely a philosophy, or even an aspiration; it is something vastly more than this.

The Hindu Swami will visit the West and discourse sweetly, in persuasive English, upon Hindu philosophy. But he will not practise his religious rites or reveal his idolatrous habits and his bondage of caste to those western people who admire him. These things would at once create a revulsion of feeling against him and his philosophy. And yet these are much more an essential part of his faith than all his moral platitudes and eloquent disquisitions.

And it should not be forgotten that this same Swami, in the very act of crossing the oceans to visit the West, violates one of the most prominent commands of his faith.

II

What, then, is Popular Hinduism?

I shall endeavour to analyze it and present some of its outstanding features, such as are witnessed all over the land.

1. That which obtrudes itself upon all sides and which is, perhaps, its most determining factor is its

caste system. In other lands, mean social distinctions obtain and divide the people. In India only, Caste is a religious institution, founded by the authority of Heaven, penetrating every department and entering into every detail of life, and enforced by strictly religious penalties. One has well said that Hinduism and caste are convertible terms.

2. Another outstanding feature of popular Hinduism is its Polytheism.

While pantheism is the essential philosophy of the land, — a pantheism which denies the existence of all beings and everything save Brâhm (the Supreme Soul), — nevertheless this pantheism has, in the popular mind, degenerated into the greatest pantheon the world has ever known. Even ten centuries ago its gods were said to number three hundred and thirty millions! And this army of deities has been multiplying ever since. Even twenty-five centuries ago, the fertile imagination of the Brahman had so peopled this world with gods and godlets of all grades that the stern and sensible mind of the great Buddha became disgusted with the whole pantheon; and he established his new faith as a reaction from the old to the extent of ignoring *any* Divine Being.

If, in these earlier days, such a man was unable to

endure this manifestation of human folly, what can we not say in these days, when, in addition to the acknowledged host of well-known Hindu deities, every family has its god, and every hamlet its protecting demons; and when trees, rivers, mountains, and a thousand other objects represent to the popular mind separate godlets? One can well say that India has gone mad in its passion for populating the world with gods.

3. Moreover, this pantheon has been incarnated. It has descended into a wild and hideous idolatry. There is no other land on earth where idolatry is so rampant as it is in India. Images are found everywhere. If the gods are numberless, how much more the idols which represent them, and which are found in every hamlet and house and upon roadsides!

In addition to those idols which are made for regular and permanent worship, there are myriad others which are made of clay and other perishable substances, to be used for the time only, and then to be thrown into the river or to be washed away by the rain.

And what hideous objects these idols of India are! The images of the gods of the ancient Greeks were beautiful, and one feels sometimes almost inclined to excuse an image-worship where ignorance weds art to religion and combines beauty with devotion.

But there is no such excuse for the idolatry of India. In all my travels through this great land I have hardly seen an image, or an idol, which is what may be called an artistically beautiful object. On the other hand, many of them are peculiarly gross and revolting in appearance. The most universally worshipped god in all India is Ganesh. His idols are found all over the land, not only in temples and shrines, but on roadsides, and in all places where people assemble. And this Ganesh, the son of Siva, is represented by the grossest and most hideous idol. This "pot-bellied god" has his body crowned with an elephant head!

Of course, Hindu taste cannot be judged by western standards. One cannot fail to recognize this fact in trying to judge types of human beauty in this land. But even Hindu types of beauty are not at all realized in their idols. It would often seem as if that which was most revolting in appearance is that which appeals most strongly to the Hindu, as an outward expression of the divine. In any case, it is true that the idolatry of India is farthest removed from the chaste, the beautiful, and the elevating.

And this evil is intensified by the fact that all worshipped idols are bathed with oil, and therefore attract all the dust, dirt, and grime of the immediate vicinity.

Educated Hindus, though they tell you that these idols are only for the ignorant masses, rarely decline to unite with their families in bringing their offerings to, and in worshipping, the same.

Some will tell us that in idolatry people do not worship the idol itself, but the god who is supposed to reside within it. Even if this were true, one could not admire such a worship did he know the character of the god which is supposed to reside therein. But their statement regarding this is not true. I have personally inquired of many of the common people who are idolaters, and I have never yet found a man whose mind, in worship, passes beyond the idol itself. I admit that the educated mind may leap in thought behind the image; but the masses of the people do not. It is, at best, a debasing worship, and drags the people down to the level of the hideous objects before which they prostrate themselves.

A well-known Hindu writer said recently, in the *Christian College Magazine*:—

"I do urge most emphatically that, whatever may

Two Hindu Idols, South India

have been the original intention, and whatever may be the esoteric meaning, the millions that perform idolatrous practice in this country see nothing symbolic behind the image and take the whole show quite literally. And can anything be more degrading to an intelligent human being? We know that all religions are necessarily more or less anthropomorphic. But our popular Hinduism surpasses everything else in this respect, too. There is a famous shrine in this Presidency where the deity's *chota hazri* [early meal] begins with bread and butter, and he goes on eating without respite till midnight, when he appropriately takes a decoction of dried ginger to help his digestion before he retires to his bedroom with his consorts; there is another famous shrine where a cigar is left in the bedroom every night for his godship to smoke; in another shrine, under the management of a nominal ascetic, fetters are applied to the god's feet whenever the temple's exchequer runs low, to extort money offerings from the devotees and pilgrims; in numerous other shrines the deity is taken out in procession and whipped publicly for having committed petty thefts; in one shrine the whole process of a highway robbery is acted out in detail during the annual festival; births, marriages, deaths, and similar occurrences are, of course, as common and frequent in our temples as in our homes. Gentlemen, can any amount of esoteric whitewashing justify these disgraceful and fairly incredible practices? Then there are the *deva dasies*, our 'vestal virgins,' of whom even small and poor temples have one or two to boast. They are the recognized prostitutes of the country, and many sociologists are of opinion that no 'civilized' human society can completely get rid of such a class. Is that any reason why we should associate them with our religion and tempt the devil himself with their presence in our holiest places and shrines?"

4. Another marked feature of modern Hinduism is its devil-worship. This is peculiarly manifest in South India. In the Madras Presidency, whose fifty million population is mostly Dravidian, nine-tenths of the people follow the faith of their ancestors, which is Demonolatry.

When Brahmanism came to South India, many centuries ago, it found intrenched among the people, everywhere and universally, this ancient cult. The Brahmans, recognizing this, did what they have always done; they said to the people: "We have not come to destroy your religion; we will take your demons and demonesses, marry them to our gods, and give them shrines and worship in our temples. Come with them and be a part of our religion. We will give to you the privileges, and confer upon you the dignity and blessing, of our great religion." The people were impressed by this offer, accepted the situation, and were absorbed, with their religion, into the Brahmanical faith. From that time forward they have been recognized as Hindus, and have, after a fashion, been loyal members of that faith.

But let it not be supposed that, by becoming Hindus, they have deserted their ancestral religion, and have ceased to be devil-worshippers. Far from it. Hinduism proper is to them a mere plaything, or a festival pastime. On special Hindu holidays, and perhaps on occasions of pilgrimage, they will visit these Hindu temples and bring their offering to the deities of Brahmanism. But their chief concern and their daily religious occupation is found in the appeasing of the many devils whose abode is supposed to be in their countless village shrines and under well-known trees in their hamlets. They have not abated one jot of their belief in the supremacy of these devils in their life-affairs; and they always stand in fear of them, and do what they can to satisfy their bloody demands.

Thus at least nine-tenths of the people of South India are, first of all, demonolaters, and secondly, but a long way behind, are Hindus. And yet a great many people in the West think of these people as the pure worshippers of the highest type of the Brahmanical faith!

And it should not be forgotten that all over India there are probably fifty millions of people who are the so-called outcasts of the land, the miserable product of the caste system of Hinduism. They are "the submerged tenth" of India. They are not only socially ostracized, they are under the definite ban of the Hindu faith. They are the hewers of wood and drawers of water of Brahmanism. They have no place in Hinduism proper; they are not permitted to enter any of its temples. They have no right to receive whatever comforts religion may confer; its rights and its privileges are entirely denied to them. But the tyranny of the religion has been such, during the many centuries of the past, as to keep this class of people not only in absolute social servitude, but also in religious dependence; and has taught them (because it has compelled them) to be satisfied with the spiritual crumbs which are the meanest remnants of what the religion professes to give its members.

I have often felt, as I have talked with these poor, miserable Pariahs, that I was incapable of understanding their willingness to remain thus loosely attached to a faith which denied to them its most elementary comforts and blessings. The mystery is doubtless to be explained by their supreme abjectness and helplessness, which have been ground into them by many centuries of bondage. The consequence is, that while these many millions of outcast people are numbered among the Hindus, and regard themselves as Hindus, Hinduism itself has for them nothing but curses, and, more than all others, they must be satisfied with the devil-worship of their fathers.

5. Beneath all these lower aspects of popular Hinduism is still found what may be called its lowest stratum — Fetichism. There are many people and tribes in India who have not ascended sufficiently high, in religious conception, to make for themselves definite images of the gods they worship. Like the African, they are content to take natural objects, such as a rock or a stone, and regard it as possessed of some spirit and worship it. Sir Alfred Lyall, that well-known authority on India, has told us that one

can find in India, as in no other land, religion of all forms and in all grades of development, — from the lowest step of animism to the most spiritual and abstruse pantheism. I myself have seen, within the area of one acre of land in South India, the instruments of these varied forms of worship, from a greasy, round stone, before which the lowest classes prostrated themselves, to an image of one of the supreme gods of Hinduism. There is not a phase of worship, however high or mystic, or however mean or degraded, which has not its devotees in this land.

6. Modern Hinduism is also guilty of harbouring and fostering immorality.

This is a cruel statement to make concerning any faith. But justice compels me to add this as one of the characteristics of Hinduism. Some of the most revered and popular writings of this religion are so full of obscenity and impure suggestion, that, to publish them in a Christian land, in the English tongue, would make the publisher liable to imprisonment. When, years ago, Lord Dalhousie, the Viceroy of India, enacted a law punishing obscenity, the leaders of the Hindu religion were so exercised by it that the government had to exempt religious writings of Hinduism, and emblems of that faith, from the action of the law.

There are many religious books in India to-day which are classical in the beauty of their language, but which the Universities of India decline to use as text-books because of their gross obscenity.

Among the most demoralizing institutions to the youth of India are the temple cars, which are found in every village of any consequence throughout the land. They are erected at great expense, by temple authorities, are most elaborately carved, and are used for the conveyance of the gods through the village streets upon festival occasions. There is hardly one of these cars, in South India at any rate, which is not disfigured by grossly sensual carvings such as ought to bring blushing shame to any decent and self-respecting community. They are open to the public gaze, and children of the village play under their shadow, and gaze daily upon their vile and disgusting sights. The government would forbid the erection of such cars to-morrow, if they had not pledged themselves not to interfere with the religion of the people!

In the Vaishnava cult of Hinduism there is at least one sect, well known throughout the land, whose worship is loaded with impurity, and whose worshippers, at certain festivals, specially, yield themselves to all forms of sexual practices such as cannot be mentioned.

Sakti worship, or the worship of the goddesses, lends itself definitely to this gross evil; and the leading Tantraic books of this cult are so filthy that they are not fit to be translated. In Bengal, where the worship of Durgai, the wife of Siva, is dominant, the Hindus themselves are beginning to protest against the lewdness, obscenity, and licentiousness which prevail at their great Holi festival, which is the annual festival of the goddess.

Another institution connected with the temple worship of India, and of which Hindus ought to be heartily ashamed, is that of dancing-girls. Little girls in their infancy are devoted and dedicated by their own mothers to the temples. They are supposed to be married to the gods of the temple, and are called "the servants of the gods." They dance in attendance upon the gods, upon festival occasions, and are an inherent part of the temple worship. But the sad thing about these women is that their own mothers knew, when they dedicated them in infancy, that they were binding them to a life of shame. For the dancing-girls are the professional prostitutes of India. There are a host of these women (twelve thousand in South India alone) who, without their own consent, and in the sacred name of religion, have been handed over to this life of shame, to corrupt and debase the youth of the land. Their life is a loud cry against their mother-faith, which systematically devotes them to destruction of soul and body. Some educated men of the land denounce this as an evil which should be stopped. But the leaders of the faith turn a deaf ear to all such cries.

7. The treatment of woman within Hinduism is worthy of attention.

Hinduism has never looked with kindness or consideration upon women. It seems to have been its settled policy to treat them with contempt and unkindness. The consequence is that the girl babe is never welcome in the Hindu family. And from the cradle to the grave woman has no independence or right within the pale of this faith. During childhood she is in bondage to her father, during her marriage she must give implicit obedience to her husband, and as a widow she remains the ward of her sons.

Look at the disabilities under which the Hindu woman labours to-day.

She is held in ignorance. Only six Hindu women out of one thousand are able to read and write. She has never been regarded as worthy of education.

Her ignorance has been regarded as her safety, and has been the studied policy of Hinduism.

She has never been regarded as worthy to know the sacred books of her own faith. It is a sin in Hinduism to-day for any man to teach a woman the most sacred truths of the faith. Her mind is not a fit receptacle for such truths.

While she has nothing to do in choosing for herself a husband, she is bound in infancy, through holy wedlock, to a child like herself. Her child husband may die before he attains manhood, when she becomes a widow. And, because her stars are supposed to have had influence in his death, she is treated with cruelty and is regarded as the evil star of the home.

Owing to this evil custom of child marriage, there are to-day twenty-six million widows in this land, of whom four hundred thousand are under fifteen years of age. It is not simply that the lot of these poor women is one of greatest hardship and contempt; they also become the prey of lustful men and fall into grossest sins. In modern times the government has tried to lighten the burdens of womanhood in the land; but the representatives of Hinduism, and its custodians, all stand in the way of any helpful legislation, and are determined to keep woman in servitude at all hazards.

8. The religious ascetic represents one of the characteristic features of modern Hinduism.

Religious asceticism has been the ideal of the Hindu life from time immemorial. The man who has given up all earthly pursuits and wanders with beggar's cup in hand from place to place, making pilgrimages to the holy places of India, or who separates himself entirely from men and devotes years to the solitude of the wilderness in the cultivation of piety, — he it is who is the admiration of the whole Hindu community. And it is for this very reason that so many men in India to-day don the yellow robe of this profession, and make capital out of this sentiment of the people.

There are millions of these religious mendicants who are entirely non-productive and live upon the common people. A few of them, doubtless, are sincere and are seeking after communion with God. But the vast majority are lazy and rotten to the core. Their life is known to be utterly worthless, and they are morally pestiferous in their influence upon the whole community. And yet the people accept them as the highest types of piety in the land. Even the poorest among them would give his last morsel to these worthless men. There are, indeed, very few in the community who would dare to refuse an offering to these beggars, because they are so ready to invoke dreadful imprecations upon those who decline to give anything to them. There are few things that an orthodox Hindu dreads more than the curse of a religious ascetic.

Thus, though these men are known to trample under foot every law of God and are utterly useless to the whole community, the people nevertheless regard them very highly and shower their blessings upon them.

In any land the maintenance of such an army would be a great burden upon the people; in India, where they are so poor, how heavy this burden must be, and how great must be the curse of such a host preying both morally and physically upon the rest of the community!

It is equally disastrous to the conception of the common people concerning their faith that so large a body of recognized hypocrites should, nevertheless, be so highly esteemed as types of piety.

The existence of this class of worthless men reveals, also, another striking fact which characterizes the religion of India, and that is the utter divorce of faith and morals. Hinduism has never recognized any connection, and least of all any essential union, between piety and ethics. As we have seen, the most pious men in the land, according to Indian ideas, may be the most immoral. This has been one of the fatal defects of Hinduism from the earliest times. Conscience has found very small place in this religion of the Brahmans.

9. Modern Hinduism, also, inculcates the spirit of pessimism among its people. The Puranas tell us, and the people universally believe it, that we are now living in *Kali Yuga*, the iron age, in which all things are evil, and in which righteousness is a thing largely unknown to the people. All the forces of this age are against the good, and it leaves no encouragement to any one to try to do, and to be, good.[1]

10. Add to this the even more potent belief of the people in astrology. The planets and the stars, the moon and the nodes are living gods, they say, which wield an influence over the life and destiny of human beings. The astrologer is perhaps the most important functionary in the social and religious life of the people. No marriage can be performed unless the

[1] See Chapter X, Kali Yuga.

horoscope of the bride and the bridegroom harmonize. No social or domestic event of importance, and specially no religious ceremony of any consequence, can be carried on save during what are called auspicious days and moments. Astrology is the right hand of Hinduism, and it has supreme authority in the direction of most of its affairs.

Add to this the belief in omens, which enters very largely into human life and thought. A Hindu will not start upon a journey save on what is astrologically an auspicious day; and if even a crow crosses his path from left to right, after he has begun his journey, it is regarded as an ill omen, and he will at once return home. He spends much of his time in watching such omens; even an ass's bray carries a significance to him. If it is heard in the east, his success will be delayed; in the southeast, it portends death; in the south, it means wealth; etc. It matters not how important it may be that a man should undertake a journey or a task at a certain time, he will not do it at that time if he finds it to be inauspicious. When the new governor of Madras recently arrived at his destination, the reception to be given to him by the Hindus had to be postponed because it was ignorantly put at an hour which was *Rahu Kala* — an inauspicious hour!

In a thousand similar ways, the Hindu people are controlled and handicapped by silly superstitions which make life a burden to them and which rob them of efficiency and sanity.

This, then, is the Hinduism of the masses; and no other people devote themselves so faithfully to their faith as do these. And none, for this very reason, are more worthy of our sympathy and of our assistance to rise to better things in the realm of faith.

CHAPTER VIII

HINDU RELIGIOUS IDEALS AS THEY AFFECT THE PROGRESS OF CHRISTIANITY

To the student of comparative religion there appear many striking consonances between Hinduism and Christianity. Many a deep note in religious thought and life finds common expression in these two great faiths. Yet their dissonances are much more marked and fundamental.

In nothing are Christianity and Hinduism more antipodal than in the ideals which they exalt, respectively, before their followers; and this conflict of ideals is the most stubborn, as it is the most pervasive, that Christianity has to face in India. The vision of God and of man, of human life and attainment, which we present before an orthodox Hindu, does not impress him as it should, simply because it does not fit into his thinking. It antagonizes his inherited prepossessions; it violates many of the most cherished ideals of religious life and spiritual endowment, which, from time immemorial, have been handed down to him.

It is an interesting question how much of this difference is of the essence of the two religions, and how much is the product of the mental and spiritual make-up of the tropical East, on the one hand, and of the more northern West, on the other. The climatic and national idiosyncrasies are more potential in the complexion of the two faiths than we are wont to think.

But whether these different ideals are, or are not, essentially characteristic of the two faiths, is not a question quite germane to my present purpose. It is enough to remember that the western conception of Christianity, which the missionary has inherited and which he is eagerly presenting, and can hardly avoid presenting, to the people of this land, is far removed from what the Hindu has always been taught to believe that a religion should bring into a man's life and possession.

It is easy enough to prove to the man of ordinary intelligence the debasing influence of idolatry, the accursed slavery of the caste system, the gross immorality of the Hindu pantheon, and the dwarfing and degrading character of the ceremonialism of modern Hinduism.

But behind and above all these, the Hindu has

inherited a number of ideals which allure and command him. They are his ultimate criteria and resort, and they conflict with those which the supplanting faith presents as the *summum bonum* of life. It is not until the Christian teacher can show to him, in a way that will move him, the excellence of the supreme ideals of Christianity above those of the old faith, that his work can be said to have achieved a triumph in his life.

Hence the great—I might almost say the transcendent—importance of mission schools of all grades through which are sown the seed of a new philosophy of life. Herein also lies the even more valued service which a sane and a strong Christian literature in English and in all the vernaculars of the land can render, and is rendering, to the cause of Christ in India. For the fight in India is, more than it is or has been in any other land, one that gathers around basal conceptions and fundamental postulates about God and man and life; and Christianity can never seem attractive to an intelligent Hindu until it has conquered his assent at these points of vital importance.

Let us consider a few of these ideals which everywhere and always obtrude themselves upon us in India.

I

The Divine Ideal

In the conception of the Godhead which obtains in Christianity and that which dominates modern Hinduism there is found a difference of emphasis which amounts almost to a contrast. To the Hindu, the Supreme Soul or Brhâm is idealized Intelligence; to the Christian God is perfect Will. To the former, He is supreme Wisdom; to the other, He is infinite Goodness. The devotees of each faith aspire to become like unto, or to partake of, their Divine Ideal. Hence the goal of the one is *brahma gnana* (Divine Wisdom); of the other, it is supreme love or goodness. Thus at its foundation the religion of India has always placed *perfect intelligence* as its corner stone, while the basis of the rival faith has been an ideal of *ethical perfection.* Hence, that process of intellectual gymnastics which so markedly characterizes the higher realms of Hindu sainthood and effort, on the one hand, and the altruistic fervour and outgoing charity of the ideal Christian, on the other. For this reason, also, the great root of bitterness which Hinduism has, from the first, sought to remove has been ignorance (*avidia*)—that intellectual blindness which persists in maintaining that the self and the Supreme Soul are separate realities and which is the only barrier to the self's final emancipation and final absorption into the Divine. To the Christian, on the other hand, the dread enemy is sin—that moral obliquity which differentiates the soul from the perfect ethical beauty of God. In consonance with this, the salvation which is exalted as the *summum bonum*, to be forever sought by the one, is self-knowledge, by the other self-realization in conformity to the Divine Will. I would not affirm that moral rectitude is absent as a desideratum from the ambition of the Hindu, nor that the Christian does not accept with his Lord that "this is eternal life to *know* God," and that he does not aspire with the great Apostle "to know even as I am known." But the supreme emphasis which is given by the one to nescience as the evil to be removed, and to wisdom as the crowning grace to be achieved, and, by the other, to rebellion of heart against God as the great sin, and to transformation to His moral image as perfected salvation, is much too marked to be overlooked by the student of these two faiths, and by the Christian missionary in the land.

And all of this comes as a natural consequence from the different concepts which the two religions have of God Himself. Indeed, these two standpoints from which the Godhead is conceived account for the deepest divergencies of Hindu and Christian philosophy and theology.

II

The Hindu and Christian Conceptions of Incarnation are similarly Divergent

Incarnation is a fundamental doctrine of the religion of Jesus. It is also an overshadowing tenet of modern Hinduism. For this reason, the Christian missionary finds in this doctrine the best leverage wherewith to raise the Hindu to our faith. Yet at this very point his efforts are largely frustrated by the very different conceptions which obtain in the two religions. The Christian incarnation must be, and is, first of all, of a perfect ethical type—an ideal of transcendent moral beauty and spiritual excellence. The least flaw or crookedness in His character would vitiate His pretensions, and would be the death-blow to the doctrine of His incarnation and divinity. In Hinduism, on the other hand, moral criteria have no application to the "descents" or incarnations of Vishnu. To his three first incarnations (of the fish, the tortoise, and the boar), moral tests are, of course, out of place; nor are they any more applicable to the grossly sensual Krishna, who is the only "full" incarnation of the god, and who is the supremely popular modern incarnation of the Hindu pantheon. Hindus have never dreamt of squaring the "going" of their incarnations with ethical demands and standards.

Whatsoever of good Vishnu, in his descent, is said to have come to achieve in the world, it certainly was not a moral or a spiritual good. So an appeal to the moral excellence, or to the atoning work and purpose, of the Christ does not, at first, in any way impress them as an argument for His divine character or heavenly origin, any more than the moral obliquity of their own "descents" argues to the contrary.

Moreover, the Hindu conception of incarnation largely resembles the Jewish. It must be a triumphant descent. Vishnu, in all his incarnations, came to destroy rather than to suffer himself to be put to death. A suffering and a dying god is to-day, to the Hindu, what it was twenty centuries ago to the Jew and Greek —a stumbling-block and a foolishness. It is true that

Buddha, who was in more recent times adopted as an incarnation, in order to win over to modern Hinduism the followers of his faith, is somewhat of an exception to this rule. But not, according to the Hindu interpretation of it.

So the two elements of glory in the incarnation of Christ — His spotless character and His Cross and death — do not ordinarily appeal to the inhabitants of this land as in any sense necessary or important.

III

Ideals of Life

From the above considerations it will be natural to conclude that the ideals of life entertained by the East and West are far removed. The conflict of these ideals is the primary cause of the many strange religious and social movements which to-day send their ramifications into every town and hamlet of this land; and it creates the mighty revolution now at work in India.

Consider first the religious ideals which dominate this land and the "Far West." Hinduism has exalted asceticism as the highest type of life and the best method of holy attainment. From time immemorial the religious mendicant, with his ideals of self-renunciation and ascetic practices, has found universal admiration among this people, and his motives and methods stand as the most highly approved in all the annals of this religion.

It is true that this was universally exalted above all other forms of life among Christians also at one time, as it continues to be among, perhaps, the majority to-day. And is not the Cross, which is the emblem of self-renunciation and self-effacement, the motive power of our faith, as it is also the embodied ideal of our Life? True; but there is this marked difference between the two faiths. In Christianity the Cross is only a means. The Cross of self-effacement is the pathway of Christ and of the Christian to the crown of self-realization. We despise the lower good in order that we may attain unto the higher.

In Hinduism, the rigours of asceticism are, indeed, sometimes a means to an end; but that end is not character or any spiritual achievement, but power with the gods. Nearly all the notable instances of religious austerities and self-torture practised by *yogis*, and recorded in Hindu legend and history, were undertaken for the purpose of accumulating thereby a great store of merit through which power might be acquired over men or gods. Thus many an ascetic is said to have so subdued and afflicted his body that nearly the whole Hindu pantheon trembled in the presence of the power thus acquired by him.

But when the Hindu ascetic has not this object in self-renunciation, his austerities are an end in themselves. He renounces all — not simply the mean things of life, but also the noblest ambitions and the most heavenly sentiments — because they are a fetter which bind him to the world. He indeed calls a good deed, or a holy thought, a "golden fetter," but it is, just the same, regarded by him as an evil which prolongs his human existence; and these human conditions must be ended as soon as possible.

The Christian, on the other hand, suppresses his passions in order that his holy desires may prevail; the Hindu struggles equally against the worst passions and the noblest sentiments of his heart; for they all delay that calm equilibrium of the *self* which is the doorway into *sâyutchia* (absorption). Thus character, or the prevalence of the nobler sentiments of our nature above the meaner, is not, and never has been, the aim of Hindu asceticism. And in consonance with this fact is the other, namely, that nine-tenths of the five and a half million ascetics, sadhus, and fakhirs of India are universally recognized as pestilential in their morals, and as distinguished examples of what the laity of the land should avoid being or becoming.

The Christian seeks, as his ideal, the perfect blending of the ethical and the spiritual in his life; in Hinduism, faith has always been divorced from morality, and there has never seemed to be any incongruity, in their minds, in the act of ascribing true saintliness and spiritual excellence to those who are known daily to trample under foot every command of the Decalogue.

Thus the ideal life which has captivated India from time immemorial, and which at this present wields a mighty influence over the people, is not the generous, the upright, and morally spotless life, so much as the wandering, the monastic, or the secluded forest life of the ascetic, regardless of its spiritual character. In other words, it is not a stern and noble victory over sin and worldliness in the common relationships of life, but a fleeing from the sin and duties and responsibilities of life into the *mutt*, or wilderness, which has fascinated the inhabitants of this peninsula as the best type of life possible.

Now, in view of all this, what shall the Christian teacher do in this land? Shall he also exalt this ideal and temper it with Christian wisdom and chasten it with Christian meaning? Doubtless the wise missionary will consider well the amount of emphasis which this aspect of life requires in India, in view of the ideal which Hinduism has presented to the popular mind. He will also, I think, hesitate, on the one hand, to bring his faith into comparison with Hinduism in the matter of mere ascetic rigour and severe self-mortification, in which the Christian has always lagged far behind the Hindu devotee and monk. On the other hand, he will not be likely to exalt over-much this type of life in a land in which, for more than three thousand years, it has ruled supremely but has had so little of moral significance and has achieved such meagre spiritual results.

Another phase of life which furnishes to the people an ideal is the *ceremonial.* Among the myriad gods of the Hindu pantheon and all the sages of its history and legend, there is not one who is worthy to be exalted as an ideal of character. The reason is not far to find. With this, however, we are not at present concerned. It is enough if we remember that this absence of an incarnate ideal in the religion has led to the exaltation of rules and ceremonies as the safeguards of — yea, more, as the very essence of — a worthy and noble life. There is no sadder fact in India at present than that of this great religion, of two hundred and thirty million souls, being largely emptied of moral content as related to the common life, and built up of numberless petty external ceremonies which harass the individual, and grip the life with a dead hand at all points. The ceremonialism of the Scribes and Pharisees in the days of our Lord and which excited His supreme wrath, was not a consequence as compared to that of Hinduism to-day. From conception even to the burning-ground, every detail of life, individual and communal, religious and social (there is no social as apart from religious life in Hinduism), is cast into a mould of ceremony or ritual which robs it of ethical content, and makes it into what an indignant Brahman writer recently called "a huge sham." To the ordinary Hindu, all of life's values are measured in the coin of external rites. Let one be an atheist if he please, or even a libertine or a murderer, and his status in Hinduism is not impaired. But let him eat beef, even unwittingly, or let him ignorantly drink water which has been touched by a man of lower caste than himself, and his doom is irrevocably sealed! Through this whole system the Hindu conscience is perverted, and the true distinction between right and wrong is buried deep under this greatest and most elaborate mass of ceremonial that the world has ever known. To a people who have thus inherited the ceremonial instinct, who are Pharisees by a hundred-fold heritage and by sweet choice, it is not an easy thing for the man of the West, with his natural distrust of all that is formal and outward in life, to present effectively his Lord, whose bitterest woes were pronounced against the formalists of His time, and whose commands are always ethical, and whose life is, first of all, and last of all, spiritual.

Another ideal of life which has too exclusive emphasis in this land is that which is denominated *quietism*—an ideal which extols the passive virtues as distinguished from the manly, aggressive ones. I would by no means claim that these two ideals are Hindu and Christian, respectively. They are rather begotten of the countries and climes under which the two religions have been, for many centuries, fostered. To the eastern and tropical Christian, the teaching of our Lord furnishes abundant warrant for a glorifying of the passive and nonresisting virtues. And I am inclined to believe that we of the West have few things of greater importance and of deeper religious significance to learn from the East than the appreciation of such graces of life as patience and endurance under evil. We stand always prepared to fight manfully for our convictions, and to obtrude them at all points upon friend and foe alike. It is not in the nature of the East to do this. We say that he has no stamina. We call him, in opprobrium, "the mild Hindu." But let us not forget that he will reveal tenfold more patience than we under very trying circumstances, and will turn the other cheek to the enemy when we rush into gross sin by our haste and ire. His is one of the hemispheres of a full-orbed character. Ours of the West is the other. Let us not flatter ourselves too positively that our assertive, aggressive part is the more beautiful or the more important. Yea, more, I question whether ours is the stronger and more masculine part of life and character; for is it not to most of us an easier thing to fling ourselves in vehemence against an evil in others than it is to sit calmly and patiently under a false accusation, as our Lord Himself did? At least it must be left an open question as to whether the impulsive and domineering vigour of the West is preferable to the "mildness" of the East.

What I wish to emphasize is the dissimilarity between our western type of life and the eastern, and to warn the Christian worker from the West against the danger of assuming that Christian life must be adorned with only those western traits and excellences of character which are foreign and unpalatable to the East — the very fault which also characterizes the Hindu on his side, and which makes him feel so superior at times and so inaccessible to Christian influence. For, let it not be forgotten that the Hindu regards what we call our foibles of petulance, arrogance, and intolerance, with the same disapprobation and disgust as we do their more frequent violation of the seventh, eighth, and ninth commandments of the Decalogue. And who is to decide as to which catalogue is the worse and the more heinous in the sight of God?

IV

The Hindu Conception of Ultimate Salvation presents Another Point of Divergence from the Christian Ideal of Life Beyond

Even in the methods and processes of redemption pursued by the two religions we see fundamental differences. In Christianity, God is the prime

Agent in human salvation. He worketh for us, in us, and through us. In our own redemption we are only co-labourers with Him.

In Hinduism, man stands absolutely alone as the agent and cause of his salvation. And, as the stupendous task rests upon his shoulders, it is no wonder that he has sought relief in the doctrine of metempsychosis, whereby it is believed that millions of rebirths furnish to him an adequate time and a sufficient variety of opportunity for the great consummation. But he has never given to himself, or to us, the first reason for believing that this endless fugue of rebirths will accomplish that which he accepts without questioning; namely, the ultimate glorification of all souls. There is nothing in this long and tedious process itself which assures us that any soul will reach final beatification rather than permanent and irremediable degradation. And yet the ultimate absorption of all souls into the Divine is assumed as a matter of course by him. This process, and that of Christianity, are expressive of the characteristics of the two faiths and of the two peoples. The slow and patient East, and the faith which it has begotten, spins out its theory of time and of human existence almost *ad infinitum*. Multitudinous births alone can satisfy the demands of the tedious process of human emancipation. But, in Christianity, one passage through this world, with human hands clasped in the Divine, suffices to open the door of eternal bliss to the redeemed soul. And this idea is consonant with the more youthful nature of the West, to whose people one birth, followed by a life of energy, furnishes an entrance into eternal joy beyond.

It is equally important that we take note of that which is connoted by the final consummation offered by each of these two faiths to their followers. To the Christian there is a conscious, blessed life beyond death — a separate, personal existence which will last throughout eternity in the sunshine of the Heavenly Father's presence and in the ineffable joy and glory of His fellowship. It is the idealized life built upon the foundation of what is best and most stirring and beautiful here upon earth. It is *life*, in all that this blessed word signifies of sweet contemplation, of blissful activity, of imperishable love, and of unspeakable joy. All the most beautiful and enticing imagery of earth has been used to portray, or rather to suggest, the "eternal life" of the Christian religion.

But what is the picture which Hinduism has drawn of the finality of life to its followers? After the weary fugue of births and re-births, with its interludes of many heavens and hells, the "self" passes on into final union with the Divine Soul. It loses all consciousness and self-knowledge; every vestige of personality and all that this implies is swept away; it is incapacitated for every emotion of joy and for every act of service. There is nothing that we associate with life at its best and sweetest which does not find here negation. It is a calm blank, a rest, indeed, but from every struggle of thought, will, and emotion. This is the consummation which India has for many centuries held aloft as an attraction to its weary pilgrims.

Here, again, we observe how appropriate to the end in view is the supreme difficulty of the way. If the highest struggle of the soul in this world is against existence and its human actions and conditions, it is to be expected that a complete riddance of life and of all its accompaniments will be the *summum bonum* of the final consummation. And if this struggle for emancipation is to continue through numberless births and earthly existences, it is natural that the coveted end should bring a loss of all that life connotes in highest sentiment as well as basest passion. I need not dwell upon the contrast between this and the anticipations entertained by every humble Christian.

This whole eschatological system of Hinduism corresponds, as we have seen, to the teaching of that faith in reference to God, man, and earthly life and conditions. And the Christian preacher's or teacher's vivid portrayal of the Christian's heaven too often denotes to the Hindu only one of the many purgatorial heavens of his religion, and rarely suggests to him the supreme test of the value of our faith as contrasted with his own. The glories of our heaven do not appeal to the stolid, weary, transmigration-ridden soul of the Hindu as they do to the youthful, hopeful, buoyant soul of the Christian. And this is a fact which the missionary would do well to keep in mind at all times.

I might continue the list of the incompatibilities of Hindu and Christian ideals. But I have gone far enough to show, I trust, that the two faiths are at many points antipodal, and that their ideals clash in matters fundamental and crucial.

Further, I wish to repeat that I do not maintain that Christian ideals are always, or even ever, represented in their fulness, or with the right emphasis, by us of the West. Hinduism is an ethnic faith, and it must be weighed and valued by the ideals which the people of this land have imbibed from it and invariably connect with it. Christianity is a world faith, and no one nation or continent can be a full exemplar, or an all-wise interpreter, of its life and ideals. Hence I claim that one of the considerations which demand closest attention from a western teacher, as he imparts his faith to the people of India, is that of the choice and emphasis of ideals which he shall present to them. Let him neither assume, on the one hand, that Hindu ideals are unchristian, nor, on the other, that our western ideals, both in their emphasis and exclusiveness, are the all-in-all of Christian truth and life. Christianity in the East, when it becomes thoroughly indigenous, will reveal and glorify a different type of life from that of the West. It will be less aggressive and assertive, but more contemplative and more deeply pious and other-worldly than anything we have been wont to see in the West.

The day has come when missionaries must study with more seriousness the religion of India, that they may understand its true inwardness and discover its sources of power. Above all, they must be conversant with its highest ideals and understand the relationship of the same to those of their own faith. And they must not forget that they must approach this study with genuine sympathy and appreciation, in order to find the best in Hinduism, as well as to be fortified against its worst features.

Never before did the educated men of this land stand up with more determination for their old ideals, and this is a matter of serious concern to our cause. On the other hand, the most encouraging fact in the realm of Christian work in India at the present time is that of the marvellous place which our Lord has found among the people of the land, especially the educated, as the ideal of life. They will have none of Him as a Saviour, and His death has no significance to them. But His blessed life has become the inspiration and the ideal of life to the cultured classes of India, in a way which is transforming their ethical conceptions and which largely eclipses all other life-influences among them. Herein lies our hope and assurance for India. But what they crave, and what they say they *must* have, is "an Oriental Christ," a Christ who is not presented in a western garb of life and thought. Herein do we learn a most important lesson for our life-work, as Christian missionaries in this land of the East.

CHAPTER IX

THE HOME LIFE OF HINDUS

The home life of a people is one of the most decisive tests of its character and its state of civilization.

In this chapter I shall attempt only to describe the home life of Hindus. And even within this limitation I can only refer to the general characteristics which obtain among nearly *all* Hindus, and shall pass by the details, which differ so largely in different parts of the country and among different castes.

It is in the home that the natural religious bent of the Hindu finds its full scope and most touching manifestations. Generally speaking, one may say that the house of a Hindu is his sanctuary, where the tutelar god has its niche or shrine to which daily worship is rendered. There is hardly any event connected with home life which is not religiously viewed and made the occasion of definite family worship. Of the sixteen events in the life of a man, from birth to death, there is not one which is not viewed from a religious aspect, and is not accompanied by an elaborate ritual.

There is hardly a respectable Hindu household in which there is not a shrine containing an idol of stone or of some metal which corresponds in value to the measure of the family's wealth. "Every morning and evening it is worshipped by the hereditary *purohit*, or priest, who visits the house for the purpose twice a day, and who, as the name implies, is the first in all ceremonies, second to none but the *Guru*, or spiritual guide. The offerings of rice, fruits, sweetmeats, and milk, made to the god, he carries home after the close of the service. A conch is blown, a bell is rung, and a gong beaten at the time of worship, when the religiously disposed portion of the inmates, male and female, in a quasi-penitent attitude, make their obeisance to the god and receive in return the hollow benediction of the priest."[1]

Even the building of the house is a matter which must be done according to the rules of faith. The selection of a site, the correct orientation of the building, the number and location of the rooms, the proper material for the structure, — all of these must be determined by the *Vastu Sastri*, or the architects, who do their business not so much on scientific lines as upon religious. They have their *Shastras*, or

[1] From "Hindus as They Are."

books of instruction, in architecture, whose basis is largely a consideration of the supposed sentiments of the gods and a proper harmonizing in the building of various religious conceits, crude superstitions, and immemorial customs.

Even the day and hour of entering and dedicating the house must be fixed by rules of faith, which are as exacting as they are multitudinous. To enter and consecrate a house at the wrong astrological moment would bring in its train a number of domestic disasters. The house may be anything, from a most primitive hut to a many-aisled palace; but in every case the astrologer must be consulted as to the time; the spiritual architect must give his rules as to the structure; and the family priest must make the house habitable by an elaborate ceremonial and offerings to the god or gods of the family.

It is only after all these have been accomplished that a householder may, with a clean conscience, enter his new home and expect a blessing upon his family therein.

To a stranger who passes through the streets of a town or village it may seem strange that no two adjoining houses have exactly the same orientation. He may think it an evidence of carelessness, or a want of taste. But to the Hindu it is the result of pious conformity to the rules of his faith. To a non-Hindu it may seem peculiar that Hindus generally enter their new homes in the first half of the year. But to the Hindu it is the only half when the gods are awake; it would be unpropitious and almost sacrilegious to dedicate a house in that part of the year when the gods are supposed to be asleep!

The Hindu home would not be, to a westerner, either pleasant or convenient. It looks dingy and dark, doors are small and massive, windows are few and generally closed. This is partly because they are intended to keep out the tropical glare, and partly because the people seem averse to occupying an airy room. A westerner would suffocate in a room in which Hindus would delight to spend a night. It has always been a wonder to the writer that they thrive on so little fresh air in their homes.

Hindus, in the main, care very little for elaborate household furniture. Even in homes of wealth, articles of household furniture are few and are chosen merely for utility's sake, save in homes where western ideas are finding their way and a growing desire to ape western manners takes possession of a family. Some years ago, a wealthy Hindu gentleman welcomed the writer into his fine new three-storied bungalow, whose front door was elaborately carved and had cost Rs. 2000. It was furnished with fantastic articles of European furniture. Mechanical toys and speaking dolls had places of prominence; and among the pictures which adorned the walls the place of honour was given to a framed tailor's pattern-plate! A full-sized painting of the late British queen was specially honoured by being kept in a dark closet! The family did not live in this house, but occupied a comfortable one-storied building in the back yard. It was adequate to their needs and in harmony with their tastes.

Hindus generally sleep on the floor. They spread a mat under them, and this suffices for the ordinary man. Many add to this a dirty pillow, which is a mark of extravagance and an evidence of degeneracy. The men of the house may sleep anywhere within, or in the verandah without, according to the season of the year. Recently, western ideas have encroached upon this primitive, sanitary custom, and cots are finding an ever increasing place in the household economy.

The Hindu family system is widely different from that of the West. Among them the Joint Family

System prevails universally. It is built on the old patriarchal idea, according to which three generations generally live under the same roof and enjoy a community of life and of interest. When a man and wife have reared a family, the sons bring to the paternal home their wives and live together and raise their families in the common home of their father. The supreme authority, in the direction of all their affairs, rests with the father. And the mother generally takes charge of the household commissariat. The whole income of all the members of the family is brought into the common treasury, out of which all expenses are met. There is no individual property, and no rights and privileges which any one can claim apart from another's in that home. In large Hindu families there is often found a small colony thus living together and dependent for guidance and instruction upon the father. This system entails a great deal of responsibility upon the head, whose authority is supreme. And so loyal is every Hindu to paternal authority that there is never any question raised by any one as to obedience to his commands.

This system has its advantages. In early times, it brought strength and security to households thus consolidated. It is doubtless favourable to general economy. And it has the peculiar merit of developing a strong sense of responsibility in the whole family for its every member, however incapacitated she or he may be for self-support. The weak and the sick and the feeble-minded have the same claim upon the resources of the family as have the others, and the claim is universally recognized. For this reason, poor-houses are not needed in India.

On the other hand, Hindus themselves are coming to regard this system as being out of joint with modern life, under the ægis of a progressive, civilized government. One of its chief defects is its encouragement of laziness in members of families. No one feels that he is responsible for his own maintenance. And no matter how industrious a member may be, the product of his labour is not his own — it belongs to the family. Such a system saps the foundation of industry and enterprise. It furnishes constant temptation to slothfulness and inactivity. In former times, this may not have been so manifest; but at present, when opportunities open wide their inviting doors, and means of accumulating wealth and influence multiply, the system has become a source of discontent and of serious difficulty in the community.

A few years ago the educated Hindus of South India were so exercised over the injustice of the situation that they urged upon the Madras Legislature a new act, called "the Gains Learning Bill," whereby every man might claim the financial results of his own labours and accumulate wealth apart from the property of the family. The matter was fully argued in the Legislature, and the injustice of the Joint Family System was so clearly revealed in this matter, that the bill was carried through. Thereupon, orthodox Hindus raised such a storm of opposition to the bill and decried it so vehemently, as a subversion of their faith and an overthrow of their most ancient and cherished institution, that the governor never signed the bill; and it has therefore never become law.

Nevertheless, the agitation against the system is increasing, and the incongruity of the Joint Family System with modern social conditions is becoming so marked that the day of its overthrow is approaching.

A well-known Hindu writer describes the injustice of this system as follows: "As one of the usual consequences of a patriarchal system, a respectable Hindu is often obliged to support a number of hangers-on, more or less related to him by kinship. A brother, an uncle, a nephew, a brother-in-law, etc., with their families, are not infrequently placed in this dependent position, notwithstanding the trite apothegm, which says, 'it is better to be dependent on another for *food* than to live in his *house*.'"

Moreover, this system fosters family dissension. It requires an ideal family, under the strong guidance of an ideal head, to live in peace and harmony under this system. The writer above quoted, himself a Hindu who had long lived under the system, expressed himself strongly upon the subject: "The millennium is not yet come. Seven brothers living together with their wives and children, under one and the same paternal roof, cannot reasonably be expected to abide in a state of perfect harmony, so long as selfishness and incongruous tastes and interests are continually working to sap the very foundation of friendliness and good-fellowship. Union is strength, but harmonious union, under the peculiar régime indicated above, is already a remarkable exception in the present state of Hindu society. On careful inquiry it will be found that women are at the bottom of that mischievous discord which eats into the very vitals of domestic felicity. Separation, therefore, is the only means that promises to afford relief from this social incubus; and to separation many families have now resorted, much after the fashion of the dominant race, with a view to the uninterrupted enjoyment of domestic happiness."

Outside of the family itself, perhaps the two most important functionaries are the family priest and the astrologer. And of these two the latter is doubtless the more influential. It is well known, as I have written on another page, that Hindus are not only firm believers in astrology, but also the abject slaves of this science, falsely so-called, in all the affairs of life. It is wonderful how many events in the life of a family come within the realm of astrological guidance and control. From birth to death, most of the important transactions of life are controlled by astrological considerations.

And with the astrologer we naturally join the soothsayer, who is frequently in demand to pronounce his incantations and utter his *mantras*, to remove all kinds of maladies and misfortune that may overtake members of the family. It is impossible for a Westerner to realize how much of the life of the Hindu, in the home and in society, is circumscribed by superstitions and directed by omens only. In the case of a man setting out upon a journey forty-three different things may happen which prognosticate good, and thirty-four which forebode evil. In household matters, the eye of the Hindu man, and very specially of the Hindu woman, is ever open to any one of a thousand indications that may reveal the will of the god or the demon as to conduct on the occasion.

The position of women in the Hindu home is fundamental, and much misunderstood by the people of the West.

It is sadly true that woman in Hinduism has suffered, throughout the centuries, gross injustice, and has laboured under a thousand disabilities. But it does not follow from this, as those not familiar with Hindu lives are too apt to conclude, that woman is therefore a nonenity and a mere helpless drudge in the family.

It is true that the great lawgiver, Manu, said, "No sacrifice is allowed to women apart from their husbands, no religious rite, no fasting; as far only as a wife honours her lord, so far is she exalted to heaven." In accordance with this, Hinduism has always consistently maintained that woman's well-being is entirely derived from her relationship to man. Her salvation is to be acquired through him. Her glory upon earth and her bliss in heaven and final emancipation depend upon her attitude to him, specially her obedience and devotion.

It is also true, that in no stage of her existence can she be regarded as independent. She is dependent upon her father in childhood, the slave of her husband so long as he lives, and subject to her son during the days of her widowhood. Hinduism leaves her no opportunity, in this human existence, for liberty and independence.

Hindu ideas of womanhood have always been low and unworthy. Rather than being considered a helpmeet to man, she has ever been regarded as his tempter and seducer. The proverbs of India are full of these base insinuations concerning womanhood. "What is the chief gate to hell? Woman." This is only one of a host of common sayings which brand the womanhood of India with shame.

It is for this same reason that woman has always been held unworthy of education. To educate a woman is compared to placing a knife in the hands of a monkey. The ignorance of the women of India to-day is not a matter of careless neglect, but rather of studied purpose to deny to them that which might change their relationship of subjection to man.

One might suppose that in matters of religion,

which is the peculiar consolation of the woman of India, a wide door of opportunity might be given to her. But here again Manu says, "Woman has no business with the texts of the Vedas; thus is the law fully settled. Having therefore no evidence of law, and no knowledge of expiatory texts, sinful woman must be as foul as falsehood itself; and this is a fixed rule."

There are texts which command kindness and respect to womanhood. But the above quotations represent the tenor of Hindu literature.

All of these represent the attitude of man toward woman in the home. In society, she has had no recognized place whatever, until the present, when, under the influence of western civilization, she is beginning to find a very limited scope for her legitimate activities.

Nevertheless, in the seclusion of her own home, and inheriting the burden of this deep reproach heaped upon her from time immemorial by men, woman has created for herself a place of power in the Hindu home. Within this sanctuary she has erected her throne and reigns a queen. Has man kept her in ignorance? She will therefore apply herself the more assiduously to works of faith and piety.

Has he heaped upon her abuse and called her "donkey" and "buffalo"? She has repaid the insult by a loving devotion to her lord, such as has conquered his pride. Whether it be as wife or mother, the women of no other land wield greater power than the much-abused women of India. There is no woman on earth who reveals, at this present time, more devotion and attachment to her husband than does the Hindu wife. The old system of *Sati*, whereby a woman immolated herself on the funeral pyre of her dead husband, what was it? It was, indeed, a custom instituted by man, enforced by religious rewards and penalties, with a view to reveal the woman as the abject subject of her husband. And yet she glorified that custom and often transmuted it into the most sublime exhibition of wifely devotion. Hear the description of a *Sati*, given by a Hindu, the subject of which was his own aunt. "My aunt," writes he, "was dressed in a red silk *sari*, with all the ornaments on her person; her forehead daubed with a very thick coat of *sindur*, or vermilion; her feet painted red with *alta;* she was chewing a mouthful of betel; and a bright lamp was burning before her. She was evidently wrapped in an ecstasy of devotion, earnest in all she did, quite calm and composed as if nothing important was to happen. In short, she was then at her *matins*, anxiously awaiting the hour when this mortal coil should be put off. My uncle was lying a corpse in the adjoining room. It appeared to me that all the women assembled were admiring the virtue and fortitude of my aunt. Some were licking the betel out of her mouth, some touching her forehead, in order to have a little of the *sindur*, or vermilion; while not a few, falling before her feet, expressed a fond hope that they might possess a small particle of her virtue. . . . In truth, she was evidently longing for the hour when her spirit and that of her husband should meet together and dwell in heaven. She had a *tulsi mala* (string of basil beads) in her right hand, which she was telling, and she seemed to enjoy the shouts of 'Hari, Hari-bole,' with perfect serenity of mind. We reached Nimtalla Ghat about twelve; after staying there for about ten to fifteen minutes, sprinkling the holy water on the dead body, all proceeded slowly to the Kultalla Ghat, about three miles north of Nimtalla. The dead body, wrapped in new clothes, being placed on the pyre, my aunt was desired to walk seven times round it, which she did while strewing flowers, cowries (shells), and parched rice on the ground. It struck me at the time that, at every successive circumambulation, her strength and presence of mind failed; whereupon the Darogah (government representative) stepped forward once more and endeavoured, even at the last moment, to deter her from her fatal determination. But she, at the very threshold of ghastly death, in the last hour of expiring life, the fatal torch of *Yama* (Pluto) before her, calmly ascended the funeral pile and, lying down by the side of her husband with one hand under his head, and another on his breast, was heard to call in a half-suppressed voice, 'Hari, Hari,'—a sign of her firm belief in the reality of eternal beatitude. When she had thus laid herself on the funeral pyre, she was instantly covered, or rather choked, with dried wood, while some stout men with bamboos held and pressed down the pyre, which was by this time burning fiercely on all sides. A great shout of exultation then arose from the surrounding spectators, till both the dead and living bodies were converted into a handful of dust and ashes."[1]

The custom of Sati has been outlawed; but the spirit of Sati still dominates the womanly heart of the Hindu wife.

It is this beautiful blending of piety and wifely de-

[1] "Hindus as They Are."

votion which has been the song of Hindu poets, and the admiration of the Hindu community, from time immemorial. It is true that a wife dare not utter the name of her husband. The name of the husband of a Hindu woman was Faith. When she came to read the Bible, she skipped this word every time it occurred in her reading. Why should she demean her lord by pronouncing publicly his sacred name?

And yet, when it comes to matters of religion, her stern piety and her religious devotion in the home are the most potent factor of the household; and husband and father will bow to her supremacy in this realm. All public life and social functions have been proscribed to her; therefore, does she see to it that in her narrow home sphere, both religiously and in the training of her children, her influence shall be supreme. And it is.

It is here that the progress of Christianity is much impeded in India. A man is often found ready to change his faith, and to abide the consequence of the same. It is much more difficult for a woman to transfer her affection. But the conversion of the husband will not abide in permanence so long as the wife persists in her devotion to the ancestral faith. The writer has often seen illustrations of this supremacy of the influence of the woman. But it is not always so. In 1823, a Brahman child was born in Calcutta. When six years old, he lighted, by torch, the funeral pyre of his dead father and living mother. When he attained manhood and had received a University education, he became a Christian. He was then not only renounced by his family, but his young wife also spurned and denied him. In accordance with her faith, she regarded and treated him as dead, performed his funeral rites, and, with shaven head, unjewelled body, and the widow's white cloth, mourned his decease as if he had actually died. For Christ's sake he had been an outcast from his people and was twice dead to his beloved. This experience has been repeated a thousand times in India in the case of Christian converts. But, in this particular instance, there was a remarkable dénouement. The young man, deserted, divorced, and ceremonially buried by his wife, married a Christian woman, with whom he lived happily for many years. But after her death he returned to his first love and *remarried the widow* of his youth, who, in the meanwhile, had relented and become a Christian. This was the experience of Professor Chuckerbuthy, of the General Assembly College, in Calcutta, who died in 1901.

Marriage among Hindus differs in many respects from the same compact among western people. It is in no instance dependent upon the initiative of the contracting parties, if such the bride and the bridegroom may be called in India. Neither of them is a direct participant in the arranging of the contract. It is all done by the parents or the guardians of the boy and girl. It is entirely a business, and not a sentimental, affair. No other system would be possible under past and present conditions in India. In the case of infant marriages, the children concerned have, of course, neither knowledge of, nor special interest in, the matter. Even in cases where the future bride and bridegroom have attained puberty, no sentiment is ever allowed to enter, as a consideration, into the matter. The first question asked is whether the parties belong to the same caste and are connected by family ties. If so, the marriage may be a suitable one. It is strange that the children of brothers and sisters furnish the most suitable marriage relationships. But the children of brothers, or those of sisters, furnish a prohibited relationship! It is regarded as improper for a boy to marry the daughter of his mother's sister, or of his father's brother, as it would be to marry his own sister. The marriage of those remotely connected by blood is rarely considered; the marriage of those not at all connected by blood relationship, never.

The next matter of paramount importance is a consideration of the horoscope of the parties. Were the boy and girl born under astrological conditions which harmonize; or does her horoscope so conflict with his that their dissonance would bring evil and misery to the family? In the latter case, a marriage will be impossible, even though all other conditions are most inviting.

Then follows the question of dowry; and here comes the great struggle. The girl's parents have to furnish, with the bride, a considerable dowry, whose size is directly related to the affluence of the boy's family, or to his education and prospects in life. The bickerings which take place in this matter are most unseemly; and the marriage compact is degraded into a sordid, mercenary transaction. Fathers of girls involve themselves in debts which they can never clear, in order to marry their darlings to sons of high families of good connection. It is this difficulty of marrying daughters, save at an intolerable expense to the family, which largely accounts for the universal and keen disappointment of Hindu families when they discover, at childbirth, that a daughter, and not a son, has been born.

The contract having been sealed by definite religious ceremony, the children wait until the girl attains puberty, which may take place at any time, from the age of ten to fourteen. Then the rites of consummation are performed, and they live together as man and wife. Until the marriage is consummated, it is the height of propriety that the parties shall be apart and strangers to each other.

It is very often the case that there is much disparity between the age of man and wife. A married woman is supposed to belong to her lord for time and eternity. A widow is therefore ineligible for remarriage, even though her husband may have died when she was an infant. The man, on the other hand, may contract any number of marriages. The rapidity and the businesslike way with which he proceeds to arrange new nuptials after the death of his wife seems appalling to a Westerner! It matters not how many wives he may have had, nor how old he has become, none but the very young is eligible to become his spouse. The consequence is that many men of matured, and even of old, age are wedded to mere girls.

This is partly owing to the fact that the Hindu has not yet realized the need, or importance, of companionship between man and wife. This is very marked among the educated men of the Hindu community. Not only by age, but also by educational and other qualifications, a wife is in no condition to be a sympathetic companion to her spouse. So that the relationship has, to them, little of mutuality in it.

The lot of the Hindu widow is, proverbially, a hard one. She is despised and hated, even though she be but a child, because her husband's family persist in believing that his death was caused by her adverse horoscope. She suffers every obloquy in her husband's home, is deprived of her jewels, has her head shaven, and is clothed only with a coarse white cloth. Her fastings are long and severe, and she is not allowed to attend any festivity; for the presence of a widow would be deemed an evil omen and a curse.

Moreover, she is the object of suspicion, and is frequently the prey of men's passions. It is a strange comment upon the religious perversity of a people of the tender domestic nature of Hindus, that they should deal with so much cruelty and such apparent indifference to the bereavement and suffering of the unfortunate widow who bears so tender a relationship to them. Religion has never wrought greater cruelty and injustice to any one than to the Hindu widow, specially to the child widow. And, notwithstanding the fact that these suffering ones are a great host in this land, there are few of their people who raise their voice in their defence or strive for their relief.

The relationship of son-in-law and mother-in-law is always a strained one. The wife's mother may live with her under very decided limitations. It is not permitted to her to eat in the presence of her son-in-law, or to enter a room where he happens to be!

The situation is still worse between the daughter-in-law and the mother-in-law. The vernaculars of India abound in proverbs which illumine this relationship and reveal its strange character. The husband's mother apparently delights in nothing more than in exercising a cruel restraint over her son's wife. Nothing that the young woman can do will please her. And the husband too often sides with the older against the younger woman. When, however, the situation becomes intolerable to the wife, she takes French leave, and goes home to her parents. This soon brings her husband to terms; and it is etiquette that he go and ask her to return, apologizing for the troubles that she has endured. And so the situation is improved, for a while, until another visit to her parents becomes imperative. It is natural enough that the mother-in-law should thus deal harshly with her daughter-in-law; for is it not her revenge for the similar treatment which she received many years ago as daughter-in-law? The real attitude of the Hindu toward his wife is doubtless more cordial than it appears to a Westerner. He seems to delight in revealing an indifference to her feelings and a contempt for her position. In the household, she is not permitted to eat with him; she must wait upon his lordship and take the leavings of his meal. Upon a journey, it would be gross impropriety for her to walk by his side. Etiquette demands that she walk behind him at a respectable distance of, say, ten paces.

The love of jewellery is a marked passion with the women of India. Millions of money are expended every year in the manufacture of female adornments. And in this work there are more than four hundred thousand goldsmiths constantly employed. The wealth of a family, especially among the middle classes, is largely measured by the amount of jewellery which the women of the household possess.

No one would grudge to these women a certain amount of these personal ornaments; but when it becomes a mad craze to convert all their wealth into such vanity, and thus to render their wealth entirely unremunerative, it becomes a serious matter. The loading down of a woman or a girl with precious stones, gold, silver, or cheaper metal, adds anything but attractiveness to the person. It gives them a gross conception of personal attractiveness as well as a monetary value to beauty, which degrades the ideals of the country. When a woman's ears and nose, the crown of her head, her neck, arms, hands, waist, ankles, and toes are made to sparkle with the wealth of the family, and to bear down the frail body of the proud victim, they cease entirely to set off the personal beauty of the woman herself, and become rather a counter attraction; and she is admired not for what she is, but for what she carries.

Moreover, it is well known that these women are not satisfied, on public occasions, to wear their own jewels only; they borrow also those of their neighbours and shine with a borrowed light, which reflects a great deal more their vanity than their beauty. Many a time has the writer seen bright little Brahman girls carrying upon their person the combined glittering wealth of several families upon festive occasions. Add to this again the fact that there are thousands of women and children murdered in India every year for the sake of these personal ornaments which they flaunt before the public, and with which they tempt criminals.

It is claimed that higher-class Hindus are cleaner in their personal habits than almost any other people on earth. This is probably true, so far as a multiplicity of ablutions can make them. The religious washings of the Brahman are so frequent as to make him largely immune to epidemics of cholera and other filth diseases. And yet the lower classes of the people, in their homes and elsewhere, have little to boast of in the line of cleanliness. They all aspire to the weekly oil-bath, which is doubtless a wholesome thing in the heat of these tropics, where, through paucity of clothing, the skin is much exposed to the sun's rays. But oil has well-known attractive powers for dust, filth, and vermin too!

It must also be remembered that the Hindu is given much more to seeking ceremonial than sanitary cleanliness. It matters not how filthy the water may be, chemically; if it be ceremonially clean, he uses it freely. If it be ceremonially polluting, it is eschewed.

As one sees a village community make all possible uses of the village pond, he wonders why the whole village has not been swept away by disease. They are saved from their folly, doubtless, by the piercing, cleansing rays of the tropical sun.

Hindu clothing is both beautiful and admirably suited to the tropical climate. The one cloth of the Hindu woman, which she so deftly winds around her body, and which is usually of bright colours, is perhaps the most exquisitely beautiful garment worn by any people. And this is altogether adequate to her needs. Unfortunately, western habits are now coming into vogue, and, in the case of men and women alike, the clothing of the West is partially supplanting that of the East. Nothing could be more unfortunate, from the standpoint of health, beauty, and economy.

The culinary arrangements and the cuisine of the Hindu home are somewhat elaborate. Well-to-do Hindus, notwithstanding many caste restrictions, are somewhat epicurean in their tastes, and live well. As we have seen in the chapter on Caste, there are many limitations placed upon the selection of food, the method of its preparation, and of eating. Meat is entirely banned by the highest castes. None will touch the meat of the bovine kind, save the outcast

Pariah. All are very particular in seeking seclusion for their meals. This is perhaps the reason why the Hindu home is, generally speaking, so much more secluded than that of other people. Hindus believe that fingers were made before knives, forks, and spoons. Consequently they eat their food entirely with their fingers. It seems offensive enough to Westerners. It has often taken away the writer's appetite as he has feasted with them, to have the cook dole out his rice to him with his bare hands! They eat entirely with their right hand, and never touch the food with the left, reserving that hand for baser purposes.

In wealthy families, household duties are performed by many servants. It is amusing to see how many servants are required in India to perform the ordinary functions of one able-bodied servant in the West. The services which a Hindu will demand from his menials are far greater than those of a healthy Westerner. His languid nature and general effeminacy make him entirely dependent upon his servant for most of the activities and amenities of life. Recently the writer heard a Hindu companion in a railway car call his servant at night from an adjoining car to come and turn the shade over the compartment lamp that he might have a nap! A well-known writer, in describing the life of a Babu, says: "The *Khansama* of a Babu is his most favourite servant. From the nature of his office he comes into closest contact with his master; he rubs his body with oil before bathing, and sometimes shampoos him,—a practice which gradually induces idle, effeminate habits and eventually greatly incapacitates a man for the duties of an active life. Indeed, to study the nature of a 'big native swell' is to study the character of a consummate Oriental epicure, immersed in a ceaseless round of pleasures, and hedged in by a body of unconscionable fellows, distinguished only for their flattery and servility."

During times of sickness, the native doctor is in requisition. This functionary is not without his merits; for it is a hereditary profession, and not a little medical wisdom and experience have been transmitted from father to son down the centuries. Nevertheless, as compared with modern science, the ignorance of these men is woful, and the unnecessary loss of life through that ignorance is lamentable. Their pharmacy is as defective as many of their remedies are absurd and disgusting. The present government, by multiplying its hospitals and dispensaries, has done much to arrest disease and remove suffering. And yet the remedies do not reach one-tenth of the population. And many of the one-tenth are so suspicious of western science that in their extremity they will pass the well-equipped government hospital and its diplomaed attendants in order to consult the native doctor and to partake of his concoctions. One of the reasons for this prejudice is the largeness of the dose which the Indian doctor invariably supplies. How can the diminutive doses of the white man and his establishment remove important difficulties and heal serious diseases? The writer has known not a few well-educated Indian Christians living under the shadow of a well-equipped missionary hospital which furnished its medicines free, sneak away a few streets beyond to consult the man who is a compound of a quack and an astrologer. And yet, doubtless, the new pharmacy of the West brings healing in its wings to millions of this people annually; and it is one of the causes for the rapid increase of the population.

At childbirth, the barber's wife is always called. She is the midwife of India, and the poor Hindu wife who is about to become a mother is the victim of the ignorance and stupidity of this woman. It is no wonder that so many die in childbirth or survive only to become invalids through the remainder of their lives. To remove this serious evil, government is putting forth strenuous efforts to bring intelligent relief to the mothers of India.

The entrance of death into a Hindu family brings, as elsewhere, inexpressible sorrow. The women of the family resign themselves to their grief, which is expressed by loud wailings, with beating of their breast and tearing their dishevelled hair. While professional wailers are rare, nevertheless friends and relatives congregate and add volume to the dirge of sorrow. The leading women mourners will often express in weird chant and appropriate words their praises of the virtues and the beauties of the departed ones. The men of the household mourn in silence, as it is not fitting that the man should audibly express his sorrow in public.

Hindus make immediate arrangements for burning or burial as soon as death has occurred; so that, usually, the funeral services are over within twelve or eighteen hours after death. This is desirable, because of the Hindu custom of fasting so long as a corpse remains in the house; and is also necessary because of the speedy decomposition of the body in the tropics. It is also made possible by the fact that Hindus do not use coffins.

It is the custom of most of the higher-caste Hindus to cremate their dead; while many of the lowest castes and outcasts resort to burial. Cremation would doubtless be the more sanitary method, if the fire were not so inadequate in many instances. The Hindu burning-ground is a place of ghastly and disgusting interest.

Funeral ceremonies do not terminate with the burning or with the burial of the body in Hinduism. The ritual connected with the dead, which is called *Shradda*, is, among the higher classes, a most elaborate and complicated one, and lasts, with intermissions, for a year. These are conducted with much effort by, and at great expense to, the oldest son of the family. And a great significance is attached to their rigid performance. It may be regarded as a part of the great ancestral worship of the East.

The function of this ceremony is also kindred to that of Roman Catholicism, which, through prayer and offerings, seeks the release of souls from Purgatory. By this ritual, which involves also gifts to Brahmans and priests, the son makes more easy the pathway of the departed parent through the shades into the realms beyond, and relieves the departed soul of its encumbrances and facilitates its progress toward bliss. By some it is claimed that these ceremonies, when rightly performed, render unnecessary his suffering in hell or his returning to this world for rebirth. It is more likely that the purpose is to reduce the suffering and to enhance the progress of the soul between this birth and the next. In any case, all orthodox Hindus regard the *Shradda* ceremonies as possessing great virtue and high importance. And this is one of the principal reasons why every Hindu man and woman is so eager for the birth of a son in their family. Without a son, who is there to relieve their soul from destruction, and to bring to them future peace and rest through the *Shradda* ceremony? Thus parents ever pray for male offspring; and the greatest disappointment in the life of a Hindu woman is not to be able to present her lord a son to solace him in this life and to assist him through the valley of death. One of the questions asked by the dutiful son, as he performs this laborious ritual, is, —

> "O my father, my grandfather, my great-grandfather!
> Are you satisfied? Are you satisfied? We are satisfied."

If any son, by the dutiful performance of offering and ritual here upon earth, can bring help and peace to his dead ancestors, the Hindu son may be expected to succeed.

The following, taken from an ancient Sutra, is regarded as a Hindu burial hymn :—

"Open thy arms, O earth! receive the dead
With gentle pressure and with loving welcome.
Enshroud him tenderly, even as a mother
Folds her soft vestment round the child she loves.
Soul of the dead, depart! take thou the path—
The ancient path by which our ancestors
Have gone before thee; thou shalt look upon
The two kings, mighty Varuna and Yama,
Delighting in oblations; thou shalt meet
The fathers and receive the recompense
Of all thy stored-up offerings above.
Leave thou thy sin and imperfection here;
Return unto thy home once more; assume
A glorious form."

CHAPTER X

KALI YUGA — INDIA'S PESSIMISM[1]

MANY nations, during the period of their infancy and ignorance, have given to Time and its divisions the power and qualities of life and have clothed them with moral purpose and attributes. Chronos was to the Greeks of old the god of time, in whose hands were the destinies of men. Even up to the present day not a few ignorant people of Christian lands are influenced, to some extent, by an inherited superstition about "lucky" and "unlucky" days. But I know of no land which is suffering more than India from traditional, false, and injurious conceptions of chronology. Time is here endowed with life and enthroned among the gods. Sivan is "*Maha-Kalan*," the great incarnation of Time, and the mighty destroyer of all things. It is also said that "Time is a form of Vishnu."

We are told that we are living in *Kali yuga*, and that we are subject to all the evil which is the permanent characteristic of this iron age. I believe that

[1] This chapter is a modified form of a lecture delivered to Hindus.

there are few things in India which so thoroughly influence the life, habits, and character of the people as do their many conceptions about chronology. And I am convinced that incalculable good would come to the country if all these old and exploded ideas were to give way to more rational ones — such as are in harmony with modern intelligence and civilization.

Consider, then, the various aspects of the chronology which all but universally prevails in India in order that we may see wherein it touches the life and moulds the thought of educated and uneducated alike.

I

The Astounding Length of the Chronological System

In ancient Vedic times there obtained here, so far as we can see, much more sober views of chronology than at present. It was much later that the imagination of Hindu writers took full wing and carried the people into the all but infinite reaches of Puranic chronology. One must wait for the elaboration of Vishnu Purana, for instance, in order to meet that apparent sobriety of mathematical detail which is utilized to add credibility to the most fantastic time system that imagination ever devised.

Christians of the West have doubtless erred on the side of excessive brevity in their theories and beliefs about the beginnings of history and especially in their attempt to locate the origin of the human race. Until recently, it was thought that our human progenitor, Adam, was created no more than sixty centuries ago, and that the whole history of mankind is consequently confined to that brief space of time. In the same way the practical mind of the West has pictured to itself the termination of human life and history upon earth at some not very remote date in the future. Science has already shown the error of the former, as history is likely to demonstrate the falsity of the latter theory.

But India has, with much greater daring and with more of unreason, carried back many billions of years the origin of mankind and has painted vividly a future whose expanse is as the boundless sea.

We are now, it is said, at the close of the first five thousand years of *Kali yuga*. And this same *yuga*, or epoch, has 427,000 years still in store for us and our descendants! Before it arrived, the other three *yugas* — *Kritha*, *Tretha*, and *Dwapara* — had passed on; and these, together, were equal to more than ten thousand divine years, or to nearly four million human years! These four epochs equal a total of 4,320,000 human years, and this is called a "*maha-yuga.*" This in itself would stagger the practical mind of the West. But it is only the very threshold of Hindu chronology! There are seventy-one of these great epochs in a "*Manuvanthara,*" or the period of one Manu, or human progenitor. And there are many of these Manus with their periods. For instance, there are fourteen of them required in order to cover the time called "*Karpa,*" or one day in the life of Brahmâ. And after Brahmâ has spent his modest day everything is destroyed and his godship spends an equal period in sleep and rest. Then begins another Brahmâic day, in which a new succession of Manus spend, with their progeny, their interminable epochs. And thus one series of epochs follows another, sandwiched in by equally long spaces of lifeless darkness. And this goes on until Brahmâ has completed his divine life of one hundred years; and then comes the final dissolution. Having gone on as far as this, there is no reason why the imagination should rest at this point; and so Vishnu *Purana*, which, of course, is composed in praise of that god, claims that one day of Vishnu is equal to the whole life of Brahmâ!

No one can bring within the range of his thought

or imagination one tithe of the years, divine or human, which are included in this marvellous chronology. A billion years are but as a day to the Hindu mind.

And if any one is anxious to know the exact place at which we have arrived in this chronological maze, the same *Purana* informs us that we are five thousand years advanced in the *Kali yuga* of "*Varâha karpa*," or the first day in the second half of Brahmâ's life. And thus we are supposed to live not far (say a few billion years!) from the middle of the Hindu chronological system. One may better realize the length of the system if he remembers that we have yet to spend of the present *Kali yuga* alone more than seventy times the whole of the old Christian chronology from Adam to the present time! And yet, as compared with the whole system described above, *Kali yuga* is less than one day in a thousand years. And that largely measures the difference between the imagination of the West and the same developed faculty in the East!

It is quite unnecessary to say that the prehistoric Manus of previous *yugas* are absolutely imaginary creatures, since history can tell us practically nothing about the head of our race, even in the present Hindu dispensation. There is not a line of history or of reliable tradition that will enable us to reach farther back than five or six thousand years in this quest for the origin of our race. There was, of course, a beginning of human life on earth; and we may, just as we please, call the progenitor "Manu" or "Adam." But, according to the Hindu chronological system, six thousand years only carries us just back into the last *yuga*, and is as but yesterday in the march of the divine æons of the past. Certainly, writers whose productions are unreliable as a guide to the events of the past century or two are only indenting upon their imagination when they descant upon the chronological data of the *Puranas*.

One of the principal evils connected with this measureless time system is found in the fact that it helps to destroy the confidence of all intelligent men in the historicity of characters and events which would otherwise be worthy of our credence. For example, the question is asked whether such a man as Rama Chandra ever existed. We at once reply in the affirmative; for does not the Ramayana dwell upon his exploits, and are there not other reasons for believing that such a hero lived in ancient times in this land?

And yet when the *Puranas* tell us that this same

Rama received his apotheosis and appeared as an incarnation of Vishnu in the *Tretha yuga*, say one or two millions of years ago, we are astounded at the credulity of those who could write such a statement as well as those who can accept it; and we are led to question whether, after all, Rama ever existed or is simply a poetic conception carried far away into an imaginary time. Thus the chronology of the land tends to cast a cloud of doubt and suspicion over all that is historical, traditional, or legendary in the literature of the people.

Still greater than this is the unfortunate influence of such a system upon the people themselves, in helping to destroy any appreciation that they would otherwise have of historic perspective. It is well known that the people of India have throughout the ages been the most wanting in the ability to write and soberly to appreciate historic facts.

They are great thinkers and wonderful metaphysicians, but they are not historians. The meagre history of India which has come down to us was not written by the people themselves. Not until recently, and then under the influence of western training, did any reliable book of history emanate from the brain and hand of a native of this land.

All that we know of the ancient history of India comes to us in two ways. It is known indirectly through the language and literature and ancient inscriptions of the past. Historians of to-day have to study the science of language, and especially the growth of the Sanscrit tongue; and, through an intimate knowledge of the same, they arrive approximately at the time in which many of the most important books of the land have been written and at the dates of the events narrated in them. Or they may be helped, to some extent, to learn this history by a study of the teachings of the books themselves, which may indicate the time in which they were written. A few inscriptions and coins give the dates of certain reigns, which thus bring us directly and briefly into the correct era of certain important events.

But the bulk of the history of India comes through foreigners. At different periods in the history of the land men of other nationalities visited India and then recorded their observations concerning the country and the people. The Greeks were great travellers and keen observers in ancient times. They came to India and left in their books such statements about the land as assist us to understand its condition at that period. Then the Chinese, in the early centuries of the Christian era, visited this land and recorded in their works much of interest about the social and religious condition of the people. Later, the Mohammedan conquest brought many foreigners into India, and some of the writers of Islam give us further insight into the affairs of the country. From the fifteenth century the Romish missionaries have conveyed, through their reports to Rome, much of information concerning the people and their life. And thus the history of India has largely depended upon the keen and careful observations and statements of men of other lands who came here for travel, trade, or religion. But Indians themselves have, at no time, contributed to this most important department of literature. We may search in vain for even one volume of reliable history out of the myriad tomes of embellished narratives which have emanated from the fertile brains of the men of India. How shall we account for this strange and very striking fact? It must be, in part, owing to the innate passion of India at all times for poetic embellishment and exaggeration. A cool, scientific, unadorned statement of a fact or of an event has never satisfied the soul of the children of the tropics. Hence, the history of the past becomes legend, human heroes are painted as divine, and epochs and eras are lengthened out to almost eternal proportions.

Now the most serious result of all this is that the people have come firmly to believe that these wild exaggerations, which were written by some dreamy poets of the past, are the sane and cool expressions of simple historic fact; and thus they have largely lost the true sense of historic perspective, are unable to distinguish between fact and fancy, and are strangers to the lessons of the past. For it must be remembered that the teachings of former ages, and especially the life-lessons and character-influences of those generations of men, have less and less of significance to us the farther we throw them back into the dim and hazy realm of the prehistoric and legendary. The near past, with its familiar voices and its heroes of real flesh and blood, brings to us an appeal to life and noble endeavour to which we are always glad to respond; while the remote characters of myth and of legend neither impress us with their reality nor inspire us to a higher and better life.

And, in the same way, these immensely drawn-out

æons of the past make it impossible for those who believe in them rightly to appreciate the significance and importance of the present. One's presence in the world and the value of his best activity for the world's good can mean something to him if he appreciate the fact that there is no great distance to the very beginning of human history. Though his span of life is small, it nevertheless has a definite relationship to the whole of history, and there is some encouragement for a man to work for the good of his race. But this encouragement dwindles into nothingness when a man believes in those many æons of human life, each æon being in itself an immense reach of billions of years.

II

The Cyclic Character of Hindu Chronology

A very unique thing about this chronology is that it revolves in cycles. Each *maha-yuga* is composed of four *yugas*, and these are ever the same series and of the same character. We pass on through the long vista of *Kritha*, *Tretha*, *Dwapara*, and *Kali* only to begin once more on the same series; and thus forever we move in this four-arc circle without ever getting outside of it. It is claimed that this cycle of *yugas* has already revolved about twenty million times and will go on spinning twenty million times more, attaining nothing and going nowhere. It is enough to make one dizzy to think of this mighty chronological wheel, spending 4,320,000 years for every one of its forty million revolutions, with nothing to vary the monotony of these ever recurring epochs!

The first question which one would naturally ask, after assuming the truth of this breathlessly long system, is whether it could forever return upon itself after this fashion. Is there no *progress* in time? Is it true, in this sense also, that "there is nothing new under the sun"? While other people are refreshed by the sense that they are moving forward and upward in the fulfilment of some great destiny, are ever adding new increments to their wisdom, and are rising higher upon "their dead selves" to ever nobler achievements, is it right that the people of this great land should be doomed to think that there is no permanent advance for India, but that she alone must forever return whence she started and repeat the weary cycle of the past?

As a matter of fact, no people can be thus tied down to any mechanical order of time. Every race and nation is either making for progress or for degeneracy. It will never return to its old moorings. The past has told upon it. It has accumulated some wealth of knowledge, of experience, of character, which, as the centuries roll, brings it farther on in its career. It is true that a nation, like a man, may have lapses by which it may fall down a step or more in the ladder of its upward progress. But this cannot be a necessity of its nature or a relentless law of its being.

This chronological system also accounts for much of the pessimism that pervades the minds and depresses the heart of the people of India to-day. It is everywhere claimed that the best things of India were found in the remote past. But, you ask, will not the *Sattia yuga* — the golden age — return again? Oh, yes, it is next in the procession, we are told. But we must not forget that there are about 427,000 long years before this *Kali yuga* comes to an end. Even supposing that the doctrine of transmigration is true, and that the soul of man must pass through many reincarnations; who can be expected to hold on to courage and hope through nearly half a million years of dreary existence? What India sorely needs to-day is a conviction that she is moving onward — that there is but one *yuga* in her calendar, and that that is the *yuga* of *opportunity to rise to higher things*. Thus alone can she be stimulated to her best efforts and most worthy activity.

In this connection we must not forget another aspect of these changing and ever recurring ages of the *puranas*. Each *yuga*, *maha-yuga*, and *karpa* is followed by a period of more or less complete destruction. The achievements of each period are forgotten, because its results are obliterated or consumed by a mighty cataclysm. And thus no gain acquired in any past age is available for the coming epoch. In this way, the whole idea of the puranic chronology is the most effective ever devised by man in any land to bring discouragement and despair into the heart of the people who live under it. Whether we look at the absurd length, the discouraging cycles, or the destructive cataclysms which are an essential part of the system, one and all bring in their train depression, stagnation, and the spirit of reckless waste. While we recognize that this chronology is a natural product of the dreamy, patient soul of the East, the most important fact for us to remember is that it also perpetuates and accentuates the very evil which gave it birth.

III

The Moral Characteristics of the Hindu Time System

This, doubtless, is the most striking feature of this chronology and gives it a larger influence than any other in the thoughts and life of the people of this land. And I really believe that it is more deleterious in its influence upon the Hindu character than anything else connected with this system.

According to this chronology, in its most elaborated form, every day, yea, every hour as well as every *yuga*, or epoch, has its peculiar moral character assigned to it. It is well known that the first era in the *mahayuga* is called *Sattia yuga*, or the era of truth. During this period the cow of righteousness stands upon four legs, and all living beings are good, beautiful, and happy. This indeed is the golden age of Hinduism. But, alas, its last departure was some four million years ago, and it will not return, they say, for nearly half a million years more. Then it is followed by "the silver age," in which the cow is said to stand on three legs only! In other words, virtue and happiness have suffered diminution, and evil and misery have crept into human life. If in the previous age asceticism was the crowning glory, in this second age knowledge is supreme. This is said to be the time of Rama's exploits and trials.

We then come into the bronze era, the so-called period of Krishna's incarnation and "goings." The poor cow of virtue has suffered still further limitations and has but two legs to stand upon in this *yuga!* This is called the age of sacrifice — the time when sacrifice has preëminence as a source of power in salvation.

Then we come down to the iron age in which we have the supposed infelicity to live. This is the time of evil, *par excellence*, in which the cow has been reduced to the last extremity and has to stand upon one leg! The gradual deterioration of the ages finds here its culmination. Of this fourth age there is a description in the Vishnu-purana, which is translated as follows: —

> "Hear what will happen in the kali yuga.
> The usages and institutes of caste, of order and rank,
> will not prevail,
> Nor yet the precepts of the triple Veda.
> Religion will consist in wasting wealth,
> In fasting and performing penances
> At will; the man who owns most property,
> And lavishly distributes it, will gain
> Dominion over others; noble rank

Will give no claim to lordship; self-willed women
Will seek their pleasure, and ambitious men
Fix all their hopes on riches gained by fraud.
The women will be fickle and desert
Their beggared husbands, loving them alone
Who give them money. Kings, instead of guarding,
Will rob their subjects, and abstract the wealth
Of merchants, under plea of raising taxes.
Then in the world's last age the rights of men
Will be confused, no property be safe,
No joy and no prosperity be lasting."

"Women will bear children at the age of five, six, or seven, and men beget them when they are eight, nine, or ten. Gray hair will appear when a person is but twelve years of age, and the duration of life for men will only be twenty years."

Now the idea in all this is that each *yuga*, or era, has its fixed character. Rather than that the men of a *yuga* should impart their character to the age in which they live, the age itself has a pronounced moral bent which is transferred to all who happen to live under it. Thus we see in the theory a perversion and contradiction of the facts; for an ethical character is assigned to days and hours rather than to moral beings, who alone are capable of such values.

Therefore, for a thorough consideration of the

system as a whole, it is only necessary that we consider the character assigned to this evil age in which we live. There is nothing more deeply wrought into the consciousness of the people of this land at the present time than the conviction that this time in which we live is indeed *Kali yuga*, that it is irremediably bad, and that it taints with its own character everything that has life.

Pandit Natesa Sastri remarks: "In India when a young boy or girl happens to break, in eating or dress, the orthodox rules of caste, his or her parents will say, 'Oh! it is all the result of the *Kali yuga.*' If a Hindu becomes a convert to any other religion, or if any atrocious act is committed, the Hindu will observe, 'Oh! it is the ripening of Kali.' Every deviation from the established custom, every vice, every crime, in fact, everything wicked, is set down by the ordinary Hindu to the ascending power of the Lord of the Kali age."

Nor is this merely a superstition of the ignorant. We remember how, in the year 1899, when it was said that great calamities were due, the Dewan of Mysore promised to place the matter of preparing for these calamities before the Maharajah. For was it not the five thousandth year of *Kali yuga?*

Now it does not occur to one in ten thousand to ask whether this is really so. It is accepted as a dogma which must not be questioned; and all the evil and falsehood which this involves must be a dread of the soul and a bondage of the mind whether it become a fact of experience or not.

But, accepting the universally received belief of India that *Kali yuga* is now five thousand and eight years old, who can tell us what was the condition of things in India before this? Everything before that time is absolutely prehistoric. The best authorities, and indeed all authorities, claim that the Vedas were first sung, that the Rishis of India came into existence, that the Sanscrit tongue and the Indian Aryans who spoke it and the religion of Hinduism which they brought or cultivated,—all of these find their origin during the last five thousand years. All the evidences of history unite to assure us that there is practically nothing existing at the present time in this land which is not in some way the child of these last fifty centuries of *Kali yuga*. Who, then, can dogmatically tell us that these centuries have been better or worse than the eras preceding them? We know no more about the *Dwapara* and the other previous eras, if any such ever existed, than we know about the inhabitants of other planets, if such there be. It is therefore futile, yea more, thoroughly wicked, to impose upon the people a chronological system which is so pessimistic and hopeless in its tenor as this.

But even looking back through the probably four thousand years which embrace all that we really know about India, what do we see to encourage this pessimistic view of our era?

Let it not be assumed that the people of India in the days of the Rishis of old were purer in life or loftier in ideals than many who live in India to-day. It is true that such evils as caste, infant marriage, and many similar customs did not exist at all in Vedic days. But it is also true that not a few serious evils of ancient times, such as drunkenness, human sacrifice, and slavery, do not generally exist in India to-day.

But if we desire to know what the condition of the present time is, we should compare this beginning of the twentieth with the beginning of the eighteenth century and see what progress has been achieved. During the last two centuries numberless crimes and evils have been swept away. I need only mention such enormities as *thuggee*, *sattee*, infant murder, etc., all of which were thriving even a hundred years ago, but which are now things of the past. And what shall I say of a horde of other customs that have cursed the land, such as infant marriage, *thevathasis*, caste, all of which are beginning to yield to the enlightened thought of the present and will soon be driven out of the country?

I need not add, however, that all of these wonderful changes and progress have not come out of Hinduism. They have been carried out and are progressing in the teeth of constant opposition from the orthodox defenders of the ancestral faith. It is the new light of the West that has dawned upon India and has brought to it a new era. Even while the people are insisting that they are in the midst of *Kali yuga* and are confident that the days are "out of joint," they are nevertheless witnessing such a revolution in religious, social, and intellectual life all around them that any people who were not under the blind spell of the Hindu time-fallacy would rejoice with exceeding joy to see it.

And herein do we find one of the great evils of this chronology: It incapacitates the people to accept or to appreciate any blessing which has or may come to them through religious and social advancement. They think that everything must be bad, as a matter of course, in *Kali yuga*, and so nothing can appear good to them, however beneficent and beautiful it may be.

This conviction that things are now out of joint, and the settled purpose that all will continue an unmixed programme of evil, has more to do with the sad and universal pessimism of India than anything else of which I know. It crushes all buoyancy and cheer out of the mind and rests like a pall upon every future prospect.

Then this expectation for the future robs men of any ambition to remedy present evils. For, they naturally will say, "Why flee from ills which are pressing upon us and which by experience we have learned to endure, if it be only to contract greater troubles in their stead; for freedom from evil is an impossibility in this age?" Is it not, to a very considerable extent, the reason why there are so few whole-hearted reformers in India? Why should a man seek, at the risk of opprobrium and enmity, to root out of the country some accursed custom if his inherited belief in the inherent badness of the present era is still with him? He must feel that all his efforts will be worse than vain; for even if he and others may succeed in overcoming this custom, it will be only to give room to another that may be worse. Hence the universal apathy in the face of crying evils and damning customs; hence also the helpless "*cui bono?*" to every effort of others to help the land out of the deep pits of injustice and ancient ills.

Out of this belief comes another equally portentous danger, viz. that of easily yielding to the temptations of the time, and of a readiness to participate in the common sins of the day. For, say many, are not these immoralities and evils an integral part of the time; and, if so, what harm is there in our partaking of them? Or, at least, is it not our best interest to harmonize ourselves with the essentially evil environment of our age rather than vainly to combat the sins of the day and to strive to no purpose to remove them?

And thus a belief in the divine order and purpose of the evil of our time and in the impossibility of changing the character of our age becomes one of the most prolific sources of sin, of weakness, and of moral and spiritual apathy in the land to-day. Do not many sin without fear and with increasing facility because they think it is the only life that best harmonizes with this *Kali yuga* in which they live?

Much of this conception of time is connected with

the all but universal belief of the people in astrology. In India, astrology is still fed by popular ignorance and superstition, and continues to rule with an iron rod in this last stronghold among the nations of the earth. It would seem as if it controlled the conduct of individuals, of families, and of society in general. It claims that for one to be born under the dominant influence, or spell, of one of the heavenly bodies is for him to be its slave ever afterwards. And thus the life of every human being is said to be largely controlled by certain planets and constellations, some of which are malign, and some benign in their character and influence.

For it must be remembered that it is not only the *yugas* that are possessed of moral attributes; even years, months, days, and hours are also classified as good and bad, auspicious and inauspicious. For one to do a thing this month is auspicious, while on the next month it will be the reverse.

In the same manner, almost every human activity has its "lucky" and "unlucky" times — occasions when effort is much less, or more safe or valuable, than at other times. For instance, the Hindu is warned against going eastward, Mondays and Saturdays; northward, Tuesdays and Wednesdays; westward,

Fridays and Sundays; and southward, Thursdays. This, we are told, is because Siva's trident is turned against those points of the compass on those particular days, and one would therefore be in danger of being transfixed by this divine weapon!

Then a man must not begin any important work on *Râhu-kalam.* This inauspicious time covers an hour and a half of each day of the week and is at a different hour every day. The only safe hour is from 6 to 7.30 each morning. That hour is free from the influence of *Rahu*, and is therefore auspicious. And what is Rahu? It is not a planet at all, as was thought years ago; nor is it a mighty snake which periodically swallows the sun or moon. It is merely the ascending node in astronomy wherein alone the eclipses can take place. And yet this imaginary monster has a very real place in the life of this great people, and the foolish dread of it converts a period daily into an inauspicious occasion for important effort.

I will present only one other illustration with a view to showing how extensively this moral attribute of time is ascribed and emphasized in the serious affairs of life in India. For instance, when a man is engaged in the performance of religious duties, it is regarded as of supreme moment that he know when certain acts are of no merit, or, on the other hand, of special merit. Now, there is a regular code of rules for this special purpose. By observing these rules carefully one may accumulate religious merit or power with the gods beyond any one who does not observe them. We are told that a rupee contributed in charity during the time of an eclipse, or at the time when the new moon falls upon Monday, brings as much merit to the contributor, with the gods, as an offering of one thousand rupees at any ordinary time. Who, then, would not choose the right time for his religious activity if time alone is the element which adds value to it, and if motive has evidently so little of importance in giving quality or value to our efforts in the religious life?

CHAPTER XI

ISLAM IN INDIA

THERE are sixty-five million Mohammedans in India. This constitutes more than one-fifth of the total population, and is considerably larger than the whole population of the Turkish Empire. There are now under the British Empire more Mohammedans than under any other government in modern, or in earlier, times. For at least ninety-five millions of the followers of the Prophet of Mecca are prospering to-day under the ægis of Great Britain; which is probably five millions in excess of the Christian population of the same empire. This is a significant fact.

And this Islamic population in India is growing, too. During the last decade it increased by 9.1 per cent, while the population of India, as a whole, increased only by 1.9 per cent.

Of the Mohammedans of India, only a small portion are descended from the Mussulmans of the West; while the remainder are the results of conversions from Hinduism.

HUMAYAN'S TOMB, DELHI

This population is scattered all over India, though North India is the home of the majority of them. Bengal, also, has a large Mohammedan element in its population. It is that part of the country where Islam has gathered in the largest number of converts; for, of the people of that Presidency, more than one-third (25,264,342) are Mussulmans. And in certain portions of East Bengal the Mohammedans are in the large majority.

In South India, too, there is a fair representation of the members of this faith. One can hardly pass through any section of the country without seeing and recognizing them by their physiognomy, costume, or customs.

I

The History of Islam in India

It is nearly twelve hundred years since the first military expedition of this triumphant faith entered this land. It is an interesting fact that the first attack of Islam (711 A.D.) upon India almost synchronizes with the end of the millennium of Buddhistic rule in India. Thus the incoming of the new Hinduism under Sankaracharyar almost coincides with the first onslaught of the western hordes of the Arabian Prophet upon the strongholds of India.

It was a pure conquest of the sword which gave to Mohammed in India, as in other lands, a place and a possession. And those early days of Mohammedan triumph are, in the main, a record of cruel butchery and of widespread massacre. They fulfilled, to the letter, the command of the founder of their faith, which says: "When ye encounter the unbelievers, strike off their heads, until ye have made a great slaughter among them; and bind them in bonds; and either give them a free dismission afterwards, or exact a ransom; until the war shall have laid down its arms. This shall ye do." (Quran (Koran), xlviii. 4, 5.)

The fanaticism and bigotry of that people carried triumph everywhere; and their triumph meant to every Hindu the acceptance of the sword, the Quran, or tribute. For some centuries, indeed, the fortunes of Islam in India wavered, and its undisputed sway was not recognized until the time of Baber, the distinguished founder of the great Mogul Empire in the sixteenth century. It is also true that, among the mild and patient population of this land, the spirit of that militant faith gradually softened until the era of Akbar the Great—a ruler who was not only illustrious as a lawgiver, but also was justly celebrated for his cosmopolitanism and religious toleration. He was succeeded by another great name, Shah Jehan, a man of wonderful administrative powers, but one of narrow sympathies and occasionally given to cruel bigotry. And yet, if he did not possess the graces for a noble character, he adorned his realm with religious edifices which still stand unrivalled in their exquisite beauty.

The cruel Aurangzeeb practically closed the Mogul dynasty by his weakness, bloodthirstiness, and uncompromising bigotry.

It is strange that during the centuries of cruel dominion, of uncompromising fanaticism, and of religious intolerance, the whole population of the land was not absorbed into Islam. But the Mogul Empire passed away. And, while it left a strong impression on the country as a whole, and affected somewhat the faiths of this land and left marvellous monuments of architectural beauty, it did not seriously change the undercurrents of the life of the whole people.

II

The Present Condition of this Faith in India

Like all other faiths in this peninsula, Islam is accepted and practised in all degrees of purity, from the orthodox worship, conducted in the grand and beautiful mosques of Delhi and Agra, to the grovelling, superstitious, heathenish ceremonies which obtain among, and which constitute the religious pabulum of, the masses of Islam in remote villages and in distant sections of the land.

Generally speaking, the religion of Mohammed is not calculated to appeal to the highly poetic mind of India. It is too severe and prosaic in its character. The mind of India delights in mystical elaborations and in the multiplication of fanciful incarnations and other divine manifestations. The Allah of Islam is almost as remote and as unknowable a deity as is the Brâhm of the Vedantist. But in the absence of a personal god the Vedantist and Hindus in general have built up a system of numberless incarnations which "play" upon the imagination of the votaries and give ample scope to the remarkably poetic genius of this people.

Mohammedanism has nothing of the kind; it denies even the possibility of divine "descent," and its animus throughout the centuries has been one of antagonism to the incarnation doctrine of other faiths.

The Quran is largely wanting in the tropical

warmth and legendary lore which is such a resource and comfort to the Indian mind, and which therefore abounds in the sacred writings of the Brahmans.

Doubtless, the simplicity and intelligibility of its creed — one God, one prophet, one book — commends Mohammedanism to the minds of many. But simplicity is not a foible of the religious mind of India. It has always craved the complex, the mystical, and the unfathomable. It delights in inconsistencies, and indulges freely in the irreconcilable mysteries of faith. Hinduism, being the child of the Hindu mind, abounds in tropical exuberance of spiritual exercise and "amusements," which seem childish and inane to all other people.

The teaching of Mohammed has, therefore, very little that can appeal with power, carry conviction, and bring contentment to the people of India.

In nothing, perhaps, is this more manifestly marked than in the conception of the deity above referred to. Islam is a most uncompromising form of Unitarianism. It is bitterly opposed to any doctrine which brings God down to men and renders Him intelligible to the common mind. It denies the possibility of the divine putting on human, or any other, nature.

Hinduism, on the other hand, is the very antithesis

of all this. At first, this was not so. But its rigid pantheism gradually necessitated manifestations of the divine, in order that faith and devotion might be made possible. And, in later centuries, the doctrine of incarnation was accepted as a haven of rest to the Hindu mind and soon became a wild passion of its soul. There is no other people on earth who have carried the doctrine of incarnation (*Avatar*) to such excess of imaginings as to create such abundantly grotesque and fanciful appearances of their many divinities. Normally, then, the Mohammedan faith, at its very core, must be unsatisfying and even repulsive to the tropical Hindu mind. It was brought here at the point of the sword; and, for centuries, it was the faith of a ruling power whose custom was to tax heavily all people who did not conform, outwardly at least, to the State religion.

After Islam had become established and secure in its success in India, when it could relax its grip upon the sword and relinquish something of the spirit of intolerance which characterized it, it had to meet and cope with a greater foe than that of the battle-field. Hinduism has always exercised a great benumbing influence upon all faiths which have come into contact and conflict with it. It has insinuated itself into the mind of the conquerors and laid its palsied hand upon every department of religious thought and life. So that, after a few centuries of prosperity in India, Islam began to forget its narrow bigotry and uncompromising severity and fraternized more or less with the religion of the country. Little by little a latitudinarianism crept in, which found its culmination in that remarkable man, Akbar the Great, who entertained the teachers of all faiths and encouraged a fearless discussion of their respective merits. Dr. Wherry writes: "The tolerance of Akbar, who not only removed the poll-tax from all his non-Moslem subjects, but who established a sort of parliament of religions, inviting Brahmans, Persian Sufis, Parsee fire-worshippers, and Jesuit priests to freely discuss in his presence the special tenets of their faith and practice, was remarkable. He went farther, and promulgated an eclectic creed of his own and constituted himself a sort of priest-king in which his own dictum should override everything excepting the letter of the Quran. His own creed is set forth in the following words of India's greatest poet, Abul Fazl:—

"O God, in every temple I see those who see thee, and, in every tongue that is spoken, thou art praised.
Polytheism and Islam grope after thee,
Each religion says, 'Thou art one, without equal,'

Be it mosque, men murmur holy prayer; or church, the bells ring, for love of thee;
Awhile I frequent the Christian cloister, anon the mosque:
But thee only I seek from fane to fane.
Thine elect know naught of heresy or orthodoxy, whereof neither stands behind the screen of thy truth.
Heresy to the heretic, — dogma to the orthodox, —
But the dust of the rose-petal belongs to the heart of the perfume seller." [1]

This religious cosmopolitanism developed into what has been called an "Eclectic Pantheism," which welcomed all men and satisfied no one.

Even though Aurangzeeb tried to stem this tide of liberalism and to rehabilitate the intolerance and cruelty of ancient Islam, his effort was not only unsuccessful, but was partly instrumental in bringing on the downfall of the Empire. And the faith of Mohammed in India has revealed, ever since, the sickly pallor and want of vigour which tropical life and contact with Hinduism necessarily entail.

When the government of this land ceased to be Mohammedan, and the sceptre passed into the hands of the British, whose glory it has been, for centuries, to protect its subjects from the bloody hand of intolerance and to vouchsafe unto all not only the blessed boon of *Pax Britannica*, but also the inexpressible

[1] "Islam and Christianity," p. 68.

right and privilege of religious liberty, — then passed away, never to return, we hope, from this motherland of tolerance, the ghastly sceptre of bigotry and fanaticism. And thus Islam ceased to be enforced and propagated by the strong arm of law and by the pointed argument of sword and spear of the legions. It has, since then, enjoyed in this land a free and an open field for the exercise of its powers of persuasion. But its increase has not been marked. And what there has been of progress has been owing to its other characteristics, which we will mention later.

Thus the faith of the Arabian prophet has lost, in India, not only its vigour, but also its prestige and purity, by contact with the lower faiths of the land, especially with the ancestral faith of India. From that religion it has taken unto itself many of the base superstitions, and not a few of the idolatrous practices, which have characterized it.

Indeed, the great mass of the converts from Hinduism, and their descendants, have had but a distorted conception of the lofty faith of Mohammed, which they have unequally yoked with their ancient superstitions and errors.

The Indian census of 1901 tells us how the pure monotheism of Mohammed has been debased by contact with worship at human shrines: "We have seen in the case of Hinduism that the belief in one supreme God, in whom are vested all ultimate powers, is not incompatible with the belief in Supernatural Beings who exercise considerable influence over worldly affairs, and whose influence may be obtained or averted by certain ceremonies. Similarly, in the case of Islam, while the masses have, on the whole, a clearer idea of the unity and omnipotence of God than the ordinary Hindu has, they also have a firm belief in the value of offerings at certain holy places for obtaining temporal blessings. Thus the shrine of Saiyad Salar, at Bahraich, is resorted to, both by Hindus and Mussulmans, if a wife is childless, or if family quarrels cannot be composed. Diseases may be cured by a visit to the shrine of Shaik Saddo, at Amroha in Moradabad; while for help in legal difficulties Shàh Mina's dargah at Lucknow is renowned. Each of these has its appropriate offering, — a long embroidered flag for the first, a cock for the second, and a piece of cloth for the third. Other celebrated shrines are those of Bahauddin Madar Shah at Nakkanpur in the Cawnpore district, and of Ala-uddin Sabir at Piran Kaliar in Saharanpur." The same writer, in his report concerning Bengal, says: "The unreformed Mohammedans of the lower and uneducated classes are deeply infected with Hindu superstitions, and their knowledge of the faith they profess seldom extends beyond the three cardinal doctrines of the Unity of God, the mission of Mohammed, and the truth of the Quran; and they have a very faint idea of the differences between their religion and that of the Hindus. Sometimes they believe that they are descended from Abel (Habil), while the Hindus owe their origin to Cain (Kabil). Kabil, they say, killed Habil and dug a grave for him with a crow's beak."

Before the recent crusade against idolatry it was the regular practice of low-class Mohammedans to join in the Durga Puja and other Hindu religious festivals, and although they have been purged of many superstitions, many still remain. In particular, they are very careful about omens and auspicious days. Dates for weddings are often fixed after consulting a Hindu astrologer; bamboos are not cut, nor the building of new houses commenced, on certain days of the week; and journeys are often undertaken only after referring to the Hindu almanac to see if the proposed day is auspicious. When disease is prevalent, Sitala and Rakshya Kali are worshipped. Dharmaraj, Manasa, Bishahari, are also venerated by many ignorant Mohammedans. Sasthi is worshipped when a child is born. Even now, in some parts of Bengal, they observe the Durga Puga and buy new clothes for the festival, like the Hindus. "Apart from Hindu superstitions, there are certain forms of worship common amongst Mohammedans which are not based on the Quran. The most common of these is the adoration of departed *Pirs.*"

In Rajputana, the Mohammedans of local origin "still retain their ancient Hindu customs and ideas. The local saints and deities are regularly worshipped, the Brahman officiates at all family ceremonials side by side with the Mussulman priest, and, if in matters of creed they are Mohammedans, in matters of form they are Hindus."

In Baluchistan, we are told of the Mohammedan that "his practice is, to say the least of it, un-Islamic. Though he repeats every day that there is one God only who is worthy of worship, he almost invariably prefers to worship some saint or tomb. The Saints, or *Pirs*, in fact, are invested with all the attributes of God. It is the Saint who can avert calamity, cure disease, procure children for the childless, bless the efforts of the hunter, or even improve the circumstances of the dead. The underlying feeling seems to be that man is too sinful to approach God direct, and therefore the intervention of some one worthy must be sought."

In South India, also, Hindus and Mohammedans fraternize not a little, especially in the religious festivities. Mohammedans do not hesitate, under certain conditions, to bring offerings to particular Hindu shrines. And it is a very common thing to see Hindus pay their respects to Mohammedan fakirs. The Mohurram, in South India, is participated in, at least in its festive aspects, by multitudes of Hindus. Many Mohammedans are feeling keenly the degradation of this contact. A well-known Mussulman writer moans over the situation in the following words: —

"The baneful influence that Hindu customs have had on Mussulmans is painful to read of. Many a Hindu ceremonial has been incorporated by the followers of the Prophet. The marriage ceremonies, instead of keeping to the simple form prescribed by the Quran, have been greatly elaborated, and include processions. Even in religious matters, Hindu and Mussulman practices have become curiously blended. Hindus take a leading part in the celebration of Mohurram. Passages from the Quran are sometimes chanted in the Hindu fashion; Mohammedan women of the lower classes break cocoanuts at Hindu temples in fulfilment of vows. Strangest of all, there is said to be a Hindu temple at a village near Trichinopoly which is sacred to a goddess called the Mussulmans' lady, who is said to be the wife of the Hindu god Ranganatha at Srirangam. These are some of the sad features which the census report has brought to light. They tend to show that, except in a few dead formalities, the life of Mussulmans in South India is nothing different from that of the Hindus. In many cases the followers of the Arabian prophet would seem to have forgotten even the root principles of their religion — the unity of God, the formless, and the unincarnate. This fact alone is more than enough to fill the mind of the true Mussulman with anxious concern with regard to the future prospects of Islam in this country. His pious soul can find no rest with the view before him of hundreds and thousands of his coreligionists sunk deep in the degrading practices of the heathen around."

In this connection it should not be forgotten that

the Sikh faith in North India is really a compromise between these two faiths. Its founder, Nanak Shah, possessed the very laudable ambition of producing a religion possessed of the best elements of both of these faiths. And though the more than two millions of his present followers have drifted very much toward Hinduism, which is the drift of all things in this land, and are hardly to be distinguished from their neighbours in creed and custom, yet the religion stands as a testimony to the mutual influence of these two faiths.

Nor should one forget what is now going on on this line among Hindus. Dr. Grierson tells us, in his recent interesting lecture, that "Allah the God of the Mussulman — the God of the Jews and ourselves — has Himself been admitted to the Hindu pantheon, together with His prophet, and a new section of the never completed Hindu bible, the 'Allah Upanishad,' has been provided in His honour."

Moreover, Hindus charge the Mohammedan faith with being the cause of the zenana system of this land. The seclusion of women began, they say, on account of the licentiousness of the Arabs. However this may be, it is true that the Mohammedan

Purdah system, which separates so thoroughly women from the other sex, found adoption, or at least emphasis, among the Hindus. In ancient times, so far as we can learn, the women of Brahmanism found considerable freedom and independence of life. Probably the truth is that, as Hinduism developed certain types of doctrine which bore heavily upon the weaker sex, the range of privilege and opportunity which women enjoyed found gradual limitation and curtailment which found marked impetus upon the advent of the Arab hordes.

And it should be remembered that the persistent attitude of Mohammedans toward slavery and toward polygamy has had a deleterious effect upon the Hindu people.

Though Islam came to India uninvited, and though its pathway has been marked with blood, it has not been without great opportunity to impress the people of this land with its nobility. But, as we have seen, the opportunity does not seem to have been improved. After twelve centuries of active propagandism and some centuries of political rule and religious oppression, this religion is still an exotic, and finds, on the whole, small place in the affection of the people. This is owing in part to its want of adaptation and inherent lack of vital power. As Sir Monier William has said: "There is a finality and a want of elasticity about Mohammedanism which precludes its expanding beyond a certain fixed line of demarcation. Having once reached this line, it appears to lapse backwards — to tend toward mental and moral slavery, to contract with the narrower and narrower circles of bigotry and exclusiveness."

Add again to this the fact, already mentioned, that its new environment in India has been deleterious to the vitality of the Mohammedan faith. "Mohammedanism, as a quiescent non-proselytizing religion, could only become corrupt and rotten. The effect of all this policy on the mass of Mohammedans was to deprive their religious sentiment of that intolerance which constituted its strength. Its moral power was gone when it ceased to be intolerant. . . . These two religions have thus settled down beside each other on terms of mutual charity and *toleration*. This does not imply any great change or deterioration in Hinduism, for its principles admit every belief as truth, and every religion as a way of salvation. All that it requires is acknowledgment of the same principle from other religions, and this is the position which it has practically forced Mohammedanism to assume in India. But such a position is utterly opposed to the principles and claims of the latter religion; and in forcing Mohammedanism to accept it, Hinduism has undoubtedly gained the triumph."[1]

And yet let it not be supposed that Islam in India is either dead or moribund. It is evidently sensible of its defects and has made, from time to time, efforts to reform itself.

Under the stress of circumstances and the sense of waning power they have even translated the Quran into Urdu, with a view to reaching the common people. This is an unique effort on their part. Like Romanists, in the use of the Latin service, the Mohammedans cling, with deathly tenacity, to their Arabic bible and Arabic worship, foolishly believing that to vernacularize their faith is to degrade and corrupt it. In Madura, where there is a mosque of some pretension, there are only two or three who can pronounce their Arabic Quran. And while they have learned to pronounce, in the ancient tongue, their beloved book, they do not understand the meaning of what they say, and merely parrot

[1] "Hinduism and Christianity," by Dr. Robson, pp. 168, 173.

the whole ritual. But a break has been made from this inane method of worship, and their holy book has now been translated into one vernacular of India.

Islam has also revealed definite redeeming qualities which seem distinctive and are worthy of enumeration.

Its prohibition of the use of intoxicating drinks is definite, and its attitude toward that accursed habit has been consistently and vehemently antagonistic. Hence, the Mohammedan of India is recognized as a sober man, faithful to his religion in this matter wherein the Christian reveals so much weakness. It is true that in some parts of the country Mussulmans are too often addicted to the use of opiates. But a drunken member of this faith is rarely to be found. In this, Islam has joined forces with Hinduism itself in proscribing a habit which is the curse and ruin of too many Christian lands. And it is a distinct blot upon the Christian Church in India that many of its followers, in this land of sobriety and abstinence, so easily fall into the temptation of the cup and become the victims of intemperance.

Islam also enforces the law of usury among its followers. With the Jew, the Mohammedan has been strictly forbidden to make money by the use of money. And though they find ways of evading this law, to some extent, the ideal which they have before them is a restraint and a blessing in a land where the usurer is a ubiquitous curse, because of his rapacity and the expertness with which he draws the common people into his net and leads millions to financial loss and ruin.

The supreme place given in this faith to the duty of almsgiving, and the effective way with which it is carried out among its members, is another praiseworthy feature. At the time of their political rule and extensive sway there was a well-known tax whose purpose was to carry relief to the poor and the suffering. And Mohammedans feel to-day that there is hardly a religious duty which is more sacred and carries with it more of reward than that of distributing alms to the poor. Far more than Christianity has it given importance and distinction to this as a special form of its religious activity.

Moreover, its command to observe the five seasons of daily prayer is important, with a view to maintaining and enforcing the ordinary forms and observances of a living faith. Many a time have I been impressed with the way Mohammedans, in this land, faithfully and boldly observe this rule and privilege of their faith by spreading their mats in most unexpected places, even in the presence of gaping crowds, and prostrating themselves in prayer with their faces Mecca-ward as a proof of their sincerity and as a testimony to the power of their religion.

But there is nothing in which Islam exerts a more salutary influence in this caste-ridden land than in its attitude toward this monster evil of Hinduism. Islam is neither founded upon race, colour, nor nationality. It has been well said that in Islam "all believers belong to the highest caste." It recognizes to the full the brotherhood of all the members of its faith. Even its slaves have been exalted to its throne and have achieved highest distinction. The last census correctly says: "On its social side, the religion of Mohammed is equally opposed to the Hindu scheme of a hierarchy of castes, an elaborate stratification of society based upon subtle distinctions of food, dress, drink, marriage, and ceremonial usage. In the sight of God and of His Prophet all followers of Islam are equal. In India, however, caste is in the air; its contagion has spread even to the Mohammedans; and we find its evolution proceeding on characteristically Hindu lines. In both communities, foreign descent forms the highest claim to social distinction; in both, promotion cometh from the West. As the twice-born Aryan is to the mass of Hindus, so is the Mohammedan of alleged Arab, Persian, Afghan, or Mogul origin to the rank and file of his coreligionists."

I admit that there are social distinctions and class cleavages among the members of this faith, as among all peoples. These are in no sense religious, however, as they are in Hinduism. Among the members of that faith there is equality of right; and every Islamite, by his own industry and character, can enjoy that right in this land. It is true that Islam has yet to learn the brotherhood of man as such, and to recognize that the non-Mussulman and the Mussulman alike are possessed of equal rights and favours in the sight of God. But within the faith itself, caste, as such, is unknown. This is much more than can be said of the Indian Christian Church at the present day, notwithstanding the spirit of our religion and its definite injunctions. The Hindu caste system has been transferred too much into the Christian fold. Most of the accessions from Hinduism to Mohammedanism at the present time are from the lowest classes of Hinduism, with a view to securing a definitely higher social status which Mohammedanism distinctly promises and invariably confers upon these newcomers. It were well if modern converts to Christianity from the outcasts could hope for and receive from the Hindus the same recognized advance in social position and esteem by becoming members of our religion, as they do by entering the faith of Islam. This is not the fault of Christianity, but the folly of its converts, who do not leave their heathenish conceptions and estimates outside the precincts of Christianity. This difference, which I have emphasized, is, as might be expected, more marked and manifest in South India than elsewhere. A Christian worker in this land cannot help envying Islam the noble stand which it has taken concerning caste.

At the present time the Muslims of India are divided into two sects, something like the Catholics and Protestants of Christianity. The Sunnis are the traditionists, and constitute the large majority of that faith. The Shiahs are the dissenters. For twelve hundred years has this division existed, and the two parties are as irreconcilable to-day as ever. There is also a sect of mystics known as Sufis.

In the seventeenth century a new sect of Purists was formed in Arabia. They reject the glosses of *Immams*, will not accept the authority of the Sultan, and make light of the great Prophet himself. They are a fanatical sect and delight in proclaiming *jihad*, or holy war, against the infidels. These are the Wahabbis. This sect was introduced to India by Sayad Ahmed Shah, and it has gained many converts. It is largely a movement toward reforming the faith from within. In spirit, it is not very unlike the movement of the fanatics known as Ghazis, whose zeal burns against all infidels, especially those of the European Christian type.

III

What is the Character of the Mohammedan Population in India?

It will be interesting to appraise them largely by comparing them with the Hindu population which surrounds them. Generally speaking, they are morally on a level with their neighbours. In South India, especially, it is difficult to discriminate between the ethical standards which obtain among Mohammedans and Hindus. In both cases they are low and unworthy. This is unexpected, as Islam has always stood for a worthy ethical standing, while Hinduism has, from time immemorial, divorced morality from piety. Nevertheless, it is a fact that those who have passed on from Hinduism to Mohammedanism have rarely ascended in the ethical standard of life.

The personal habits of the Indian Mussulman are not clean, to say the least of them. In this they are a contrast to the Brahmans, and to some other high-class Hindus, whose ceremonial ablutions are many. In South India, the Mohammedan is described by a vernacular expression which is as uncomplimentary as it is filthy, and which is intended to classify them among the lowest in their habits. When cholera and similar epidemics prevail in the regions with which I am familiar, the Mohammedan, with the Pariah, on account of unclean habits, becomes the first victim of its ravages.

Add to this their strong belief in fate, which leads them, during these epidemics, to neglect or to decline the use of medical remedies. Many a Muslim perishes during such times because of his fatalistic convictions.

They are also among the most ignorant of all classes in India. While, in the total population of the land, hardly more than 5 per cent are, in any sense, literate, the Mohammedans, as a class, have only 3 per cent. And of the Mohammedan population nearly all the women are analphabet. In the educational system of India the government places Mohammedans among the "backward classes," and every effort has been made by the State, even to the doubling of educational grants, to stimulate the members of this faith on educational lines.

It is one of the most discouraging facts connected with the Muslim population that while they are brave in bearing arms and loyal to the government, they have an apparent aversion to the schoolhouse, and can with difficulty be induced to secure even an elementary education. This bears very heavily against their prosperity and influence. Public offices in India are wisely placed in charge of those who are competent, by a thorough training and a broad education, to well fill them. The consequence is that the Mohammedan has been gradually driven out from nearly all public positions of trust by the intellectually more alert Brahman, and even by lower-class Hindus, who are availing themselves of the opportunities for higher education.

It is not strange that the political influence of this community has correspondingly waned, so that only a very small number relatively of Muslims is found to-day in the councils of the Empire.

A new ambition, however, seems to be taking possession of the community. They have recently organized many schools under the direction of "The Society for the Aid of Islam." These schools, without neglecting the study of the Quran and their sacred language and the tenets of their faith, give instruction on western lines, and in the English language.

They have established, also, under the inspiration of the late Sir Sayid Ahmed Khan, a college at Aligarh. Though the rationalistic teaching of the founder causes the institution to be discredited by orthodox leaders, the college has developed wonderfully, and is beginning to assume the proportions of a Muslim University. Of this institution a learned Mussulman remarked in an address:—

"We want Aligarh to be such a home of learning as to command the same respect of scholars as Berlin or Oxford, Leipsic or Paris. And we want those branches of learning relative to Islam which are fast falling into decay to be added by Moslem scholars to the stock of the world's knowledge. And, above all, we want to create for our people an intellectual and moral capital—a city which shall be the home of elevated ideas and pure ideals; a centre from which light and guidance shall be diffused among the Moslems of India."

Much may be expected from the institution. But what is one such school among the many millions of this community in India? Government is anxious to aid and inspire the community on these lines; and the present success of the institution is, in good part, owing to the smile of the State upon it.

The recent organization of the Pan-Islamic Movement is full of hope. The leading representatives of the community in India seem anxious and determined to rouse their coreligionists from their lethargy and to create within them a new ambition for a higher and a more honourable place in intelligence and official usefulness. This is much needed, because the community has reached its lowest ebb of influence among the people.

In the present unrest Mohammedans mainly stand with the government against the Hindu Extremists. They wisely realize that the British Raj presents to them, as a community, far better opportunity and larger favours than would accrue to them under any other possible government, even though their warlike traits might lead them once more to subdue and rule the land themselves.

IV

Christian Effort in India in Behalf of the Mussulman

Missionaries have everywhere presented to Mohammedan and Hindu alike the Gospel Message. The follower of Mohammed has never been ignored in the proclaiming of Christ and in the work of the Mission school.

Generally speaking, they are a very hard class to reach; they very rarely seem impressed, or are willing to consider the message as a personal call to themselves. The high character of their faith above that of the surrounding people partly accounts for this. Moreover, the religion itself inculcates intolerance, and naturally narrows the vision of appreciation and sympathy amongst its followers.

It is also, in some measure, due to their supreme ignorance of the teaching of their own faith. They have many fantastic notions about Islam, such as intelligent members of their faith repudiate, and such as make them inaccessible to the Christian worker.

And yet they are not reached and impressed with more difficulty than are the Brahmans and some other high-class Hindus. Though conversions from among them have been relatively few, accessions from Islam to the Christian faith have been continuous during the last century. There have not been many mass movements among them. It has been largely the struggle of individual souls from the trammels of one faith into the liberty of the other. Dr. Wherry informs us that: "In the North, especially the Punjab, and the Northwest Frontier Province, every congregation has a representation from the Moslem ranks. Some of the churches have a majority of their membership gathered from amongst the Mussulmans. In a few cases there has been something like a movement among Moslems toward Christianity, and a considerable number have come out at one time. But perhaps the fact that tells most clearly the story of the advance of Christianity among Moslems in India, is this, that among the native pastors and Christian preachers and teachers in North India there are at least two hundred who were once followers of Islam. Among the names of those who have gone to their reward (many of them, after long lives of faithful service), some of my readers will recall the names of the Rev. Maulvie Imaduddin, D.D., Maulvie Safdar Ali, E.A.C., Munshi

Mohammed Hanif, Sayyad Abdullah Athim, E.A.C., the Rev. Rajab Ali, Sain Gumu Shah, the Rev. Abdul Masih, the Rev. Asraf Ali, the Rev. Jani Ali, and Dilawur Khan. These faithful servants of God have left behind them memories which still live. Many of them have bequeathed volumes of literature, which have added much to the literary wealth of all the churches. They give an index wherewith to guide us as to what the strength and character of the Church of the future will be when the strong champions of the Crescent shall have become the Champions of the Cross."

We are also told by the Rev. Maulvie Imaduddin, D.D., of North India, that "117 men of position and influence have become Christians, of whom 62 became clergy and leading men in many of the Indian Missions, and 51 are gentlemen occupying positions professional and official. Out of 956 baptisms of the Church Missionary Society in the Amritsar District, 152 were Mohammedan converts. In the Punjab there are at least two congregations made up entirely of Mohammedans, while in Bengal there is a body of more than 6000 Christians composed almost entirely of Mohammedan converts and their descendants, a large number having come over *en masse* some years ago. These last were converts in the first instance from Hinduism to Mohammedanism, and hence were not bound so strongly to Islam."

In South India, less attention has been paid to Mohammedans as a class, and the results therefore have been very meagre. A few individuals, here and there, have accepted our faith, and that is practically all. This is not strange when we remember that out of the eleven hundred Protestant missionaries, male and female, in Southern India, perhaps not a dozen have any special training and aptitude for work among Mohammedans, and hardly more than that number are giving themselves entirely to the work.

The difficulty of this work should appeal more than it does to the heroic element in missionaries and missionary societies alike. The above facts indicate that there is encouragement for one who gives himself heartily to this people. In no other land has missionary effort for the members of this religion achieved greater results than in India. If their numbers are few, they are more resolute and pronounced in their Christian character than many others. In the roll of honour among the converts from Islam have been found the names of a number of distinguished pastors and able writers.

In the recent Conference of Missionaries, held in Cairo, a new purpose was manifested to take up with more discriminating and pronounced zeal and better methods the work of reaching and converting the Mohammedans of the world.

In India, a better organized and a wider campaign for the conversion of Islam is needed. Men and women who are to take up work in their behalf must not only be well trained for this specific work by a thorough knowledge of both faiths; they must also be imbued with abundant sympathy for the people, and with a sympathetic appreciation of the vital truths which have thus far animated the Mohammedan faith. The constructive, rather than the destructive, method of activity must increasingly animate all. The Mohammedans are peculiarly sensitive; and there is so much of contact between their faith and ours that through the pathway of the harmonies of the faiths men must be led to know and feel the supreme excellence and power of the faith of the Christ.

CHAPTER XII

THE CHRIST AND THE BUDDHA

THE study of the life and the character of noted and noble men is the most helpful and inspiring of all studies. It not only illustrates life at its best, it also fills men with an ambition to pursue the same noble purposes and to achieve the same lofty results in life. In presenting a brief glimpse of the two most powerful personalities that ever impressed themselves upon the world, I desire to place them side by side that we may appreciate the assonances and the dissonances of their wonderful lives and rise through the study into a true conception and love of the most perfect Life ever breathed upon earth.

I have no apology to offer, as a Christian, for comparing the life of our Lord with that of any human being; for, though Divine, He was also supremely human; and human glory and achievement appear in their fulness only when we gaze upon Him as one of the mighty human forces of history.

Christ and Buddha lived their brief lives upon earth

The Greatest Image of Buddha (183 feet long)

many centuries ago; and yet never did they grip so many by the magic of their attraction as they do at present. Nearly two-thirds of the whole population of the world to-day acknowledges the lordship of the one or the other of these and loves to be called by their names. The influence of the one dominates all the life of the West, while that of the other is supreme in the East. And it is a curious and interesting fact that Buddha has not only been exalted as the ninth incarnation of Vishnu in the faith which he aimed to overthrow, he has also been adopted into the Roman Catholic Calendar and is worshipped on the 27th of November as a Christian saint under the title "Saint Josaphat."

I am also convinced that the influence of the lives and teachings of Buddha and Christ will react upon each other with ever increasing power during the coming years. Indeed, we are now witnessing this very influence developing before our eyes.

I

Let us first observe the conditions under which these two lived their earthly lives.

One was born into royal prerogatives and splendour and was surrounded in youth with all the luxuries and blandishments of an Oriental court. The other, though of royal lineage, was born in poverty, cradled in a manger, earned a meagre subsistence as a carpenter, and was able to say at the end of His brief career that the foxes had holes and the birds of the air had nests, but that He had not where to lay His head.

Sidhartthan early married and became a father, but later renounced all the pleasures and responsibilities of a *grihastan life.* His great renunciation is one of the most striking and impressive acts in the history of mankind, and his subsequent asceticism was of the most thorough and rigid type.

Jesus of Nazareth avoided the entanglements of married life and had a supreme contempt for the wealth and the pomp of the world. Yet He was not an ascetic. So freely did He associate with men, participating even in their festivities, that His enemies falsely charged Him with being a "glutton and a winebibber." He never countenanced the idea that highest sainthood must come through asceticism.

He found His intimates not among the ascetic Essenes, but among householders and men of affairs.

Both these great souls were similarly oppressed by the prevalence and the tyranny of an exclusive ceremonialism. In the one case, it was the innumerable bloody sacrifices and the all-embracing and crushing ritual of the Brahmans which roused the anger and opposition of Gautama; while, on the other hand, the myriad rites, the childish ceremonies, and the hollow religious hypocrisy of the Scribes and Pharisees filled Jesus with hatred and led Him to a denunciation of that whole class. "Woe unto you, Scribes and Pharisees," was the oft-repeated expression of wrath which He heaped upon them.

Thus the religions which both established were, in part, reactions from the religious excesses and errors of the days in which they lived.

It is strange that neither Christ nor Buddha left any writings behind them, even though writing was a known art in their times. Their mighty influence was through oral teaching and example. This was different from the method of other such world-leaders as Moses, Mohammed, and Confucius. It proves that whenever any one has truths of saving power to commit to the world, there are many who, as his messengers, are ready to convey them. Better indeed than to convey one's thoughts by printed page is it to impart them through the living voice to disciples who will thrill the world by the message coloured by their own mind and transfigured by their own enthusiasm. This was the method of Christ and Buddha.

Both were surrounded by an Oriental environment. Their antecedents and their prepossessions were of the East, eastern; and at their births they were introduced to scenes and began to breathe the atmosphere of the Orient. All the great founders of the World Religions were men of the East. This was doubtless because the East kept more closely than the West in touch with deepest religious thought and was animated with highest religious emotions and heavenly aspirations. Certainly the world owes more to ancient Asia for its religious life and spiritual attainments than to all the other continents put together. And Asia is to be thanked, above all, because she gave to mankind the Christ and the Buddha. For the eastern flavour of their messages and the Oriental tints of their life we are deeply grateful. To those of the West, these have always brought quiet restraint and a hallowed, peaceful repose to counteract the hurry and worry of life to which they are so much exposed and which are a part of their very being.

II

The Common Principles which controlled their Lives

Both were men of deepest sincerity. All sham and hypocrisy were foreign to their nature; they held insincerity in any one to be the meanest and most deadly sin. To this intense loyalty to the truth, Jesus bore emphatic testimony by an early martyrdom; while Gautama gave the same unwavering witness by a long and holy life. They both stood in the midst of communities which were rotten with hypocrisy and which were using religion as a sacred garb of duplicity and were raising temples of dishonesty to enraged deity. They stood like prophets in the wilderness and pronounced woe upon all hypocrites.

Moreover, both Christ and Buddha were profoundly ethical in their teaching. They found that humanity was not only rotten with insincerity, it was also deceiving itself with the vain delusion that moral integrity and ethical nobility can be bartered for a multitudinous ceremonial. Men have always been prone to exalt ritual in proportion as they have neglected the eternal demands of conscience and the ethical foundation of character. The myriad-tongued ceremonial of the Brahmans of twenty-five centuries ago was the old evasion of righteousness in human life. Gautama saw this, and his noble soul rebelled against a faith which proclaimed that salvation was a thing of outward religious forms and not of the heart within.

> "To cease from all sin,
> To get virtue,
> To cleanse our own heart,
> This is the religion of the Buddhas."

These were the words with which he enunciated his new principles and carried forward his campaign of reaction against the faith of his fathers. Nothing less than, or apart from, purity of the soul within satisfied his requirement.

Indeed, he exalted so much the more highly this banner of heart purity and holiness, the less he had to say of the spiritual claims upon the soul. He had tried elaborate ceremonial and had found it wanting; he had practised the most severe religious austerities, but they had availed him little. In the quiet light which had dawned upon him under the sacred Boh tree he found that nothing wrought so mightily and beneficently as *Dharma*, or righteousness.

> "The real treasure is that laid by man or woman,
> Through charity or piety, temperance and self-control.
>
> *   *   *   *   *   *

> The treasure thus hid is secure, and passes not away;
> . . . this a man takes with him."

> "Let no man think lightly of sin, saying in his heart, 'It cannot overtake me.'"

These are only a few of the many noble ethical deliverances of this great man's creed.

And during all his life, subsequent to the great renunciation, he embodied in himself the ethical beauty of all that he had taught.

And what shall I say of Jesus, the Christ? In the noble integrity of His heart, in the sublime ethical ideals which He ever exalted, in the moral rectitude which He practised and enjoined upon all His followers, who was like unto Him? In His day, also, men had forgotten the true foundation of character; and the religious leaders of the people were placing supreme emphasis upon human traditions and upon man-made rites as the way of salvation.

They "tithed the mint and the cummin" and forgot the weightier matters of the law. To eat with unwashed hands, to consort with a Samaritan, to carry a load or raise a sheep from the ditch on the Sabbath, —this was a sin which, to the Pharisees, would weigh a man down to hell itself; while to lie or to use other foul language, or to trample under foot the whole decalogue was, by comparison, a venial offence. The whole moral code was rendered impotent by them, while ceremonial cleansing was the be-all and end-all of their system. Christ was daily thrown into conflict with these "blind leaders of the blind"; His soul abhorred their whole religious system. He characterized them as "whited sepulchres." He showed that it is the heart which defiles a man, "for out of the heart proceed evil thoughts, murders, adulteries, fornications, thefts, false witness, blasphemies." "Blessed," says He, "are the pure in heart, for they shall see God." "It was said to them of old thou shalt not kill;" but Christ equally prohibited anger, the cause of murder. He not only denounced adultery, but the lustful look which is the source of adultery.

To His followers He said "unless your righteousness exceed the righteousness of the Scribes and Pharisees ye shall not enter into the kingdom of heaven." He prayed the Father that He would sanctify His own, and added that for their sakes He sanctified Himself. Holiness was a passion with Him, and at the basis of His teaching He enjoined moral cleanness and ethical integrity. And His life in this, as in other things, was a perfect exhibition of the virtues which He taught. And from that day to this

His precept and example have mutually supported each other. In Him were wedded faith and conscience, piety and character. So that, where Christ is best known and most loyally followed to-day, there do we find a perfect sense of human relations and a supreme desire after ethical perfection.

Furthermore, these two great souls were consumed with a broad and universal charity. Their environment was perhaps the most averse to general benevolence that the world could then show. In India, there had already grown to great power the caste system with its multiplying ramifications. Then, as now, it narrowed the sympathies of men, it arrayed one class against another, it cultivated pride and fostered mutual distrust and dissension.

When Sakya Muni came upon the scene, he saw the terribly divisive system sending down its root like the banyan tree on all sides and absorbing the life and thought of the people. It repelled him, and, with all his mighty intellectual and moral energy, he attacked it. He proclaimed all men brothers and worthy of human sympathy, love, and respect. He opened the door of his faith to all classes on equal terms. He vehemently opposed every effort to divide men except upon the ground of character. He enjoined upon his disciples not only love and kindness to all men, he also insisted upon a similar attitude toward all forms of lower life.

The fact that Buddhism is to-day one of the three great Missionary Faiths of the world, seeking all men that are in darkness, is the best proof that the founder of that faith had a heart which embraced the whole realm of life in its love. He felt that no man, however humble or however far removed in ties of race and kinship, should be deprived of the blessings of his love and sympathy. It is an interesting fact that nearly all past religious reformers in India — both those inside and outside the pale of Brahmanism — were anti-caste in their sympathies and teaching. But it is only Buddha who consistently maintained the broad foundation of a universal brotherhood and incorporated it into his faith as a cardinal principle.

In like manner, Jesus of Nazareth lived His earthly life at a time of narrow sympathies, and with people who were among the most exclusive that ever lived on earth. The Jews believed themselves to bc the specially favoured sons of Heaven. And, what was more they thought that they were exalted because they were *worthy*, because they excelled all other people. Hence, they stood aloof from other nationalities and despised them as their inferiors, a social and physical contact with whom would be pollution. There is in many respects a strange correspondence between the Jewish social code of twenty centuries ago and that of Hinduism to-day — the same haughty mien and abjectness of spirit — the aloofness of pride and the cringing meanness of social bondage — representing the two extremes of society. Christ also turned His face like a flint against this mean artificial classification of men. He had a burning contempt for the proud Pharisee who lived upon the husks of his own contempt of others, and who trampled under foot men that were infinitely superior to himself, so far as character was concerned. But He consorted often with the outcast Publican who revealed an aspiration after better things. And He even chose men who were thus socially ostracized to enter His own inner circle of disciples and to be the standard-bearers of His cause upon earth. He taught that the most abject and socially submerged man upon earth is a son of God, and that at his moral and spiritual renovation there would be joy among the denizens of heaven. And it was while thinking of this same class that He said unto His own, in describing the judgment scene at the last great day, "Come, ye blessed of my father, inasmuch as ye have treated kindly and lovingly one of the least of my brethren ye have done it unto me, enter ye into the joy of your Lord." Though He was born a Jew, He opened wide the portals of His religion and invited all men of all conditions. "Come unto me, all ye that are weary and heavy laden, and I will give you rest." He sent forth His followers into all lands to disciple and bring to the truth all nations. And in all lands His method of procedure has been to reach first the lowest among the people and then gradually to rise to the highest, until He has taken possession of the whole land. His universal heart of love took in all men of all social strata. All that He asked was that men should come to Him with purpose sincere and with a longing for light and truth.

III

The Principles and Teachings which differentiate and separate Christ and Buddha

Thus far we have seen these two great leaders of men standing side by side and revealing the same traits and principles.

But they also revealed fundamental differences which it were well for us to consider.

Though much united them, and that when more than five centuries and thousands of miles held them apart, we also discover that a gulf wider than that of time or space opened between them.

Their lives and their doctrines and the faiths which they promulgated reveal strangely diverse contentions and tendencies.

(1) First of all, and at the root of all, lies their attitude toward the Divine Being. Jesus was preëminently a God-intoxicated Being, while the most manifest mental attitude of Gautama was his agnosticism. Christ never ceased speaking of and communing with His Father in heaven. He was wont to retire regularly from human society in order that He might enjoy the Heavenly Presence whose very radiance shone in and upon Him daily. He declared that He did nothing without consulting with and receiving direction from God. And this was natural enough when we remember His declaration that He came into the world to reveal the Father unto men. Listen to His words, "My meat is to do the will of Him that sent me and to finish His work." "The Father that dwelleth in me doeth the work." "The Father is glorified in the Son." "I love the Father and go unto Him." "Believest thou not that I am in the Father and the Father in me?" "Oh, righteous Father, the world hath not known Thee, but I have known Thee."

In all His expressions of oneness with God, of His living unto God, and of His drawing His daily strength from God, His experience was eminently unique. He lived more in heaven than on earth in those days of His incarnation. Apart from any consideration of His Divinity, He can truly be said to be a man of God whose soul was in harmony with the Father.

How different the words and experiences of Gautama Rishi! Many have spoken of him as an atheist. I do not believe that he denied the existence of God. Yet it is evidently true that he has no use in his philosophy, any more than in his religion, for a Divine Being. There was doubtless reason for this in the conditions of his time; for it may be regarded as the reaction of a strong mind against the extreme spiritualism and polytheism of the day. For, in those days, the deep spirituality of the Brahman had overflowed its banks and had created a multitudinous pantheon which repelled this man of stern mind. It was to him only a short step from a disbelief in the *many* gods to a doubt as to the existence of *any* god. And in this agnosticism he was doubtless aided by his fondness for the *Sankya* school of thought, which is Indian Agnosticism. In any case, his deliverances and his established religion, if such it really can be called, are such a reaction from the Theosophy of India as to lead one to wonder how, even with all its other excellences, it could have become in .India a State Religion for any length of time. A religion without a God, a sacrifice, a priest, or a prayer, is certainly a dreary wilderness to a God-seeking soul. And yet, this is what the Buddha conceived and promulgated among his disciples. Under the stress of a growing consciousness of the ills of this life his mind did not, like that of others, rise to heaven for relief; but his salvation was to be a self-wrought one. With his own right arm of virtue he wished to carve his way into eternal life — or, shall I say, eternal death? Is it strange that under such a godless religious system its votaries should react from this fundamental error and deify and worship that very Buddha who had not a place for God in his whole scheme of life?

At any rate, Christ and Buddha stand before us in striking contrast in this matter; the glory of the teaching of the one was that He caused His adoring disciple to fall upon his knees with uplifted eye and to say in filial reverence and trust, "Our Father who art in heaven." While the other taught his followers to lean only upon self, and to seek speedy relief from life itself, declaring that heaven returned only an empty, mocking echo to the helpless wail of the human soul.

(2) Corresponding to this difference was another difference in their conception of human life. Jesus maintained that the human soul came from God, was made for God, and that God Himself was forever seeking to bring it unto Himself. According to His theory of life, man is not left alone at any stage in his career. He may decline to entertain God in his life. He may lead a life of rebellion against his Maker and Saviour; he may even deny the very existence of the Father of his being. But God, in the riches of His infinite patience, does not desert him to his own base thought and life. He follows him like a shepherd searching for his lost sheep. He longs for his return like a tender, forgiving father for the return of his prodigal son. Human life, according to this view, may be mean and sordid and may be spent in the grossest sin; but there is hope. All is not lost while there is a spark of life left. God is still seeking and trying to bring the soul to new life. The million agents of His loving will conspire to help man; and so the possibilities of his life are still great. Thus, to our Lord Christ, the vision of human life was a bright

and optimistic one. God will not leave man to himself. He will bring all the resources of heaven and of earth to the work of saving him. "God is in His heaven, All's right with the world." Yes, all is hopeful for man because the Father is still seeking him.

How different from this was Gautama Rishi's view of human life. According to him, man is a lone, helpless creature tossed on the sea of destiny. He is the only captain and steersman of his barque, and his own reason is his only compass; he must battle alone with the waves of circumstances and find for himself the unknown harbour of peace. There is no heaven above to hear his cry, no help or redemption outside of self. Is it a wonder that life is a weariness, and existence itself an unspeakable burden to such a man?

Thus the Buddha sought in vain for light and cheer in life, and pessimism became to him, as it continues to be to his followers, the very atmosphere of life. Even as in Dante's vision of the Inferno, so in the Temple of Buddha's scheme of life there is inscribed above its portals the words: "Abandon hope all ye who enter here."

I care not who the man may be, I humbly maintain that his scheme of life is seriously wrong if it be a cheerless, uninspiring one; and it is perfectly natural that men should prefer to follow a confident, buoyant leader rather than a heartless, despondent one. If God rules over the destinies of man, we have a right to expect that success and blessing will crown the efforts of the sincere seeker after a better life. Man has received life not that he may destroy it, but that he may cultivate it and find in it life abundant.

A young mother whose child had died carried the dead body to Buddha, and, doing homage to him, said, "Lord and Master, do you know any medicine that will be good for my child?" "Yes," said the teacher, "I know of some. Get me a handful of mustard seed." But when the poor girl was hurrying away to procure it, he added, "I require mustard seed from a house where no son, husband, parent, or slave has died." "Very good," said the girl, and went to ask for it, carrying still the dead child astride on her hip. The people said, "Here is mustard seed;" but when she asked, "Has there died a son, a husband, a parent, or a slave in this house?" they replied: "Lady, what is this that you ask? The living are few, but the dead are many!" Then she went to other homes, but one said, "I have lost my son;" another, "I have lost my parents;" another, "I have lost my slave." At last, not being able to find a single house where no one had died, she began to think, "This is a heavy task that I am on." And as her mind cleared she summoned up her resolution, left the dead child in a house, and returned to Buddha. "Have you procured the mustard seed?" he asked. "I have not," she replied. "The people of the village told me, 'The living are few, but the dead are many.'" Then Buddha said, "You thought you alone had lost a son; the law of death is that among all living creatures there is no permanence." Little comfort in these words!

Of course, we can see how these two conflicting views of life found acceptance and expression in these two great leaders of mankind. For, to Jesus, the keyword of life was divine grace or atonement, while to Gautama it was *Karma*—that word which has for so many centuries been to all India the truest expression of its philosophy and of its life.

Christ taught that the grace of God was at the service of every man for his success in this life and for his redemption in the world to come. He ever emphasized the inspiring message that God's work and man's effort constitute the warp and woof of the life of every man. In His whole scheme of salvation there is no place for discouragement; for, walking through the path of life hand in hand with God, man can overthrow every enemy to his progress and achieve the best and highest in God's purposes for him.

But when the Buddha adopted the doctrine of *Karma* as the foundation of life, he and his system were doomed to despondency, gloom, and discouragement. It is indeed a noble truth that every man must drink, to its last dregs, the fruit of his own action — that the law of *Karma* works with relentless force in every life in the world. Only let us understand that God may enter into each life to enable man to face successfully that law, and it is all right. But condemn man to everlasting isolation; cut away from him every ray of Divine help, and the working out of his *Karma* becomes a terrible and an almost unending tragedy — a Sisyphean task with no hope of release save in the wiping out of life itself. And this is what the great Soul of the East believed and taught. He faced boldly the problem. He had, at the beginning, ignored the very existence of God, and thus denied himself the least hope of external aid in his own emancipation; and thus he held that stern, cruel, relentless *Karma* became the all-controlling and universal law of life.

To a Christian, among the most pathetic words ever spoken are those spoken by Buddha to his beloved cousin and disciple as death drew near— "O! Anantha, . . . My journey is drawing to its close. I have reached eighty years, and just as a worn-out cart can only with much care be made to move along, so my body can only be kept going with difficulty. . . . In future *be ye to yourselves your own light, your own refuge; seek no other refuge. . . . Look not to any one but yourselves as a refuge.*"

And that which farther, and very naturally, widens the gulf which separates them is their view of the adequacy or inadequacy of the present human life to satisfy the laws of their being.

The law which Jesus believed to prevail, and which He constantly promulgated and emphasized, was that of the finality of the human life—that man has once only to pass through this earthly life and that then comes death, which introduces him to an eternal future corresponding with the character of his choices and life on earth. According to Him, this brief earthly existence, which will not be repeated, is a training school for the glorious life beyond. Blessed is he who faithfully submits himself to this training and passes through the gate of death prepared for an immortality of joy in God's presence beyond.

Indeed, Jesus never gives the first intimation of any future birth or life, save that which would be permanent and eternal in heaven or hell.

He felt the adequacy of this life as a determiner of the eternal destiny of all men. And He felt that the salvation which He wrought and offered to all was able to carry man through the single portal of death into unending bliss. Why another entrance into this world, if by passing through the world God could bring into the life the seed and power of His own grace and life which would blossom and bear fruit in the soul throughout eternity? "Marvel not," He sayeth, "the hour cometh in which all that are dead shall hear his voice and shall come forth; they that have done good into the resurrection of life; and they that have done evil into the resurrection of judgment." And as He described the final judgment upon all men after one earthly life He says that "these shall go away into eternal punishment, but the righteous into eternal life." Moreover, in describing the condition of the dead He makes the faithful Abraham say to the soul of a dead sinner, "Between us and you there is a great gulf fixed that they who would pass hence to you may not be able to pass and that you may not cross from thence to us." That is, He claimed that the life which we live here so fixes the destiny of men that eternity will carry its impress. Hence the urgency and the supreme importance of this one life to all men. The universal succession, according to His teaching, is life, death, resurrection, judgment, and eternal reward.

To the Buddha, who, as we have seen, held that man is the only architect of his own destiny and that he must therefore abide the working of his *Karma*, a single brief apprenticeship in the school of life seemed altogether inadequate as a test of character and as a reliable foundation for the edifice of one's eternal destiny, or as a basis for the one irrevocable judgment. It is but natural, therefore, that this great Indian Rishi should have adopted as his own the doctrine of metempsychosis, or transmigration, and that he should add great emphasis to it. To him, life was a penitentiary rather than a school, a place, or an occasion, for eating the fruits of past action rather than a training for the future eternity which awaits every one.

It is true that Gautama must have had some idea of the corrective influence and disciplinary character of this earthly existence; for there is a quiet assumption that in some unexplained and unintelligible way the soul is improved by this multitudinous process of reincarnation. And yet I fail to see any reason for expecting such a development. Philosophically and morally, the *raison d'être* of the doctrine of reincarnation is to explain the inequalities of life; and it does it not, as Jesus would do it, by means of the doctrine of heredity, but by the retributive power of *Karma*, or actions pursuing the soul through successive births and compelling it to reveal by its conditions and reflect by its experiences in each birth the experiences of the previous birth. The moral influence of such a doctrine is rendered all but impossible by the fact that there is no consciousness (the true basis of moral continuity) to connect one birth with another. I know of no one but Mrs. Besant who claims to know what his previous, assumed birth was, and I have not yet met any one who believes her claim in this matter. There is no moral discipline for one in his being punished for a thing of which he has absolutely no conscious knowledge.

We must further consider the character of Gautama's philosophy. It was, as is well known, thoroughly materialistic — the antipodes of the orthodox Hindu philosophy, which is highly spiritual. To Buddha, there was no such thing as a soul apart from the body. What was there, then, to connect one birth with another, according to his teaching? In Brahmanism the doctrine of transmigration is at this point very clear, for there is the eternal *Atma*, or self, to connect and unify all its incarnations. But Gautama, who denied the separate existence of the soul, maintained that it was not the self, but the *Karma*, which passed from one birth to another; and thus there became the oneness of *Karma* without an identity of soul passing through and uniting the myriad incarnations of the person involved. How can one substitute here a sameness of *Karma* for identity of soul? Behold, then, the insuperable difficulties which such a materialism interposes to a belief either in the possibility or in the wisdom of the doctrine of reincarnation.

And yet let it be remembered here that so long as one accepts the doctrine of *Karma* he cannot evade the sister doctrine of reincarnation. They belong to the same system, and must be accepted or rejected together.

If, however, we emphasize divine grace as an element in the solution of human problems and in the salvation of man, then it is natural to conclude that one earthly life will suffice for God and man together to prepare the soul for the consummation and beatification which awaits it beyond death. But if the whole problem is to be solved and the whole work of redemption achieved by man himself, apart from God, then Buddha must have been justified in believing that an inconceivable number of births and human lives are necessary in order to accomplish this.

It was just at this point that Christ and Buddha faced the opposite poles. And it is just here, for this very reason, that the faiths which they promulgated represent, the one the perpetual buoyancy and cheer of youth, and the other the weariness of discouraged age.

Christianity claims to do its work for the soul, so far as settling its destiny is concerned, in the brief life of a few years; and under the inspiring influence of this conviction the pulse quickens, youthful hope and energy multiply, and the whole soul is kindled by a close vision of its speedy triumph and release. The Buddhist, on the other hand, knows that it is a long, lonely conflict—the interminably long processions of births weary him and the dim vision of a release which is far away brings no inspiration. Life palls upon him, courage fails him, his steps grow shorter and his pace slackens.

(3) This brings us to the ideals which these two world-leaders entertained. Often men's ideals are a better revelation of their life and character than are their achievements. These ideals which I wish to point out are two—that of inner attainment and that of final consummation.

And what was the chief ambition for personal achievement sought by Jesus and Gautama? I believe that the very names which they acquired and which are at the head of this chapter answer this question for us. "Christ" and "Buddha" are not the personal names given in infancy, nor are they tribal designations. They primarily represent their official titles. "Christ" means "the Anointed One," and "Buddha" signifies "the Enlightened One"—the one is a term expressive of spiritual powers for service, while the other means intellectual enlightenment for communion. One sought and found the baptism of the spirit of God which touched and transfigured His character; the other was seeking more light on the problems of life; and for that light he sought with a wonderful longing and perseverance until the dawn broke on that remarkable day under the sacred Boh tree and he found the light and was hence called "the Enlightened One."

Thus, in the Christ-life, the emphasis was upon ethical and spiritual attainment, while, in Buddha, the thing sought was the clear vision and transcendent illumination.

Let me not be misunderstood. There is a sense in which the consecration and the vision are in the same line. It was Christ Himself that said, "This is eternal life, to know Thee the only true God and Jesus Christ whom Thou hast sent." Spiritual knowledge is the pathway to the highest life—it is life itself. It must be, in large part, acquired through spiritual experience.

At the same time, it is an interesting fact that Buddha laid, as India has always laid, emphasis—*undue* emphasis—upon knowledge as the consummation to be sought. *Brahma Gnana* is the *summun bonum* of life. To rightly know myself in my relationship, this, they say, is the only qualification for beatification. On the other hand, Jesus insisted always upon a right moral and spiritual attitude and relationship to God as the highest point of human attainment in life. Listen to the beatitudes which he uttered: "Blessed are the poor in spirit; for theirs is the kingdom of heaven. Blessed are they that mourn; for they shall be comforted. Blessed are the meek; for they shall inherit the earth. Blessed are they that hunger and thirst after righteousness; for they shall be filled. Blessed are the merciful; for they shall obtain mercy. Blessed are the pure in heart; for they shall see God. Blessed are the peacemakers; for they shall be called sons of God. Blessed are they that have been persecuted for righteousness' sake; for theirs is the kingdom of heaven."

These are the beatitudes of His Kingdom, and all refer to the spiritual graces which He Himself exemplified and inculcated, and none refer to enlightenment.

Thus in both we have, if not a contrast, a different outlook, which has not only impressed the student with a sense of divergence; but that which is more important — it has given to the devotees of these two faiths widely different aspirations, and has given to the two types of lives produced very dissimilar traits.

But, that which is of more consequence, in these ideals, is their conception of what life tends to and must ultimately attain unto. The final consummation of life meant nought else to Jesus than God-likeness, which He called "Eternal Life." To have grown to the perfection of those moral and spiritual characteristics which adorn God Himself; to have the human will so subdued and directed until it runs parallel with the Divine will; to have the soul consumed with a love of all that He loves and with an abhorrence of all that He hates,—this is life indeed and the highest realization of the human soul. Yea, more, to pass out of this life into the conscious bliss and eternal felicity of the life to come, to dwell with God—one with Him in purpose and character, and yet living a separate conscious existence, basking in the eternal sunshine of His Presence and favour,—this is the fulness of blessing which Christ presented before His own as the end to be sought and the consummation which God placed within their reach.

On the other hand, Nirvana is the word which holds condensed the whole realm of Buddha's ideals. It is not my purpose to discuss the original meaning of this word. I gladly concede that it meant a state of moral achievement when the powers of the soul were at equilibrium and when resultant peace pervaded the life. But we also know that it meant, preëminently, that state in which the soul had passed beyond contact with body, in which contact alone it found consciousness and sensation and human activity; when the soul, freed from births, had returned to its elemental condition of semi-nothingness, with neither thought, emotion, nor volition. This was a condition in which was found only the negative blessing of release from the turbulence and surging distresses of life. Without calling it non-existence, we claim that it is wanting in every element that we connect, or can conceive connected, with human existence.

There is nothing in it to inspire hope nor to invite cheer. All we can do in its presence is to ask — is this all that man, the flower of God's universe, is to arrive at? Is there nothing better for him than to end his long, dreary existence in such an abject failure? Must he descend from the plain of even a wretched human life to this the lowest reach of existence, if such we must call it?

In the eyes of Christ, there issues out of the mighty conflict of life a purified, glorified human being fit to dwell forever in the presence of His Father and adopted to enjoy that presence for evermore. To Buddha, this same human life ends in failure and must rest forever under the dark pall of oblivion, and robbed by Nirvana of all the possibilities of good and of joy that were implanted in it.

In the absence of higher satisfaction, all that Buddha could do was to glory in his achievements, because of their pervasive influence upon the lives of others during all future time. We might imagine him joining with George Eliot in her noble aspiration: —

> "O! may I join the choir invisible
> Of those immortal dead who live again
> In minds made better by their presence: live
> In pulses stirred to generosity,
> In deeds of daring rectitude, in scorn
> For miserable aims that end with self,
> In thoughts sublime that pierce the nightlike stars,
> And with their mild persistence urge man's search
> To vaster issues . . .
> This is life to come."

But Christ gave us a larger hope and a loftier purpose than this, even the conscious possession of abundant life ourselves and the growing knowledge of the boundless good which our earthly life has done for others. To live in men is joy indeed; but that involves an ability to feel that joy; and this, again, is a part only of the Eternal Life which He gives to all who believe in Him.

It is His disciple only who can say:—

"Beloved, now are we the Sons of God. But we know not what we shall be; but we know that when He shall appear we shall be like Him, for we shall see Him as He is."

CHAPTER XIII

MODERN RELIGIOUS MOVEMENT

In matters of faith, India has always been ultra-conservative. This is largely owing, not to any fettering of thought, but rather to the Hindu Caste System, which has been the most rigid guardian of the Brahmanic faith and the doughty opponent of any new and independent movements.

India has offered to her rishis and reformers unbounded latitude of thought. And, as a consequence, her faith possesses within itself every shade of religious speculation and philosophic conclusions. The many antipodal and conflicting doctrines, theories, tendencies, and institutions which obtain under the all-embracing name of Hinduism, seem astonishing to every western investigator of this faith.

Even in matters of ritual, Brahmanism has always had its protestants, sectarians, and "come-outers." During this stern dominance of the Caste System, which is the most rigorous, if not the most cruel, inquisition that the world has known, there have always been men free to think and determined enough to push forward their ideas and their new religious methods. And these have added picturesque variety to the history of faith in India.

It is, however, a remarkable tribute to the power of caste and to the unheroic character of Hindu reformers, that, of the myriad reforms and protests against Brahmanism which have bristled throughout the centuries, only one — Buddhism — has stood apart in persistent isolation, and has maintained a separate identity and usefulness through more than two millenniums. Of all these protesting creeds, it alone has had sufficient masculine power and moral earnestness permanently to impress itself upon the world as a great religion. It has achieved this, however, not in the land of its birth, but in other lands and among other peoples. Like all other attempts to reform, or overthrow, the mother faith (and even after it had largely accomplished this for ten centuries), Buddhism finally yielded to the mighty absorptive power of Brahmanism, was overthrown as the dominant religion of India, and lost all power and acceptance among the people. This was because most of its vital teachings were appropriated by the rival faith, and Buddha himself was adopted into the Hindu pantheon as the ninth incarnation of Vishnu. Henceforward, it had no distinctive mission or message to the people of this land, and died a natural death.

The well-known passion of Hinduism for absorbing the faiths that come into contact with it, and the maudlin tendency of the people of India to yield to pressure and to sacrifice all in behalf of peace, has been the grave of many a noble endeavour and many an impassioned attempt for new religious life and power.

Nevertheless, there is no reform movement which has entered the arena of religious conflict in India, whether it still remains entirely within the Hindu faith or has possessed vigour and repulsive energy enough to step outside the ancestral faith, which has not left more or less of an impress upon Hinduism, and which does not to-day exercise some power or other over certain classes of the people.

I

All of the many modern sects of Hinduism were originally protests against the dominant Brahmanism of the day. The most popular Vaishnava sect, in South India,—the *Visishdadvaitha* sect of Ramanuja,

—was first a vigorous protest against the austere pantheism of Sankaran. It was the demand of a thoughtful and an earnest religious man for a personal God which could bring peace and rest to the soul, in contradistinction to the unknowable, unethical, and unapproachable Brâhm, which the dominant Vedantism had thrust upon the people.

The *Madhwachariars* went one step farther and inculcated a dualism, which many to-day accept as the basis of their faith.

In the region of Bengal, that other sect of Vaishnavism, which was inculcated by Chaitanya four centuries ago, is to-day the popular cult. It is a revivalism full of wild enthusiasm and ecstatic devotion; yet it attracts, in a remarkable way, many of the men of culture and learning throughout that Presidency.

The Saivite sectarians, who call themselves *Sangamars*, were, a few centuries ago, a mere uprising against the supremacy of the Brahmans and the dominance of caste.

Indeed, nearly all religious reformers in India propelled their reforms as anti-caste movements. But, later on, they have, with very few exceptions, been drawn again into the maelstrom of caste.

The Sikh religion, itself, was originally a religious reform, which found its germs in the mind of the great Kabir, and afterward attained birth in the brave reformer, Nanak Shah, during the fifteenth century. It is a shrewd, an amiable, and also a brave attempt to harmonize Mohammedanism and Hinduism. At the present time, this also is gradually yielding to caste dominance and to the fascination of Hindu ritual.

Thus every century has produced its reformers, and the banks of this great river of Brahmanism is strewn with the wrecks of protesting sects, while many other such barques are to-day adopted as the faithful messengers of orthodox Hinduism and are carrying its message to the people.

II

Modern movements of religious reform in India have not been wanting in number or vigour. And they have been largely movements away from Polytheism, on the one hand, and from Pantheism on the other, toward a modern Theism. Many intelligent men, and many uneducated, but earnest souls, have grown weary of their multitudinous pantheon, and of its hydra-headed idolatry, which charms and debases the masses. In like manner, many of them have ceased to be satisfied with the unknown Brâhm of Vedantism, and are seeking after a personal Deity, who can meet the demands of their craving hearts.

There is much of this thought and sentiment still inarticulate among the upper classes; but it is manifestly growing with the increase of the years.

This theistic movement, as a growing search after a personal God, is to be traced definitely to the growth of western thought, and especially to the direct influence of Christianity. This is no less true of those theistic movements which are by no means amiably disposed toward our religion.

The modern theistic movement first found definite expression and impetus in the life and teaching of that noble son of India, Ram Mohan Roy, who hailed from the Brahmanic aristocracy of Bengal. He was born in 1774 — just before the birth of American Independence. He studied well the ancient writings of Hinduism and translated some of the most important into English. He also searched eagerly and enthusiastically the Christian Scriptures; for which purpose he made himself familiar with the Greek and Hebrew languages. So mightily did the New Testament and its precepts grip him that he wrote and published, in

1819, an excellent tract, "The Precepts of Jesus the Guide to Peace and Happiness." This is a remarkable testimony to the ethical preëminence of the Bible. He later declared that he "believed in the truths of the Christian religion."

Being unwilling to abide alone in this discovery and in these convictions, he established, in 1815, the "Atmâ Sabhâ," or "Soul Society," in his own home. This soon developed into a small church, for which a suitable edifice was erected, that they might worship the one God free from the contaminating influence of popular idolatry and Hindu ceremonial.

This truly great man, without the aid of any European missionary, in the quiet solitude of his own heart, and under the influence of the Spirit of God, rose to some of the highest truths of Theism, and, under the mighty influence of Christian literature, became a reformer of the first order among his people.

But, during a visit to England he sickened, and died in 1833; and the theistic movement weakened and waned for a few years, deprived of his leadership and inspiring presence.

It was in 1843 that the Brahmo Somaj of Ram Mohan Roy was united with another *Sabha* organized by another great soul, Debendra Nath Tagore. Under the guidance of this sturdy reformer, the Brahmo Somaj movement put on new life and energy. Debendra Nath was very devout and courageous. He was opposed to the religion of his fathers, as practised by the people. Nevertheless, he was somewhat anchored to the past. He still clung to the Hindu scriptures and regarded the Vedas as infallible. Later, however, as these Hindu writings were studied with more care, his faith in them was considerably shattered, and he began to deny their supreme authority.

He and the other members of the society here entered upon a great struggle which ushered them into an "Age of Reason." The Vedas were abandoned as an ultimate authority, and the Brahmo Somaj, for a time, became "a Church without a Bible," and without any anchorage but the higher reason of its members.

In 1852, the society was reorganized. Reason was soon found to be inadequate as the foundation of faith; and they passed on to an intuitional basis. That again seemed to be even more unsatisfactory than reason itself. After a few years, the movement gradually developed a doctrine of inspiration, when the utterances of the leaders themselves were regarded as inspired and became the voice of God to the members. Thus, within a few years, Brahmo Somaj moved almost in a circle, in its search for a stable anchorage to its faith; and it returned to a point dangerously near to the Hindu position which it had left a few years before.

The rapid movement above indicated was chiefly owing to an ardent youth, who rallied to the support of Debendra Nath, and who gradually took the reins into his own hands. This young man was Keshub Chunder Sen; and he soon became the leading figure, certainly the most striking, in the whole theistic movement of India. He acquired growing influence over Debendra Nath, became the controlling spirit, and continued until his death to be the central figure of Theism in India.

Chunder Sen was a great enthusiast, full of intellectual resource, and, withal, a man of deep spirituality. He was an Oriental of the Orientals; his mind was of a thoroughly mystic type, and, like the devout Hindu, he loved the rigours of asceticism, and, in not a few instances, yielded to the fascinations of the methods of the Yogi.

He was a restless soul. Hinduism had so much

that was repulsive to him; and he felt that polytheism and idolatry had so crushed out of his people all the beauty of a living faith that he longed to hasten communication of his message of truth and of life the new and glorious day of Theism for India. His pace was so much faster than that of Debendra Nath that it took but a few years to make their separation a necessity. This took place in 1865. Thereupon, the old society became known as the "*Âthi Somaj*," — "The Original Somaj," — while Sen and his party formed a new organization, which was pretentiously known as "The Brahmo Somaj of India." This happened in 1866.

The old society settled down into inactivity, lost much of its spirit of reform, and has never since accomplished much in the realm of theistic advance.

The new Somaj, however, soon acquired prominence and became the life and embodiment of the Indian theistic movement.

But Chunder Sen had his serious dangers; and those lay in the very excess of his virtues.

Hurried on by his intense nature, exalted to power by his brilliant intellectual qualities, and yearning with a passion for the release of his beloved India from the religious and spiritual thraldom which he witnessed all about him, he acquired irresistible charm and power with his followers, and his words became their undisputed law; and his deliverances were surcharged with what they regarded as divine inspiration. And there is no doubt that he soon came to believe himself to be a direct vehicle of God in the communication of his message of truth and of life to the world.

Under the influence of this conviction or delusion (whichever one may choose to call it), he was swept on, and carried with him most of his followers, into startling novelties of ritual and of organization.

Finally, however, he became so extreme and radical that some of his principal followers became frightened and grew restless. The occasion of another split was found in the marriage of Chunder Sen's daughter to the young Maharaja of Cooch Behar, in 1876. Chunder Sen had worked heroically for the enactment of a new marriage law for the members of the Brahmo Somaj, whereby no bride should be married before fourteen and no bridegroom under eighteen years of age. Yet, in the marriage of his own daughter, he ignored this law, which was passed chiefly through his own energy. Notwithstanding the fact that the leader claimed divine guidance in this affair, his leading followers attributed the marriage to his weakness and pride.

This led to another secession, in May, 1878, whereby the majority of the societies and their members broke away from the Sen party and established the *Sâdhârna Somaj*—"The Universal Somaj." This schism was a terrible blow to Mr. Sen; and yet it released him from the trammels which the dissatisfied had hitherto thrust upon him, and gave him, among the remnant, an opportunity to launch out on new projects, and to introduce many religious vagaries, which to most men were striking and, to many, were shocking. Under the banner of the "New Dispensation," he practised a varied liturgy and cultivated an unique ceremonial which seemed to be a close imitation, and almost a mockery, of some of the most sacred institutions of Christianity and of other religions.

The schismatic weakness of the theistic movement did not reach its consummation in this last division. It was almost immediately upon the death of Keshub Chunder Sen, at the beginning of 1884, that his immediate family and a few of his followers proclaimed that his spirit still abode in the Mandir, where he so often spoke, and that no one should succeed him or speak from the Mandir hereafter!

Within these few short years a new cult had begun to grow around the person of Chunder Sen, like those around a thousand others well known in the history ot India. He became to some of his followers not only a great religious teacher, but also something of an incarnation on his own account, so that it seemed to them blasphemy for any living being to aspire to speak from the pulpit of the beloved dead master.

His natural successor was Babu Protap Chunder Mozumdar. He protested against this apotheosis of the departed leader, and insisted upon the fact that their movement must be open to new light, and must seek after ever increasing progress and advance. But the family were obdurate, and the new split became inevitable; and thus Chunder Sen has passed into the ranks of the Mahatmas of India and will erelong be promoted to a place among the incarnations of their deities.

Mr. Mozumdar was, intellectually, not inferior to Chunder Sen himself; and he was possessed of deep earnestness of spirit and of a beautiful English style (both as a writer and speaker) which commended him and his cause to the public, and especially to English and American Theists. He visited the West more than once, and charmed many an audience of Christian men by his deep sincerity and eloquence.

III

The progress of this Brahmo movement has not been very encouraging.

We have already seen its tendency to schism. There seems very little in the movement which makes for peace and unity. Any little pique or difference of views has not only created internal dissension, but also engendered new sects.

The leaders of the movement have been both able and absolutely devoted to the theistic cause; but they have not revealed the highest qualities of leadership, especially that quality which exalts above the leader himself the principles and the cause which he advocates. Nor have they imparted to the members of the Somaj that altruistic fervour which enables them to deny themselves in behalf of their common cause and purpose.

Numerically, the progress of the Brahmo Somaj has been most disappointing. At the last census there were only 4050 members. And, of these, more than three-quarters were in Bengal.

This, however, by no means represents the strength of the movement; for it is said, with truth, that many who do not register themselves as

Brahmos are in deepest accord with the movement. And it must, moreover, be remembered that the influence of the society is far in excess of the numbers represented. For the movement has drawn its membership, almost exclusively, from the upper class; and the majority of Brahmos are men of education and of position in society. Moreover, they joined this movement under the deep conviction of the utter worthlessness of Hinduism as a way of salvation, and with a purpose to seek after that which is best in thought and life.

It is this aristocratic character of the movement which has largely militated against its popularity. Its appeal has been mainly to men and women of English training. It has not been possessed of any passion for the multitude; nor has it adequately appreciated the importance, for its own well-being, of a united endeavour to reach and bring in the man of the street.

Nevertheless, the movement has been thoroughly permeated with an Indian spirit. The leaders have been particular in their desire to exalt and emphasize the Oriental aspect and method, as distinct from the Occidental. This is the reason why it has been so frequently and bitterly criticised. It has been judged by western standards and criticised because it has not squared with western ideals. From time to time missionaries and other Christian men, seeing no reason, from their standpoint, why these Brahmo friends should not come over in a body into the Christian fold, have been impatient with their lack of response. They failed to understand that, with these western principles and admiration, there were also eastern thoughts and prepossessions, and the invaluable inheritance of a past that kept them aloof from the foreign faith and led them frequently to deliver themselves vehemently against its most western manifestations. Even their conception of Christ was a distinctly Oriental one. And they denied that a man of the West could compare with them of the East in the deep appreciation of the Christ-character and in loving attachment to their "Brother" from the East —Jesus of Nazareth.

Yet, the Christian basis of this movement is unmistakable. We have seen how Ram Mohan Roy received a new baptism of thought and life upon studying the Christian Scriptures. It gave a new direction and inspiration to his theistic conceptions.

Chunder Sen found nearly all the inspiration from the Bible; and he lived under the spell of Christ's own power, and with a passion, such as few Christians possess, to follow Him and to be a full partaker of His blessings.

The writer will never forget his own brief visit to Protap Mozumdar, not long before the latter's death. It was on the eve of Good Friday. He found this devout man with eighteen of his disciples (one of them an Oxford graduate) studying together the tender words of our Lord uttered to His disciples in the Upper Room on the night in which He was betrayed. They were thus qualifying themselves properly to commemorate His death on the coming morn. And Mr. Mozumdar gave a strong lecture on "The Suffering Christ" to a large audience in one of the city halls on the morrow. The thought occurred to us, how many Christians had met together that same evening, like these Brahmos, for the purpose of studying our Lord's Words upon that memorable occasion and bringing themselves thus *en rapport* with Him whose atoning death they were to commemorate? As we parted, it was hardly necessary for that man of God to say to the writer in pathetic tones, "O, sir, I only wish you knew how near we are to you in these matters!" Some may have read that remarkable book, named "The Oriental Christ," written and published by this same gentleman in 1883. In the preface, he gives this strikingly beautiful account of his conversion:—

"Nearly twenty years ago, my troubles, studies, and circumstances forced upon me the question of personal relationship to Christ. . . . As the sense of sin grew on me, and with it a deep miserable restlessness, a necessity of reconciliation between aspiration and practice, I was mysteriously led to feel a personal affinity to the Spirit of Christ. The whole subject of the life and death of Christ had for me a marvellous sweetness and fascination. . . . Often discouraged and ridiculed, I persisted in according to Christ a tenderness of honour which arose in my heart unbidden. I prayed, I fasted, at Christmas and Easter times. I secretly hunted the book-shops of Calcutta to gather the so-called likenesses of Christ. I did not know, I cared not to think, whither all this would lead. . . . About the year 1867 . . . I was almost alone in Calcutta. My inward trials and travails had really reached a crisis. It was a week-day evening, I forget the date now. The gloomy and haunted shades of summer evening had suddenly thickened into darkness. . . . I sat near the large lake in the Hindu College compound. . . . A sobbing, gusty wind swam over the water's surface. . . . I was meditating upon the state of my soul, on the cure of all spiritual wretchedness, the brightness and peace unknown to me, which was the lot of God's children. I prayed and besought Heaven. I cried and shed hot tears. . . . Suddenly it seemed to me, let me own it was revealed to me, that close to me there was a holier, more blessed, most loving personality upon which I must repose my troubled head. Jesus lay discovered in my heart as a strange, human, kindred love, as a repose, a sympathetic consolation, an unpurchased treasure, for which I was freely invited. The response of my nature was unhesitating and immediate. Jesus, from that day, to me became a reality whereon I might lean. It was an impulse then, a flood of light, love, and consolation. It is no longer an impulse now. It is a faith and principle; it is an experience verified by a thousand trials . . . a character, a spirit, a holy, sacrificed, exalted self, whom I recognize as the true Son of God. According to my humble light, I have always tried to be faithful to this inspiration. I have been aided, confirmed, encouraged by many, and most of all by one. My aspiration has been not to speculate on Christ, but to be what Jesus tells us all to be. . . . I shall be content if what I say in these pages at all tends to give completeness to any man's ideas of the life and ministry of Jesus Christ. . . . In the midst of these crumbling systems of Hindu error and superstition, in the midst of these cold, spectral shadows of transition, secularism, and agnostic doubt, to me Christ has been like the meat and drink of my soul. His influences have woven round me for the last twenty years or more, and, outside the fold of Christianity as I am, have formed a new fold, wherein I find many besides myself."

Chunder Sen also abundantly expressed himself concerning the Christ, His mission, and message. But to him, again, it is an Asiatic Christ; and He must be accepted in a truly Oriental, yes, even in a Hindu, way. He says:—

"It is not the Christ of the Baptists, nor the Christ of the Methodists, but the Christ sent by God, the Christ of love and meekness, of truth and self-sacrifice, whom the world delights to honour. If you say we must renounce our nationality and all the purity and devotion of eastern faith for sectarian and western Christianity, we shall say most emphatically, No. It is *our* Christ, *Asia's* Christ, you have come to return to us. The East gratefully and lovingly welcomes back her Christ. But we shall not have your Christianity, which suits not the spirit of the East. Our religion is the religion of harmony."

In further enforcement of this Oriental character he continues:—

"Was not Jesus Christ an Asiatic? Yes, and His disciples were Asiatics, and all the agencies primarily employed for the propagation of the Gospel were Asiatic. In fact, Christianity was founded and developed by Asiatics and in Asia. When I reflect on this, my love for Jesus becomes a hundred fold intensified; I feel Him nearer my heart, and deeper in my national sympathies. . . . And is it not true that an Asiatic can read the imageries and allegories of the Gospel, and its descriptions of the natural sceneries, of customs and manners, with greater interest and a fuller perception of their force and beauty than an European? . . . The more this greater fact is pondered, the less, I hope, will be the antipathy and hatred of European Christians against Oriental nationalities, and the greater the interest of the Asiatics in the teachings of Christ. And thus in Christ, Europe and Asia, the East and the West, may learn to find harmony and unity. . . ."

And let it not be supposed that Mr. Sen was altogether wanting in an appreciation of the higher significance and vicarious efficacy of the death of Christ. Concerning this, he observes:—

"Humanity was lost in Adam, but was recovered in Christ. He was the world's atonement. . . .

"His death on the cross affords the highest practical illustration of self-sacrifice. He sacrificed His life for the sake of truth and the benefit of the world. In obedience to the will of His Father, He laid down His life, and said, Thy will be done! And surely there is deeper meaning in the fact than even the orthodox attach to it, that the death of Christ is the life of the world. . . ."

In many of the lectures which he gave, and in many of the articles which he wrote, we have evidence of the wonderful place which Christ had in his heart and of the power which He exercised over his thoughts. He exclaims:—

"Blessed Jesus, immortal Child of God! For the world He lived and died. May the world appreciate

Him and follow His precepts! . . . All through my inner being I see Christ. He is no longer to me a doctrine, or a dogma, but, with Paul, I cry, 'for me to live is Christ!'" On another occasion he says:—

"Where, then, is Christ now? He is living in all Christian lives, and in all Christian influences at work around us. . . . You cannot resist His influence; you may deny His doctrines, you may even hate and repudiate His name, but He goes straight into your hearts, and leavens your lives."

Other leaders of this movement are imbued with the same spirit. The editor of the New Dispensation remarks:—

"As a matter of fact the Brahmists have accepted Christian truth in a more special sense than Hindus, or even some Christian sects, have any idea of. . . . The organization of the Brahmo Somaj of India is framed upon an essentially Christian basis. Its missionary staff is Christian, being guided entirely by the principle of 'Take no thought for the morrow.' In its mission office, mottoes are found upon the walls which are all Christian. Almost every Brahmo household has a picture of Christ. The only Life of Jesus in Bengali is by a missionary of the Brahmo Somaj of India. Its truly evangelistical work, the life and conversation of its members, breathe distinctly the spirit and influence of Christ. . . ."

Another Theist writes:—

"Reverently have I sat at the feet of the Jesus of the Gospels to learn the exalted ethics of the Sermon on the Mount. But Jesus, other than a moral force, *the truer and higher Jesus*, long remained a sealed book to me. Who could know the veritable Christ of God without light from above? . . .

"Jesus forms the heart-blood of many a Brahmo. . . . We are ready to sacrifice anything if only by that we are enabled to love and cherish Jesus in our hearts. . . . The Brahmo Somaj is born to honour and revere Jesus, whatever the result may be."

From these quotations, which might be multiplied indefinitely, it may be seen that the movement has been, to a considerable extent, under the Christ spell and imbued with much of His Spirit. Inasmuch, however, as the movement is an avowedly eclectic one, the Brahmoist was never willing to rest completely under the Christ influence. He gave to Christ, perhaps, a supreme place, but not a unique position, in his life and thought. Jesus was to him one of many, though perhaps a *primus inter pares.*

It is this eclectic character of the Brahmo Somaj

which has robbed it of much of its power. It may seem, at first, a very fine thing to collect, classify, and codify the best from many religions and dignify them as a religion. But that can never become a unified message of life to any people. It may be ethically immaculate, but it has no vital power. The distinctive, life-giving, and inspiring element of every faith has been eliminated, and only the common, unimpassioned, and uninspiring elements have been retained.

Moreover, Brahmos have failed to realize that Theism, as such, has never satisfied any people as a way of salvation. It is doubtless a correct apprehension of the Divine Being. But religion requires a great deal more than this in the way of exhibiting the characteristics of the Deity, and especially of revealing His attitude toward, and His work for, mankind, before it can possess and reveal the potency of a saving faith.

It would seem as if this movement, up to the present time, has just missed its mark and failed of achieving greatness and power. As we have seen, the leaders have exalted our Lord in a wonderful way, and have exhibited even a passion for Him in some ways. And yet they have robbed Him of the distinct uniqueness of His nature and of His work for man. They are first eclectics, and then they are rigid Unitarians, and lastly they are Christians. They need to reverse this order so as to add efficiency and potency to the Brahmo Somaj.

It is a significant fact that Chunder Sen, with all his declared love for Christ and his great admiration for Him and His work, mentioned neither the name nor the saving work of Jesus in the final creed of the New Dispensation. That creed is as follows:—

> "One God, one Scripture, one Church.
> Eternal Progress of the Soul.
> Communion of Prophets and Saints.
> Fatherhood and Motherhood of God;
> Brotherhood of Man and Sisterhood of Woman.
> Harmony of Knowledge and Holiness, Love and Work;
> Yoga and Asceticism in their highest development.
> Loyalty to Sovereign."

It must not be forgotten, however, that this movement deserves much more our commendation than our criticism. It is a noble endeavour to pass out of an inherited bondage, a debased creed, a demoralized pantheon, and an all-embracing superstition, into the full wisdom and blessing of a correct vision of God and Duty. If they have failed of the best, they are, nevertheless, with their faces turned toward it. And there is every hope that a kind Providence, through the instrumentality of Christian thought and western civilization, will lead them unto it. If they have not accepted our western Christianity, it may be that God has something better in store for them, in training them toward the realization of that form of Christian life and thought which will not only be more in consonance with Indian taste and ideals, but will also grip the country in such a way as the western type of our faith has not yet been able to do, and *seems* incapable of doing.

IV

The Arya Somaj is a movement somewhat kindred to the Brahmo Somaj, in so far as it is a definite protest against modern Hinduism and is theistic in its teaching. The Theism of this Somaj, however, is quite different in character from that of the Brahmos.

Dayanand Saraswati was a Brahman, born in the Gujarati country about 1825. He developed into a man of keen intellect and of deep convictions. He also studied the Christian Scriptures and was slightly versed in the Hindu Shastras. He became dissatisfied with the Pantheism of his mother faith; the caste system grated upon his nerves, and the idolatry and the superstitions of the land, and especially the gross immorality of the people, roused him to deep thought and activity. He appealed to the Pandits, but found no sympathy or help from them. He found his Theism in the Vedas themselves, and ever after proclaimed, with great vehemence, that the God of the Vedas was one and was a personal God; and he found an easy way of interpreting those ancient books in harmony with his convictions!

Jesus Christ did not appeal to him in the least. Indeed, he indulges in very cheap and gross criticism of the life of our Lord. His attitude toward Christianity was not at all kindly; indeed, the movement, up to the present, has been distinguished for nothing more than its hostility to the Christian religion. Nevertheless, it is doubtless true that some of the best ideas that Dayanand possessed were gleaned from the Bible; and the Arya Somaj has learned and inculcates some of the important lessons of our faith.

When Dayanand found no encouragement in his appeal to the Pandits, he turned ultimately to the people and founded, in 1875, the Arya Somaj at Bombay. And from the first the movement has been a popular one, addressing itself to the masses and seeking to bring them over to its way of thinking and living. In this it has been, as we have seen, entirely removed from the Brahmo Somaj, which has been too content to remain a religion of the classes. Like the other movement, however, it has been largely local in its spread and influence. Of its one hundred thousand members at the present time, more than 70 per cent are in the United Provinces, and nearly all the remainder are in the Panjaub.

Moreover, it has recently gathered its recruits mainly from the educated classes, among whom the higher castes largely prevail; nearly four-fifths of the Aryas are said to be of the twice-born castes, which is a very significant fact. So that both in its popular character and methods, as well as in the high social position and educational training of its members and in its rapidly growing numbers, the Arya Somaj is a movement of considerable importance.

The principles of this Somaj, as enunciated in its creed, are not such as to grip men with power. They emphasize the unity of God, the infallibility of the Vedas; and the general aim of the Somaj is "to do good to the world by improving the physical, social, intellectual, moral, and spiritual condition of mankind." Its moral code is of a high order.

It is thoroughly national in its spirit, and makes much capital out of the present spirit of racial antagonism. It is a significant fact that during the recent season of "Unrest" the government regarded the Arya Somaj as a hotbed of sedition and a nourisher of hostility to the West and to western things.

The Arya Somaj is awake to the importance of training men as messengers of its Gospel of Theism. It has established a *Guru Kula* at the foot of the Himalayas, where quite a number of young men are being trained in its doctrines and supplied with its enthusiasms. From this theological seminary many have already gone forth, in the orthodox style of religious mendicancy, to impart their teaching and spread their movement far and wide, without any expense to the society.

There is to-day, in North India, no enemy to the Christian cause so wide awake and so bitter as the Arya Somaj. It is so thoroughly national in its spirit, is so compactly organized, and lends itself so easily to the racial and political agitation of the day, that Christianity finds in it its greatest foe in those regions.

Let it not be thought, however, that we do not appreciate the living spark of theistic truth which this movement represents, combined, as it is, with hostility to the caste system, which is India's greatest curse, and its antagonism to many of the superstitions and unworthy ceremonials of the ancestral faith.

That movement must not be condemned too severely which is a bulwark against drink, caste, idolatry, early marriages, and which vigorously promotes female education, the remarriage of widows, and various philanthropic institutions.

V

It may not be improper to close this chapter with a reference to the Theosophical Society in India. It is true that the leaders of this movement, which was established in America in 1875, and transplanted into India a short time afterward, disavow its claim to being a religion; though that claim was definitely made and warmly pushed a quarter of a century ago. It is now extolled by its members as "the cement of faiths," "the harmonizer of religions." It is said that Arya Somaj became affiliated with it in 1879, though we have seen no result of this affiliation.

The objects of Theosophy are said to be three: (1) The establishment of a universal brotherhood. (2) The study of ancient languages. (3) Investigation of the hidden mysteries of nature and the latent psychical forces of man.

These aims seem thoroughly worthy, though the last mentioned, under its original founders, led to mystical claptrap, and to the abuse of the strong superstitious instincts of India.

The society was founded by a Russian adventuress, Madame Blavatsky, and by an American soldier, Colonel Olcott, who was the easy tool, if not the accomplice, of his clever and unscrupulous associate.

In the early history of the movement, at its headquarters in Madras, Madame Blavatsky gathered around her a numerous coterie of ardent Hindus, whom she duped with various tricks and séances. This was with a view to convincing them of her constant communication with *Koothoomi* and various other Tibetan Mahatmas, of whom she seemed to be the special agent! These and other similar performances might have continued had it not been for her

French accomplices, who quarrelled with her, because she did not pay them adequately, and who exposed her mercilessly. The whole matter was published in the *Madras Christian College Magazine*, and the Russian lady was speedily sent away from India to the West for a judicious season of rest. The leaders of Theosophy have never been unwilling to impose upon the stupendous credulity of their Indian followers.

Nevertheless, it is undeniable that, with all its failings, Theosophy has exercised considerable influence upon the educated classes in this country. This has resulted largely through its readiness to utilize the recent movement of the people toward higher political privileges and their deep spirit of religious unrest.

Since the advent of Mrs. Besant, the society has been largely moulded by her erratic powers. She has not hesitated to use her ability and influence toward the creation and the development of a strong reactionary religious spirit throughout the land. She has bitterly denounced every tendency among the people toward Christianity. By her eloquence, which is remarkable, she has extolled the faith of India, and has revived and embalmed many of its worst features which were rapidly passing away; and has even defended idolatry and kindred evils by trying to harmonize them with modern and scientific ideas! She has herself become practically a Hindu, expounds Hindu doctrines, and practise Hindu ceremonies. She has persistently maintained eastern thought and customs as against western, and has thus endeared herself to English-speaking Hindus, who regard her as the goddess Saraswati herself, and are willing to give her a place in their pantheon as one of the great defenders of their faith against the mighty influences of the West!

In this matter, Mrs. Besant may be said to have caused irreparable injury to the people, as she has helped to arrest the tendency toward religious reform and progress, and has rendered articulate and given power and expression to the reactionary spirit which is now so rampant in India. More than any other person, and chiefly because she is of the West, and speaks in the accents of the West, she has antagonized progress in this land, not only religiously but also socially, and has done the greatest disservice to the people of India. In her eyes, Hindu philosophy and ritual, Hindu institutions and domestic life, have practically nothing to learn from the West, and need only to be known in order to be appreciated and loved!

This, doubtless, in good part, accounts for her present popularity.

Yet, one cannot fail to recognize the value of some things which she is doing. She has recently begun to speak with some emphasis upon lines of reform. She has been instrumental in stirring within the people a wider desire for higher education; though one can hardly understand why she has done so much for the establishment of a college for men, and has done practically nothing to advance the educational interests of her much-neglected sex in India.

Upon the death of Colonel Olcott, the President Founder of Theosophy, in 1907, Mrs. Besant became his successor. So far as the Indian vote was concerned, this was a foregone conclusion; since her avowed sympathy with Hinduism in all its forms had gained for her a strong place in the Hindu heart.

The method by which she was elected, however, is suggestive of the future course of the movement in India.

When nearing death, Colonel Olcott was induced by Mrs. Besant to invoke and to consult the "Masters" — the convenient ghosts of the dead — with a view to a choice of his successor in office. There was no doubt about his preference for the Englishwoman.

The Mahatmas wisely agreed with the Colonel and Mrs. Besant, and a powerful fulcrum was secured for lifting her into the presidency. And Mrs. Besant to-day claims that it is better for her to have been chosen by the dead than to have been elected by the living. Upon her inauguration, she insisted upon it that all Theosophists must cling to the "Masters" and adhere to their decisions.

If we mistake not, this marks the beginning of a new era in Theosophy, — at least in India, — an era during which the movement will be entirely directed and worked by those who are the authorized mouth-pieces of the glorified dead! Thus the movement is fairly launched upon a course which will inevitably lead it to something very much akin to a religion, with its accumulated mysteries and with a host of propelling superstitions of its own. More than any other land, India will lend itself admirably to the development and the propagation of such a cult.

Theosophy is not represented by a very large number of organizations and members. But the movement has the sympathy of many who have not taken upon them its name; and the society, at the present time, is certainly in favour with a large number of the educated classes.

Orthodox pandits, however, are thoroughly suspicious of the movement; and Mrs. Besant's recent attempts to thrust upon them her own interpretations of certain Hindu doctrines — interpretations, too, which are foreign to their own — has led to a spirit of opposition, where but recently appreciation and favour existed.

Theosophy, as a harmonizer of faiths, is not likely to accomplish much that will be permanently good. Religions to-day have lost much of their asperity one toward the other. The study of Comparative Religion has led men everywhere to magnify the assonances, rather than the dissonances, of the Great World Faiths. Theosophy magnifies into a cult this function of bringing religions together. It ignores, however, the fundamental differences which exist, brings all faiths into the same equational value, and assumes that they are equally effective as ways of salvation.

With such profound ignorance of the essential qualities of the faiths which are to be harmonized, and with a placid assumption that these religions are of the same efficacy, only to different peoples, it is impossible to see how Theosophy can ever render a service to any of the faiths or to the people who are their adherents which will not ultimately prove a disservice to all. Peace without truth, like peace without honour, will not ultimately redound to the promotion of religion or to the salvation of men.

Whatever Theosophy may render toward the development of an Oriental literature will depend largely upon its attitude toward truth and religion in general, and toward Hinduism and Christianity in particular. Its bitter attitude toward Christianity in the past does not encourage one to believe that hereafter the literature fostered by it will be either very impartial or very sane. And yet we shall be thankful for anything it may accomplish in the preservation of Sanskrit manuscripts and in the development of a wholesome literature of any kind on lines purely Oriental.

CHAPTER XIV

THE PROGRESS OF CHRISTIANITY IN INDIA

I

FOR at least seventeen centuries Christianity has found a home in India. The Syrian Church was the first to gather converts, and it still exists as a separate sect of 300,000 souls in a small part of Malabar. Roman Catholicism, also, has had here its six centuries of struggles and varied fortunes, and now claims its 1,500,000 followers. On July 9, 1906, the Protestants celebrated the bicentenary of the landing of their first two missionaries at Tranquebar, on the Coromandel coast. Ziegenbalg and Plutscho were truly men of God, and inaugurated a work which to-day has its ramifications in every part of this vast peninsula.

They introduced a new era of missionary effort for India. Former endeavours were ecclesiastical. Great men, indeed, had wrought for Christ in this land; but their chief aim had been to establish a religion of forms and ceremonies. In the matter of ritual in religion, Hinduism has little to learn from, and has much to suggest to, western ecclesiastics. The early failure of our faith to secure marked and permanent success in this land finds its chief cause here.

Ziegenbalg began in the right way. He identified himself with the people; he studied well their language, and hastened to incarnate his faith in vernacular literature; and, above all, he proceeded at once to translate into the language of the people the Word of God. Never before had the Bible been translated into an Indian tongue. After thirteen years of service, this great missionary died; but he left to his successors the heritage of a vernacular Bible, which has wrought mightily in South India for the redemption of the people. He also set the pace for subsequent missionaries of his persuasion, who, in these two centuries, have practically translated God's Word into every important Indian dialect. The Bible in his own vernacular lies open, inviting every native of India to-day; and in many vernaculars the translation has been revised more than once. This stands as a notable triumph of Protestantism during these two centuries in India.

The writer has a copy of one of the earliest Tamil books prepared by these pioneers of our faith. These books have already grown into a large library — the best-developed Christian literature in any vernacular of the East. All over the land mission presses are annually pouring forth their many millions of pages both to nourish and cheer the infant Christian community, and to win to Christ the multiplying readers among non-Christians. The press has already become, perhaps, the most important agency in the furtherance of Christian thought and life in this land.

One is impressed with the manifoldness of the work which began in so much simplicity two centuries ago. The missionary is no longer the preacher under some shady tree, addressing a few ignorant, ill-clad peasants. He is actively engaged in all departments of Christian effort. A Protestant mission is an elaborately organized activity, pursuing all lines of work for the elevation of the people. It has not only churches which engage in varied forms of pastoral effort; it has also its staff of evangelists and Bible women who carry the message of life to all the villages. In these missions there are not only 10,000 day schools, with their 375,000 scholars, besides 30,000 youth who are in the 307 higher institutions. There are also thousands of young men and women, in many institutions, undergoing careful preparation as teachers and preachers.

A Christian Village School in South India

There is also the medical host who treated 2,000,000 patients last year; there are industrial institutions under well-trained men, peasant settlements for the poor oppressed ryots, and schools for the blind and the deaf-mute. There is hardly an agency which can bring light, comfort, life, and inspiration to men which is not utilized by modern missions in India.

But the progress of these two centuries has been chiefly on lines which defy the columns of the statistician and elude the ken of the ordinary globe-trotter.

The number of people that have been brought to Christ, and who now represent Protestantism in this land are, indeed, far fewer than might have been expected. A round million of a community after two centuries of effort among a population of 300,000,000 is not a thing of which to boast. And this may seem the more discouraging when it is remembered that there are now engaged in this work ninety-one different missionary societies of many lands, and supporting a missionary force of 4000 men and women. There is also a native Pastorate of 1100 ordained men, with a total Indian agency of 26,000 men and women.

So great a force of workers would, indeed, warrant us in expecting larger results in conversions.

But it should be remembered that this agency is

chiefly the product of the last few decades only, and is now multiplying in numbers and increasing in efficiency at a very rapid rate. At the present time, fully 200 of the Indian agents of our missions are university graduates, and a still larger number are of partial college training.

The Indian Christian community itself, though in the main of low social origin, has made remarkable progress in education and manly independence. It is, already, perhaps the best-educated community in India. And it is feeling increasingly its opportunities and its obligations. It was only recently that its growing sense of national importance and its duties led it to organize a "National Missionary Society," which is directed by Indian leadership, supported by Indian funds, and its work is to be done by India's own sons. This society enters upon its career very auspiciously, and is not only symptomatic of present conditions, but is also pregnant with hope for the Indian Church of the future.

It took many years to lay deeply the foundation of our mission organization. Indeed, the foundation is not quite completed. And yet the work of superstructure has already begun, and more rapid results may now be expected.

But the more hidden and indirect results of Protestant Christian efforts in this land encourage the Christian worker more than all the direct results.

During the last century, at least twenty laws have been enacted with a view to abolishing cruel religious rites and removing revolting customs and disabilities, such as Hinduism, from time immemorial, has established among the people. These laws were enacted in the teeth of opposition from the religious rulers of the land, and, in more cases than one, led to serious riot and religious fanaticism. But the growing spirit of Christ in the land could not tolerate these heathenish customs; so they had to go.

The new spirit which has taken possession of the classes in India is in striking contrast with the spirit of the past. The new education, imparted on modern lines, in thousands of institutions scattered over the land, has brought its revenge of sentiment upon former thinking and believing. Western philosophy has had a noble share in the achievement; and the schoolmaster has been a pioneer in the work of transforming the sentiments and ideals of the people. The holy men of India, — the ecclesiastics, — by their conservatism, have lost all influence over the many thousands who have passed through the universities, and who represent the intelligence, culture, and advancing power of India.

It is no empty boast to claim that our mission schools and colleges have had a conspicuous share in this work of enlightenment, and in the transformation of popular and fundamental thoughts and sentiments.

The religious unrest of the day is one of the most prominent features of this advance. It is true that, during the last few years, there passed over India a peculiar wave of religious reaction in favour of old Hindu conceptions and ancient rites. But these are entirely the result of a new and vigorous, though not sane, patriotism. A loud cry of "*Swadesha*" (home-land) has swept over the country. It demands affection and acceptance for everything that is of the East, and the opposite sentiments for things western. All that is of Hindu origin, and everything of eastern aspect, is, for that very reason, regarded as sound and delectable. Of course, this reaction has found its widest utterances in matters religious; and Hindu men of western culture to-day will applaud, though they will *not* practise, religious customs and ideas which were laughed at by their class a quarter of a century ago. As a matter of fact, however, this wild Orientalism is a thing which should neither be discouraged nor condemned. It needs balance and sanity; but it is a true expression of the awakened self-assertion and the dawning sense of liberty among the people. In time, the movement will become chastened, and will throw off much of its present folly. It will then render for India and its redemption more than anything else has in the past.

In the meanwhile, however, there is a quiet revolution, both religious and social, doing its blessed work in all sections of the community.

New religious organizations have sprung into existence and are winning followers among the best members of the community. The Brahmo Somaj and various other Somajes furnish, as we have seen, asylum and rest for many men of culture who have abandoned polytheism and all that pertains to it. The Arya Somaj appeals to, and gathers in, men from all ranges.

Social reform has its organizations and its gatherings all over the land where the Hindu orator finds abundant opportunity to denounce the social evils which are a curse to all the people; and, alas! then returns to his home, where he meekly submits to these same social tyrannies which dominate his own family. What India needs to-day, more than anything else, is even a small band of men who are imbued with convictions and who are willing to die for the same. India's redemption will be nigh when it can furnish a few thousand such men banded together to *do* something or to *die* in the cause of reform.

It is Protestantism which has laid growing emphasis upon the ethical, rather than the ecclesiastical, aspect of our faith; and to this fact can be attributed most of its influence in the development of this new life and thought.

Of course, the British government has politically and socially represented and promoted these ideas. It could not do otherwise and be true to its own principles. Its influence has been the most pervasive and marked in the development of what is best in thought and truest in life.

Perhaps no change has overtaken Protestant missions during these two centuries greater than that which has transformed the missionaries themselves. There is a wide gulf between Ziegenbalg and Carey. There is a still wider one between the Carey of a century ago and his great-grandson who is a missionary in North India to-day. In devotion and zeal for the Master, they are all one; but in their conception of Christianity, of Hinduism, and of the missionary motive, they are much wider apart than many imagine.

It should also be remembered that Protestant missionaries, as a body, are no longer isolated from each other and animated by mutual suspicions and impelled by petty jealousies, as in the past. Their development in amity, comity, and organized fellowship, even during the last decade, is marvellous. Federation and organic ecclesiastical union are becoming the order of the day. Four denominations of America and Scotland are now perfecting such a scheme in South India; and this is only the beginning of an ever expanding movement for Christian fellowship all over the land. No one knows what grand results it will achieve. We all know, however, that the fraternal regard, sympathy, and confidence is far removed from the sad divisiveness of the past, that it is pregnant with blessing in the coming of the Kingdom of God, and that it is far in advance of the spirit of union which prevails in England or America. In this we believe that the East is to open the way for the West.

These and many other facts encourage those who look to the speedy Christianizing of this land. And yet we cannot, I repeat, ignore the fact of the relative meagreness of the results. It is a sad truth that the total Protestant Indian community, at the present time, is only one three-hundredth part of the population!

I would not be pessimistic, however, even in this matter of numerical growth. In the past, we have too much made a fetich of figures, and our faith has been too much pinned to statistics.

But the lessons of history must be well learned and thoroughly digested, if the future of Christianity is to improve upon her past in India. For, be it remembered, Christianity never met with so doughty a foe as that which confronts it in this land. The ancient faiths of Greece and Rome, which Christianity overcame, were infantile and imbecile as compared with the subtle wisdom and the mighty resistance of Brahmanism. The conditions of the conflict in India are different from those ever met before by our militant faith. The subtle and deadening philosophy of the land, the haughty pride of its religious leaders, the great inertia of the people, the mighty tyranny of caste, the debasing ritual of Hinduism and its debauching idolatry,—all these constitute a resisting fortress whose overthrow seems all but impossible.

II

And yet I strongly believe in the ultimate triumph of our faith in India. Under God this mighty fortress of Hinduism will capitulate. Nor do I think that the day of Christian dominance is so far away as many missionaries are inclined to think. There is an accumulation of forces and a multiplication of spiritual powers which are now operating in behalf of our faith and against the ancestral religion of India, such as will work wonders in the future religious development of the land. But this conquest of our faith will not be that which too many of us are wont to anticipate and to pray for. The religious forms of life and of thought, which we of the West have inherited and in whose environment we have grown up, we have come to identify with the *essence* of our religion; and it seems all but impossible for us to think of a Christianity apart from these outward forms. I believe that there is to be a rude awakening for our children and grandchildren, if not for ourselves, in this matter.

The western *type* of Christianity will not survive the conflict in India. Western modes of thought and forms of belief will be supplanted by those better suited to the land. Occidental doctrines and aspects of our faith will give way to those conceived from the Oriental standpoint. I believe, for instance, that the most mischievous doctrine of pantheism will surrender its elements of truth (for it has an important admixture of truth) to the formation of a new conception of God, which will appeal to and captivate the Indian mind and heart. Indeed, we are witnessing, this very day, even in the far West, the influence of India in her monistic overemphasis upon the divine immanence, working toward a new Christian conception of God. Modern interchange of thought is thus giving to India, even in America, her influence in the shaping of modern belief. And if it be thus in matters of fundamental belief, much more will it be so in matters of outward expression and in the unessential forms of Christian truth. Some of us of the West are seeing increasingly the serious incongruity which exists between our way of thinking and of putting our thought into living form, and the way of the people about us. And we are not convinced, as we perhaps once were, that it is the obtuseness, or the religious perversity, of the Indian mind which is the cause of this. The sooner the better we realize that between the people of the East and of the West there is a wide mental gulf which may, indeed, by our associating together, be narrowed, but never eliminated. And the outward type of Christianity, after western pressure has been taken away from this land, will depend upon the mental make-up and peculiar spiritual aspect of the Indian Christian. And until he is able to furnish and to enforce this, which I call the Oriental type of Christianity, he will never be able to make his faith appeal to his brothers, and to make it an indigenous faith in India.

Nor do I think that the Christianity which is to prevail in India will be encased in the present ecclesiasticism which assumes and claims monopoly of our faith. I can conceive the possibility of there being a vast amount of Christianity — a living and a self-propagating Christianity — outside the pale of organized and institutional Christianity in India. It is so in the West to-day. The organized churches of the West have within themselves an ever diminishing portion of the vital Christian life and aspirations of the country. Christianity has overleapt ecclesiastic bounds. Its spirit is overflowing, in living streams, into the life of a thousand organizations which are altruistic and philanthropic, outside the limits of ecclesiastical Christianity. It will be so in India, and throughout the world. And the Christian

Church must take this into account and shape its policy accordingly.

However this may be, East Indians will increasingly claim, as the Japanese are now claiming, the right to decide for themselves the forms of polity and the types of ritual which they will choose and cultivate as their own.

I do not say, of course, that the present forms will be entirely discarded. But they will be so modified and supplemented that they will present an ecclesiastical type of their own.

And why should they not, if our faith is to fit well the Oriental mind, and is to become a gracious power in its life? The growing opposition among the educated men of India, at the present time, is not really antagonism to Christianity itself, but to its western garb and spirit. And there is much reason for this attitude of mind. Conciliation and adaptation has not been the characteristic of the mind of the West in presenting its faith to the East. This did not make so much difference, so long as the Indian was submissive and had not waked up to the spirit of self-assertion. But to-day, when that spirit is so rampant, and when a new nationalism and a half-spurious patriotism glories in everything eastern and is annoyed by all that is western, the matter of adaptation has become all-important.

The relative barrenness of our faith during past centuries in India was largely, if not entirely, due to its foreign ecclesiastical forms and its shibboleths pronounced in foreign tongues. The Christianity of the future in India must breathe of the spirit, and speak forth in the language and life, of the people.

I am inclined to believe that the battle cry of the Christian Church will soon be lost in the ever swelling tide of enthusiasm for the Kingdom of God. Christians will seek less to promote this or that denomination, and more and more to cause to come in power the Kingdom of Heaven. And India is a land which will lend itself very readily to this transfer of emphasis. There is much in the mystical type of the Hindu mind that leads us to anticipate preëminence for India in this change of emphasis from outward organization to deep-working spiritual forces and realities.

India, which has been the most prolific land in giving birth to religions, and in being at present the asylum of all the great faiths of the world, will not be slow to give to Christianity that form and aspect which will most please her.

It is therefore important that all the Christian leaders of India should not only take note of these facts, but should also do their utmost to help in the desired consummation, and make Christianity in India a faith that will appeal to every man and woman in the land.

III

The conquest of our faith in India will be not the less, but the more, thorough, because it will be not only of the letter but also and chiefly of the spirit.

There are a few things which are fundamental to our faith, and which will become the universal and permanent possession of India.

1. The spirit and principles of Christianity will prevail and will dominate the land. Christian, as distinct from Hindu, principles are already making wonderful headway in the country. Many new institutions have been organized in the land, whose principles are those of Christ, and not of Manu. Even the oldest institutions of the country are becoming affected by the desire to appear modern, which really means an ambition to introduce Christian methods and principles. Educated Hindus, especially, add to this the peculiar weakness of interpreting things Hindu by a Christian terminology. The philosophy

which they have imbibed and the standpoint to which they have been accustomed are western and, chiefly, Christian. So that when they study their own faith they do so with these Christian prepossessions; and even when they defend their ancestral religion, they really defend not the indigenous product of India, such as is taught by the Hindu pandit and believed by the mass of the people, but Hinduism Christianized and clothed in the garb of the West and spoken in the accents of a Christian.

Hindu Swamis, who have been educated in Christian mission schools, and have spent a few years in the far West, surrounded by a Christian atmosphere, imbibing Christian sentiments, and unconsciously adopting the Christian viewpoint, return to India upon a wave of popular excitement and give public addresses and receive the plaudits of their grateful countrymen. But what is it that such men as Vivekananda and Abhedananda, and all the rest of the *Ananda* tribe, teach upon their return to India? It is certainly not an orthodox Hinduism, nor is it the pure philosophy of the East. It is rather a strange compound in which Christianity figures as prominently as does Hinduism, and, perhaps, more conspicuously. What was the caste system recently enunciated by Abhedananda in Madras? It is certainly not a thing known in India by that name. And I have no doubt that his whole audience smiled when he presented his conception of a caste system so foreign to all Hindu ideas and practice. It is just so with his Vedantism, and with his interpretation of all the religious teachings of this land. They are now construed in terms foreign to the rishi and to the pandit. But (and this the point I wish to emphasize) these interpretations meet increasingly with the applause and acceptance of educated Hindu audiences. In other words, a Christian colouring and glamour thrown over Hinduism is adding to its popularity in the land.

In the general way of looking at religious things, and especially of apprehending religious thought, there is to-day almost as wide a gulf between the educated and cultured Hindu, on the one hand, and the authorized religious instructors of India, on the other, as there is between the same learned man of the East and the thoughtful man of the West.

Or, if we look at the multiplying institutions of the country, which truly represent the thoughts and sentiments of the leading people of India, we can easily see that they are imbued with non-Hindu, if not anti-Hindu, ideas and motives. The various Somajes and other religious movements, which mean so much in the life of India to-day, are more or less an endeavour to interpret life from a non-Hindu standpoint, which often means a Christian standpoint. In any case, the religious reform movements of India at the present time breathe largely the spirit of rebellion against old Hindu conceptions.

When we think of such important movements as that of Social Reform, we can see the spirit of Christianity completely dominant, and in sharp antithesis to Hindu teaching and ritual. The Social Reform movement in India is the spirit of Christianity, trying to express itself with as little offence as possible to orthodox Hinduism, and yet constantly antagonizing its deepest principles and eating into its very vitals.

The two forces which, next to direct Christian effort, do most for the promulgation of Christian principles in this land, are the public schools and the government itself. The educational system which now prevails, and which is growing in power, is distinctly a promoter of Christian thought and principle. We often call these schools godless; but we do them an injustice. Their work may be largely negative; but their teaching turns the mind of the young away from the silly superstitions and the absurd practices of popular Hinduism, and establishes modern conceptions, which, indeed, are Christian conceptions of life and of conduct.

The government is, in an important sense, established upon Christian principles; and in all its administrative processes exemplifies the Christian, as distinct from the Hindu and Brahmanic, view of justice and of right conduct; so that, if one were able to perceive clearly the spiritual forces at work in the institutional and social life of India, he would see not only that the foundation, but also that largely the superstructure, is becoming Christian in its character.

2. In the second place, the Christ Ideal of Life is acquiring ever increasing attraction and power in the land. India has never possessed an incarnated ideal of her own. No god in all her pantheon, and not one among all her noble sages, has ever posed before the followers of Hinduism, or has ever been thought of by Hindu devotees, as the exemplar of men and the ideal of human life. To many thousands who are outward members of the Hindu faith, and who would not dream of being baptized into institutional Christianity, Jesus Christ has become the Ideal of Life. He represents to them that moral type of per-

fection and ethical nobility of manhood to which they daily aspire. Krishna may be praised by the millions, notwithstanding his immoralities; and Rama may be extolled and even loved for his limited virtue; Yudhistra may be called "Dharman," notwithstanding his unrighteous passion for the dice. But Christ only, in the eyes of modern educated India, stands the perfect test of character. All over the land, Hindus of culture, of serious thought, and of ambition to reach after high ethical standards see in Jesus Christ the only inspiration and immaculate example of life that all history, myth, and legend present. And there is not a town in India to-day where there are not found these men of power and influence who are studying eagerly the life of Jesus, are pondering over the Gospel narratives; and are reading such books of Christian devotion as Thomas à Kempis's "Imitation of Christ." This last-named book is now being translated by a Brahman gentleman, a friend of the writer, and published by a Hindu firm for its Hindu readers! I have known such men for many years, and am assured that their tribe is increasing; they are men who for the first time have found the deepest yearnings of their soul answered in the example of Jesus.

Ask any of them for their reason, and they will tell

you that Christ is of the East, like themselves, and that His example appeals to them with unique power.

In India, the ideal of life has been one of restraint. Starting with the conviction that human life is an unmixed evil, the restraint of passion and the elimination of every human emotion (the best as well as the worst) has been to the Hindu the goal and consummation of life. Nothing can be more inadequate than this; and the Hindu is beginning to feel it. Jesus represents Culture *and* Restraint. With him the restraint of the lower passions is with a view to the culture of the higher. The man of sin must die, that the man of God may live and prosper. This is the Christ ideal, as opposed to the Brahmanic. And the leaven of this ideal of life is spreading all over India and is transforming the aspirations of millions. There is nothing more inspiring or comforting than the assurance which we have that the Christ life is becoming the dominant ideal among the classes of India, as it is to a less degree among the masses.

A Brahman gentleman had the presumption to say to me, recently, that he and his fellow-Brahmans and other Hindus were able to understand the Christ much better than we of the West. He also claimed that they could understand the deep significance and the delicate shading of His thought better than we who are not of the East, like them. As a man who had taught and had tried to live the Christ in this land for more than a quarter of a century, I smiled at the audacity of his remark. And yet I knew that that man had visions of Christ that I had not; and that he has a fondness for Thomas à Kempis's book, beyond, perhaps, what I myself possess. There are aspects of the teaching and of the life of Jesus which appeal more powerfully to his Oriental and deeply mystical nature than they can possibly to the minds of all western men. Of one thing, however, I am assured; namely, that there is a growing host of Hindus in high position, and in low, who are enamoured of that ideal of life which our Lord taught and exemplified; and the fact that they interpret that life differently from myself causes me less sorrow than it does a desire to understand better their standpoint of appreciation.

3. I believe also that the Incarnation of our Lord, in its uniqueness and supreme power as the true manifestation of God, is finding rapidly increasing appreciation among the people of India.

India is the land of a myriad incarnations. The doctrine has run to seed, as it were, among this people. They are burdened with the excess of their eagerness to find God, and with their manifold imagination in giving Him form and earthly existence. There is no doctrine in Hinduism which has been carried to such a *reductio ad absurdum*.

Hindus to-day would gladly accept Christ as one of Vishnu's incarnations, if Christians would permit. I am not sure but that the tenth incarnation of Vishnu was meant to represent Christ. In any case, their growing familiarity with Him is gradually creating in their minds a disgust with the monstrosities of their own incarnations. Many of them are learning that God's Incarnation in Christ is the only one which has "descended" to the earth for the spiritual uplifting and redemption of our race; and, therefore, that it is the only incarnation which has within itself the seed of permanence and of universality. The petty, grotesque, and local "descents" of India will satisfy no one in these days of growing breadth and union, when the people are aspiring after an all-India nationality.

In Christ only is India finding the perfect revelation of God, because He alone revealed Him as the Father of boundless love; God, the Father of all men, loving them with an infinite passion and seeking them even unto death, — that is the message of the Christian

Incarnation. And how strangely does it contrast with the moral obliquity and selfish indifference to human interest which characterize Hindu incarnations! In Christ do we find that God is the ever present, personal, loving Father, seeking to bring home again His lost children. He is supremely just and holy as Ruler and Provider; but His justice and holiness are illumined and transfused by His love. And as the Eternal Spirit He is striving in the hearts of men to bring them to Himself. This is the incarnation which is gaining ever increasing power in this land and whose worship is spreading from Cape Cormorin to the Himalayas.

4. The cross of Christ will be accepted in India as the highest expression of God's love to man.

It is true that, among many Hindus to-day, as among the Greeks and Jews of old, the cross of Christ is an offence and a stumbling-block. The idea of vicarious atonement runs counter to the long-cherished doctrine of *Karma*. And it is possible that the universal prevalence of the *Karma* doctrine in the land will give to the doctrine of atonement the same one-sided aspect which it has obtained among many Christians of the West, in the present day, whereby the element of vicariousness, or its God-ward efficiency, has been considerably eliminated. They may remain content to consider the cross merely as a supreme manifestation of love, as that part of the divine example which has infinite power to attract men toward the highest life of lowest service and self-effacement. However this may be, at present, the cross in India has more significance than the trident to the Hindu. And the language of the cross appeals with increasing force to all men of thought. And I am encouraged to think that the modern commendable habit, among educated Hindus, of harking back to the oldest and the best of their religious writings, may carry India away again from its emphasis upon *Karma* to the original, pre-Buddhistic idea of vicariousness, when, for instance, in the *Purusha Suktha* of the Rig Veda, the *Purusha* is represented as being sacrificed by the gods. In the *Brahmanas*, also, it is said that the *Prajabathi* sacrificed himself in behalf of the gods.

Indeed, it has been well said that the doctrine of *Karma* itself, as connected with the doctrine of transmigration, carries within itself a strong element of vicariousness; since the person suffering in this birth knows nothing of the experiences of a supposed previous birth, and is, therefore, suffering for a past of which he is ignorant and for which his conscience cannot hold him responsible.

5. I believe, also, that the Christian conception of sin is gaining ever widening acceptance in India and will ultimately prevail as against the Hindu idea.

The doctrine of atonement and the doctrine of sin are intimately related; where the atonement is ignored or slighted, the conception of sin is apt to lose its ethical content and to become formal. India, through Buddha, abandoned, largely, its long-cherished principle of vicariousness and the multiplicity of its sacrifices. The consequence has been the gradual emasculation of the principle of atonement, until the word has become emptied of content and degraded so as to mean only the eating of a filthy pill because of a certain ceremonial uncleanness, which all the best people of the land know to be no uncleanness whatever.

It is natural, under these circumstances, to see the idea of sin also cease to have reference to moral obliquity and violation of ethical principles, and to refer only to intellectual blindness and (more commonly) to ceremonial laxness and ritualistic malfeasance. It is not surprising, therefore, that under this double departure from the truth, conscience should have lost its place of importance and of authority to so large an extent in this land.

But the day of better things has dawned upon India.

The ethical concept and the moral significance of life are beginning to grip India very thoroughly. And I believe that the day will soon come when sin will cease to be connected with intellectual delusion and ignorance, and also with ceremonial irregularity, and will be recognized in its true moral hideousness as a thing of will, and not of intellect, a thing of deepest life, and not of puerile ritual.

Thus, with the coming of Christ and the emphasis of western thought and western civilization upon moral integrity and nobility of character, there is growing also a vision of sin in its right colour and perspective. The gradual training of the people in British law and in the social ethics of the West, and in the true meaning of the righteousness of the Kingdom of God as promulgated by the Christian faith, will, ere-long, drive out the old pantheistic idea proclaimed by Vivekanada, when he said that the only sin that man was capable of was the sin of regarding himself as a sinner! It will also make it impossible for murderers to excuse themselves, as one did recently to our knowledge, as he was led to be executed, by saying that it was not he, but the god within him, that slew the man!

India is really passing through a quiet, but, nevertheless, a mighty ethical revolution. Its fundamental principles of morality and of religion, as the interpreters of life, are being rapidly transformed. Christianity is sowing everywhere its seed of life and of character, as they are exemplified in the perfect life of Jesus, and are elaborated in the four Gospels, in comparison with which the message of the four Vedas and of all subsequent Hindu literature is but as the dark and feeble groping of the blind after light.

These, then, are the five fundamental aspects of our faith which are among the eternal verities and which have come to India smiling with the impress of universality, and which are finding gradual acceptance in all portions of the land. These represent what one has aptly called "Substantive Christianity," as distinct from "Adjectival Christianity," which men are prone to overemphasize and to exalt unto the heavens. This latter we may love and cherish and promote with all our hearts; but it is sectional, partial, and transitory. The former, on the other hand, is abiding, and will shine throughout the ages of eternity. It will grow in influence and increase in its prevalence throughout this land until we all can say, with the late Chunder Sen, and with much more assurance than he, "None but Jesus is worthy to wear this diadem, India; and He shall have it."

INDEX